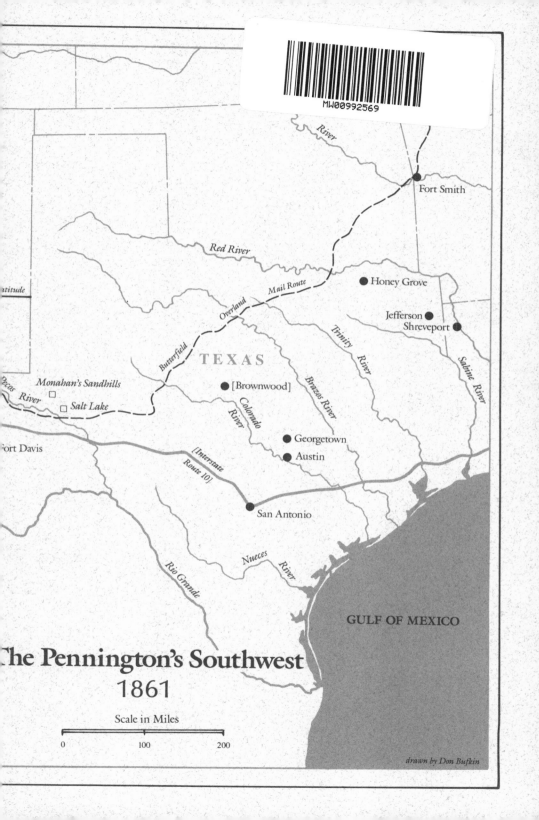

River

Fort Smith

Red River

atitude

Mail Route

Honey Grove

Overland

Jefferson
Shreveport

Butterfield

TEXAS

Trinity River

Sabine River

Monahan's Sandhills

[Brownwood]

ecos
River

Salt Lake

Colorado River

Brazos River

Fort Davis

Georgetown
Austin

[Interstate
Route 10]

San Antonio

Rio Grande

Nueces River

GULF OF MEXICO

The Pennington's Southwest
1861

Scale in Miles

0   100   200

drawn by Don Bufkin

"Whatever Arizona had to show of frontier life they have seen. They paid to see the show with their own blood, and with the blood of kindred and friends. . . ."

Tucson Post, August 3, 1907

BUEHMAN,   TUCSON, A. T.

Larcena Pennington Page Scott, 1870.

WITH THEIR OWN
BLOOD
A Saga of Southwestern Pioneers

Virginia Culin Roberts

Fort Worth: Texas Christian University Press

Library of Congress Cataloging-in-Publication Data

Roberts, Virginia Culin.
    With their own blood : a saga of southwestern pioneers / by
Virginia Culin Roberts.
        p.   cm.
    Includes bibliographical references and index.
    ISBN 0-87565-090-2 : $24.95
     1. Pioneers—Arizona—Biography.   2. Pennington family.
3. Frontier and pioneer life—Arizona.   4. Arizona—Biography.
I. Title.
F810.R64   1991
979.1'04'0922—dc20
[B]   91-15195
                                     CIP

Contents

For three beautiful people,
Carol, Jim, and Marcia

Preface

I was intrigued by frontier woman Larcena Pennington at first glimpse — a brief mention of her in Bernice Cosulich's 1951 book, *Tucson*. It started me on a twelve-year search for facts about her. The Penningtons, emigrants from Texas, proved to be the venturesome, hard-working, persistent kind of people who dared to push America's frontiers westward. No one had yet compiled all the scattered, colorful fragments of their story. It was a pioneer saga that richly deserved telling.

Early in 1854, the United States added the Gadsden Purchase to New Mexico Territory. It was not until the fall of 1856 and the spring of 1857, however, that there was any Anglo-American settlement between the Rio Grande and the Colorado River. A few American men had infiltrated Tucson, formerly a Mexican village, but that was still largely Mexican in population and character. In those nine months, four troops of United States cavalry, a few enterprising members of the Sonora Exploring and Mining Company, and perhaps sixty to a hundred other Anglo-American immigrants, including the Penningtons, established themselves well south of Tucson. Most of these settlers were single men. They clustered loosely within thirty miles of Mexico, along the Santa Cruz River and Sonoita Creek. In this wilderness, an occasional crumbling ruin testified silently to earlier habitation by Spanish colonists routed long before by marauding Apache Indians. The old Spanish road from Sonora to Tucson was a long, thin, ragged scar across this land.

Larcena's residence began six years before the separation of Arizona Territory from New Mexico and spanned more than the Territory's forty-nine years. She seemed the thread with which I could weave actual persons and events into a narrative documenting the harsh realities of that perilous frontier. She exemplified the inspiring power of the human spirit to endure and overcome adversity. Those are the aims of this book. It does not attempt to argue right or wrong in conflicts between Anglo-American pioneers—a small but vigorous minority—and natives of the region they settled, although those conflicts shaped the Penningtons' experiences. The point of view, however, is admittedly that of the settlers.

The Penningtons' names appear in an 1858 petition to Congress, in early newspapers, in military reports from the first United States army officers stationed in the Gadsden Puchase, in land and probate records of the Arizona Territory, and in census returns. These credible sources confirm that almost at once Larcena, her family, and their neighbors encountered grinding hardships and a series of turbulent, dismaying events that time and again forestalled their prosperity.

In 1919 the Arizona Archaeological and Historical Society published a booklet, *The Penningtons, Pioneers of Early Arizona,* by Robert H. Forbes, Larcena's son-in-law, a distinguished scientist and university professor. He based it on his personal trips to Pennington homes, interviews with Larcena, members of her family, and other old-timers. It is a reliable, though limited, resource. Forbes' Pennington files, preserved by the Arizona Historical Society in Tucson, contain valuable primary materials.

The books of Constance Wynn Altshuler, specifically *Latest from Arizona! The Hesperian Letters, 1859-1861* (1969), *Chains of Command: Arizona and the Army, 1856-1875* (1981), and *Starting with Defiance: Nineteenth Century Arizona Military Posts* (1983), describe many events that impinged on the Penningtons. They were extremely helpful sources.

At least eleven frontiersmen—such well-known Arizona characters as William Kirkland, Charles Genung, James Tevis, and John Spring—saw fit to mention Larcena Pennington in their memoirs. Even William Alexander Bell, a British geographer exploring the southwestern United States, described an encounter with her, in *New Tracks in North America* (1869).

Persistence and remarkable luck led me to Pennington descendants, now widely separated, who generously shared old family records and photographs and undertook research on my behalf. They provided significant data for this book. I give heartfelt thanks to Marshall Lee Pennington of Lubbock, Texas, Eunice Rader of Georgetown, Texas, and her sister, Ruth Lesesne (now deceased), all grandchildren of Larcena's brother John Parker (Jack) Pennington; to Marjorie Handy Hart of Piedmont, California, Larcena's great-granddaughter; and to Mrs. Hart's daughter Margo Hart Anderson of Piedmont. I thank Nelle Drummond of Midland, Texas, great-granddaughter-in-law of Mary Frances Pennington Randolph, and Shirley Nichols Brueggeman of Loma, Colorado, great-granddaughter of Caroline Pennington's second husband, Abner Nichols.

Chief among persons who assisted me was C. L. Sonnichsen, author of many books on the Southwest. He provided encouragement and occasional research leads and most generously critiqued my entire manuscript. Others who contributed in various ways include Walt Roberts, Carol S. Williams, Jim and Pam Scott, Mark Roberts, Lynn Hansen, Virginia Callicotte, Mark Sawyer, and authors Elizabeth Brownell, L. Boyd Finch, Betty Leavengood, Alberta Cammack, and James E. Officer, all of Tucson; Marcia S. Hayes, Jonathan Miller, and War Hayes of Marin County, California; Agnes Haywood of Port Angeles, Washington; Fern and Ben Allen of Phoenix; Marvin Cook of Eugene, Oregon; Sarah Bunnett of Santa Cruz, California; author Darlis Miller at New Mexico State University; and author/librarian Helen Lundwall and museum director Susan Berry, both at Silver City, New Mexico. Numerous strangers and friends graciously answered my letters requesting information or opinions.

I consistently received expert and courteous help from personnel at the Arizona Historical Society, Pima County Archives, University of Arizona Library, and Pima County Courthouse, all in Tucson; as well as the Arizona Historical Foundation in Tempe; the Arizona State Library and Archives in Phoenix; New Mexico State University Library and the Doña Ana County Courthouse at Las Cruces; and the Sharlot Hall Museum and Yavapai County Courthouse in Prescott, Arizona. Doubleday & Company of New York graciously gave permission to reprint the quotations from Norman Vincent Peale. Finally, I wish to thank A. Tracy Row, my editor at TCU Press, for the enthusiasm, consideration, and expertise he has demonstrated.

The Elias Green Pennington Family
Pioneers of Texas and Arizona

The Parents

Elias Green Pennington: born 16 April 1809, South Carolina; married Julia Ann Hood, 8 September 1831; killed by Apaches, 10 June 1869, in Sonoita Valley, Arizona Territory.

Julia Ann Hood: born 12 February 1815, North Carolina; married Elias Green Pennington 8 September 1831; died September 1855 at Honey Grove, Texas.

Their Twelve Children

James (Jim): born 8 May 1833, Tennessee; never married; killed by Apaches 27 August 1868 near Tucson, Arizona Territory.

Laura Ellen: born 12 November 1835, Tennessee; married Underwood C. Barnett 25 April 1867 in Arizona Territory; died 30 December 1869 in Tucson, Arizona Territory.

Larcena Ann (Tid): born 10 June 1837, Tennessee; married John Hempstead Page, 24 December 1859 in Tucson, New Mexico Territory; widowed after Page mortally wounded by Apaches, 20 February 1861 near Tucson; married William Fisher Scott 27 July 1870; died 31 March 1913 at Tucson, Arizona.

Caroline M. (Caz): born 16 December 1838, Tennessee; married Charles M. Burr 12 May 1859 in New Mexico Territory; married Abner J. Nichols about 1863 in Arizona Territory; died, date unknown, in Austin, Texas.

John Parker (Jack): born 24 December 1840, Honey Grove, Texas; married Emily McAllister 6 March 1877 in Texas; married Isabelle Purcell 24 January 1882 in Texas; died by his own hand, 1 December 1904, Georgetown, Texas.

Ann Reid: born 20 January 1843; never married; died of malaria 3 July 1867, Sópori, Arizona Territory.

Margaret Dennison (Mag): born 17 July 1844, Honey Grove, Texas; never married; died 5 April 1872 in Georgetown, Texas.

Amanda Jane (Jane): born 7 February 1846, Honey Grove, Texas; married William W. A. Crumpton 27 October 1874 at Georgetown, Texas; died 12 November 1919 at Santa Cruz, California.

Elias Green, Jr. (Green): born 27 July 1848, Honey Grove, Texas; never married; killed by Apaches 17 June 1869 in Sonoita Valley, Arizona Territory.

William Henry (Will): born 25 February 1850, Honey Grove, Texas; never married; died 20 July 1929 in Brownwood, Texas.

Mary Frances: born 28 December 1852, Honey Grove, Texas; married William M. Randolph 18 June 1877 at Georgetown, Texas; died 20 December 1935, Martin County, Texas.

Sarah Josephine Elizabeth (Josie): born 27 October 1854, Honey Grove, Texas; married Charles A. Gordon 6 October 1880 at Georgetown, Texas; died 30 October 1935, Brownwood, Texas.

Part I: Independent and Unsubdued

It was never easy. I believe it is almost impossible for us pampered children of the twentieth century to conceive of what it was like — say — to clear and plough an acre of virgin forest, or plod with a wagon train across the mountains and the deserts. But hardship, challenge, and struggle — painful in themselves — can also unlock tremendous reservoirs in the human spirit, if that spirit is independent and unsubdued. That was the spirit they had, the spirit that built America.

Norman Vincent Peale
Sin, Sex and Self-Control
(New York: Doubleday & Co., 1965)

ONE: CAPTURE

On a crisp Friday morning, March 16, 1860, a slender brook danced and twisted around live oaks and huge half-buried boulders in Madera Canyon in the Santa Rita Mountains of what is now southern Arizona. Blonde Larcena Pennington Page, age twenty-two, had no premonition of danger as she bent to fill buckets at the cold clear stream fed by winter snow melting on higher peaks and ridges. She and her ten-year-old companion, Mercedes Sais Quiroz, were alone beside a flickering campfire.

The day before, Larcena's young husband, John Hempstead Page, and his friend William Randall had brought her and the little girl by ox-wagon from Canoa ranch in the valley below. They had pitched their tents beside the creek. The two men were associated in a logging operation in the high recesses of the large canyon. They felled trees and sawed them into lumber sorely needed by settlers in this remote Gadsden Purchase region of New Mexico Territory. After breakfast, Randall had disappeared among the trees to hunt a deer for dinner and Page had hiked up to "the pinery," where his crew was already at work.[1]

Larcena could hear the faint, reassuring thud of axes on wood, higher in the canyon. Other sounds were peaceful and pleasant: the burble of the brook, the screech of bluejays, the happy laughter of Mercedes, who was playing with Larcena's little dog. Five months earlier, twenty Apache renegades had raided

Collumber's ranch near the pinery, making off with clothing, blankets, provisions, and an ox.[2] But that incident was almost forgotten.

Larcena felt secure in this lovely spot and thought for a moment of why she was here. She and John Page had been married just eleven weeks earlier in the village of Tucson. After the wedding, Larcena stayed on there while her husband returned to the sawmill in the pinery where he and his partners had a business arrangement with rancher William Hudson Kirkland. Kirkland, then a twenty-seven-year-old, tall, thin Virginia-born bachelor, lived about thirteen miles from the pinery at the Canoa ranch on the Santa Cruz River. There he and Richard M. Doss dealt in lumber sales to the military and to the public. Page and his partners hauled the lumber they whipsawed to various places as Kirkland or Doss directed.[3]

In Tucson, Kirkland engaged Larcena to teach his young ward, Mercedes, to read. Daughter of a Mexican widow, she was a bright, promising little girl, and Kirkland felt she deserved an education.

Page made the forty-mile ride from the Santa Ritas to town to be with his young wife as often as he could, but the infrequent, brief visits and the tiring trips made him determined to bring Larcena closer to the sawmill.[4] Page now proposed to Kirkland that he move Larcena into a rude unused cabin near the Canoa ranch house. The rancher objected because of the risk of raiding Apaches, and he had another concern: he wanted Mrs. Page to continue tutoring Mercedes.[5] John Page persisted, however, and finally got his way. Kirkland went to Tucson and sent Mercedes by stagecoach to Larcena at Canoa.[6]

Shortly after arriving at Canoa, Larcena developed chills and fever, a common ailment along the rivers and streams of southern Arizona. Knowledgeable persons advised her that if she would get up into the higher mountain air she would soon improve. She asked John Page if he would take her with him on his next trip to the lumber camp. Her husband was willing to do even more: he would build a cabin for her up there.[7]

Against his better judgement, Bill Kirkland agreed to let Mercedes go with Larcena. Page loaded a wagon with tools, a few furnishings, bedding, clothing, provisions and other supplies.[8] He, Larcena, and Mercedes left Canoa in the wagon on Thursday morning, March 15. William Randall, "an experienced frontiersman" and one of Page's sawmill partners, accompanied them on horseback. They rumbled slowly uphill as their oxen pulled them into Madera Canyon along a road that Kirkland had made from Canoa to the lumberyard. Bill Kirkland speculated later that even then the five Tontos who captured Larcena and Mercedes the next morning may have been observing them.[9]

• •

Larcena finished her simple chores, then showed Mercedes the smooth, hollow balls that grew on the oaks. The curious child began to collect them eagerly. Larcena stretched, easing a persistent ache in her back. She was tall for a woman of that time. She turned her gray-blue eyes westward, where brushy canyon slopes widened to frame a magnificent view. Spread before her lay the panorama of the Santa Cruz Valley — the golden desert plain three thousand feet below, basking in sunlight under a cloudless spring sky. Azure mountains curved the far horizon. But the sight failed to inspire her this morning. She felt listless, a condition she hoped would soon improve in the invigorating altitude. She glanced back at the girl intently gathering oak balls and decided that the reading lesson could wait a few minutes. The men would not be back in camp for some time.

Larcena ducked into her tent, leaned back in the rocking chair John Page had brought along for her, and closed her eyes. Her little dog curled up beside her. Only a moment later he growled and jumped up barking. She scolded him and told him to lie down, but sudden, terrified screams from Mercedes brought Larcena to her feet, just as a black-haired, copper-skinned Apache burst through the tent flap.

Larcena lunged for the Colt revolver hidden in the bedding. A rough brown hand snatched it from her. She darted from the tent, but the Indian caught her arm. Mercedes shrieked again and started to run toward her, but another brave, emerging swiftly from behind the trees, seized the child.

For most of her life Larcena Pennington Page had lived in danger of being captured by Indians. Now all at once she was surrounded by five Apaches, obviously unfriendly. Their black eyes gleamed in their swarthy faces. They indicated by sign language and in Spanish that they had just killed her husband as he drank from a spring in the canyon above and that the saddle they carried was his. She choked off an involuntary, anguished scream of denial as she felt a spearpoint prick her breast.

The Indians facing Larcena were a long way from their tribe's domain north of the Gila River. They were wiry, short-statured men of the Tonto band, with shoulder-length hair cut in a bang across the eyebrows. They wore breechcloths and high-top buckskin moccasins. Their slim, nearly naked bodies showed little of the muscular development possessed by the sturdy lumbermen. Each carried a bow, quiver of arrows, and a lance.[10]

Terrified and numbed by the thought of John Page dead, his young bride watched as the Tontos proceeded to loot and vandalize the camp. What they did not choose to take, they ruined. White clouds rose where they slashed open heavy flour sacks and dumped the contents on the ground. They strewed other supplies and food in mingled heaps. They took Larcena's feather bed up on a knoll — the bed she and John had shared the night before — and shook it until feathers flew. At that, she screamed again in sudden anger. Again the lancepoint silenced her.

The Apaches gathered up their booty and pushed the woman and girl ahead of them uphill in a northerly direction. They climbed rapidly through the oaks over a ridge and into another canyon. The slopes were steep and rocky, dotted with thorny agaves, clumps of wild grass, small shrubs, and trees. The brush beside the narrow path caught at Larcena's apron and long, bulky skirt. Her "spencer," a form-fitting jacket which she had needed in the morning chill, soon felt too warm. Her fair face grew flushed and her breathing labored.

She tore off and dropped pieces of her apron and broke twigs from trees, when she could do so unobserved. Furtively, she told Mercedes to do likewise. However, the Indians soon separated them to prevent their talking. One took Mercedes on ahead; another dropped back to watch for pursuit.

• •

William Randall returned from his deer hunt at noon and found Larcena and Mercedes gone, the camp devastated. He rushed uphill to the pinery where Page and his crew were felling trees. Bill Kirkland later reported that upon hearing the dreadful news Larcena's husband jumped onto Randall's horse "and raced at breakneck speed . . . to Canoa where the horse fell dead from the exertion."[11] There, Kirkland dispatched a fast rider eastward over the mountain passes to Fort Buchanan, the region's small military post, with an urgent plea for help. He himself prepared to ride to Tucson, forty miles north, to organize another search party. Meanwhile, Richard Doss accompanied John Page as he hurried back to the lumber camp and, with several companions, set out on Larcena's trail.[12]

• •

All day the tireless Tontos hurried their captives over "a rocky and mountainous trail, penetrating deeper and deeper into the mountain."[13] Here patches of snow lay in the shade of taller trees. The Indians had to shove, poke, and threaten in order to make Larcena keep up, weak as her illness had left her. At times the Apache carrying her "six-shooter," as she called it, aimed the pistol at her head. Seeing their dissatisfaction with her progress, she grew more and more afraid for her life. They taunted her repeatedly in broken Spanish. Mercedes understood enough to comprehend that they were planning to kill her teacher. Sobbing, the little girl managed to fall back and tell Larcena.

At last the Apaches halted briefly. One old Indian handed Larcena a cup of melted snow, which she and Mercedes drank gratefully. Another hid behind bushes and rocks and "made believe he was shooting white people."[14] Larcena felt sure he was communicating his intentions toward her. The Indians, who showed no sign of fatigue, relentlessly forced their victims onto the trail again. Larcena exerted herself, convinced that if she did not maintain their rapid pace they would kill her; but her strength was so diminished that she continually fell behind.

At sunset they climbed a narrow ridge that fell off sharply on one side. They had now come perhaps fifteen miles from the lumber camp. The Apache in the rear came running up to say that he had seen pursuers in the distance. The Tontos renewed their demands for speed, but Larcena was too exhausted to comply. One of the Indians suddenly bent toward her. Locking a forearm behind her knees, he quickly straightened, hoisted her over his shoulder and proceeded along the trail with scarcely a pause. When he tired, another of her captors carried her.[15]

The lumbermen, however, continued to gain on them. The Tontos suddenly halted. They forced Larcena to remove her heavy clothes. Obeying their commands, she stripped down to a thin chemise. They took her shoes, chattering at her all the while. She thought they were saying that many "of their people had been killed by her people . . . pong! pong! pong!"[16] Then they impatiently signaled her to move ahead on the trail.

As Larcena turned and took the first weary step, a lance thrust seared her back. She stumbled off the edge of the ridge. Some of the Apaches followed down the steep slope, spearing her repeatedly and hurling boulders at her head. A large pine tree blocked her fall and she lodged against it, senseless. The Indians dragged her to the far side of the tree and returned to the trail, leaving her to die, or thinking her already dead. One of them swooped up the wailing Mercedes, another put on Larcena's shoes and snatched up her clothes, and they all vanished quickly from the spot.

It was twilight when the sound of her dog barking on the trail above her aroused Larcena. "Here it is, boys!" rang out a voice that she recognized with joy as her husband's.[17] He and his companions were going back and forth on the ridge above her, trying to solve the riddle of the tracks on the trail. Page had just found the print of her shoes, now worn by one of the Apaches. Larcena tried to call out to him, but she was so nearly lifeless that she could neither make an audible sound nor move. In the gloom, the lumbermen did not see the evidence of her tumbling into the ravine. Following her shoeprints slowly in the dim light, they resumed their pursuit of the Indians. Despair overwhelmed Larcena. She lapsed again into unconsciousness as dark as the cold night that swiftly and silently closed in around her.

TWO: THE PENNINGTONS

The battered, bleeding woman lying in the mountain snow had married twenty-six-year-old John Hempstead Page on Christmas Eve, 1859. They were a vigorous, confident young couple ready to face frontier hardships together. Chance had led them by widely separated paths, thousands of miles from their native states, to the Gadsden Purchase where they first met.[1]

Larcena was born in Tennessee on June 10, 1837, the third child of frontier farmer Elias Green Pennington and his wife, Julia Ann Hood. From these two stalwart pioneers she inherited strength, a firm religious faith, and a cheerful, optimistic outlook on life. Her parents, both of English descent, originated in the Carolinas.[2] About the time of their marriage in 1831, they moved to Tennessee. There, before Julia was twenty-three, she gave birth to their first four children — James, Laura Ellen, Larcena Ann, and Caroline. Elias had some education, but Julia, apparently, could neither read nor write.[3] However, her character might be glimpsed in her twelve children, who, with one exception, were mutually loving and loyal, the sons kind and considerate toward their sisters.[4]

Elias, too, had much to do with that. He was good-humored, quiet, sober and hard-working. He loved his wife and was an affectionate father. Even in later years when people referred to him as "Old Pennington," he was physically impressive—"large, tall, with a fine face and athletic frame."[5] By then he was clean-shaven, although bearded in earlier years, with fair hair, blue eyes, and an aquiline nose.[6] J. Ross Browne, a traveler who met him in Tucson in 1864, described him as eccentric: when other Arizona settlers had fled the rampaging Apaches, Elias and his family had remained, "seeming rather to enjoy the dangers than otherwise." Nevertheless, Elias Green Pennington was "apparently a man of excellent sense," according to Browne, who stated that he had never seen a better example of the fearless American frontiersman.[7]

A Pennington family tradition holds that Elias and his brother John were the sons of one Elijah Pennington. Elijah, they say, had been a soldier at Valley Forge in the terrible winter of 1777 and had received a large bounty land grant in Virginia as a reward for his Revolutionary War service. There he reared eight boys and eight girls and became wealthy growing fine tobacco. He had a stern belief in self-reliance. When a son became twenty-one, Elijah gave him a rifle, a dog, a horse and saddle, and $2100 in silver, then told him to go out and make his own fortune. As each daughter married, he endowed her to an equivalent extent, instructing her that divorce or separation was sacrilegious and that she should not expect to return to his house under such circumstances.[8]

Elias' children did not hear this legend — true or mythical — from him. He made few if any references to his background and seldom if ever heard from relatives. There may have been an estrangement, some emotional distance even greater than the miles that separated them.[9]

When Tennessee became too populated to suit Elias, and when he heard of vast frontiers opening in the new Republic of Texas, he moved his family there. They reached the region that is now Fannin County, just south of present-day Oklahoma and the Red River, in November, 1839. Elias homesteaded 640 acres on Bullard's Creek, a branch of the Bois d'Arc.[10]

It was good, well-watered farmland, with lovely, mature trees — pin oak, Spanish oak, hickory, hackberry, hawthorn, and persimmon—which the surveyor used as markers.[11] Elias built his cabin about seven miles west of "the Honey Grove," an area which soon developed into a small town. The first settlers had come to the region only three years earlier, finding friendly Kickapoo Indians and Shawnees to the north and Caddos to the south. But the Cherokees and other bands had been hostile from 1837 through 1839, when they were soundly defeated by the whites.[12]

There was peace while Elias and Julia built their home and when their fifth child, John Parker Pennington, was born on December 24, 1840.[13] Three-year-old Larcena, holding fast to James, who was seven, could safely romp out to the field which their father cleared, plowed and planted in the spring. That freedom was curtailed, however, when Indian raids began again. Although a treaty is said to have forever eliminated the danger of Indian attack there by 1843, that cannot be entirely true, for hostilities hit near the Pennington farm at least three years later. Overconfident of their security, settlers had grown careless.[14]

Ten of the Pennington's neighbors formed the Honey Grove Baptist Church in 1846. Elias was the first to join after its organization. They met for worship at each other's homes; in October, 1848, they met at Pennington's. But six months later, meeting at a school near his cabin, they dissolved their church because some members had been murdered by Indians and others had left the vicinity.[15] On that disappointing day, the elders gave Elias a certificate affirming his good standing in the congregation, dismissing him as an orderly member, and giving him up "to the Lord or any Baptist church of the same faith."[16] He later carried that precious document with him into Arizona, where no Baptist church existed until years after he died, stretched out in a plowed field with Indian arrows in his back.

Larcena Pennington grew to young womanhood on this rapidly developing Texas frontier. Good-natured and uncomplaining, she became accustomed to hard work and danger, never knowing another way of life. Her father drove his wagon to Shreveport and Jefferson when his farm work was slack and freighted goods back to Bonham and Honey Grove to earn extra cash.[17] She felt anxious while he was away, relieved when she saw his oxen plodding back down the lane.

About every two years Larcena had a new baby brother or sister to play with and care for, usually a sister. After John there were Ann, Margaret, Amanda Jane, and Green (Elias Green Pennington, Jr.). Then William and Mary Frances. Sarah Josephine Elizabeth, the last child, was born in October, 1854, making eight girls and four boys in the overflowing cabin.[18] Some of them acquired nicknames. Larcena was "Tid," possibly short for "Tidder"—a baby's attempt to say "sister." In later years she was still "Aunt Tid" to her nieces and nephews. James was "Jim"; Caroline, "Caz." John became "Jack" and Margaret was "Mag." They shortened William to "Will" and the baby's long name to "Josie."[19]

Julia Ann Pennington had a hard life, bearing and rearing this large family, even though the children, as they grew, shared the work of house and farm. She must have been pleased when a school was built nearby, so that Larcena and the older children could go and learn skills that she couldn't teach them.[20]

By 1855 Elias felt the urge to move on. The Texas Republic had now been a state for nine years and civilization was closing in on Fannin County. It seemed almost as crowded as his house. The newly organized Texas Pacific Railroad Company planned to lay track just a mile south of his property.[21] This was not good news for a man who depended on ox-freighting for a living. Elias had already sold off parcels of his land periodically. In February, 1855, he sold the last of it, and shortly afterward, leaving his family at Honey Grove, he rode west to explore for their new home.[22]

Larcena, at eighteen, experienced her first great loss while her father was gone. Julia Ann had never fully recovered from the birth of Josie, her twelfth baby in twenty-two years. Now her health gradually declined. Jim Pennington, a tall, raw-boned, ruddy-faced young man of twenty-two, took charge of the farm in his father's absence. Ellen, Larcena, and Caroline did the household chores and tended the younger children. They all gathered around Julia's deathbed in September, 1855, just a month before

Josie's first birthday.[23] One can imagine their apprehension and sorrow when their mother lay dead at forty; the long, anxious days of waiting and yearning for their father; Larcena's quick, hopeful glances down the road whenever she heard the sound of an approaching horseman. Joy and grief mingled when Elias finally returned and had to be told of his wife's death.

The loss of Julia reinforced Elias' determination to leave Honey Grove. Larcena was soon packing barrels, crocks, jars, sacks, boxes, and trunks, making painful decisions about what must be left behind. She and Ellen set out the utensils, bedding, and furniture that would be needed in their new home and unlikely to be available in a less settled area. They put the necessities in, and in the niches between they fitted cherished possessions they could not bear to part with. Among these were Elias' Bible and the school books the older children had studied — Ellen would use them to teach the young Penningtons. Elias, Jim and Jack arranged all these things, as well as farm implements and seed for the next crops, in three large wagons, allowing for sleeping space, too.[24]

After a final moment at Julia's grave, the thirteen Penningtons started on the trail, followed by dogs and livestock. Larcena, Ellen and Caroline were strong and capable of driving wagons and herding cattle, taking turns with their brothers. They trekked slowly about 150 miles through the densely thicketed Lower Cross Timbers and beyond, to the site Elias had selected. He took them to a place he called Keechi in what is now Jack County.[25]

No town by that name exists today in Jack County, although there is a Keechi Creek.[26] The Penningtons left no traces of their short stay there. They farmed for a year and a half before loading up again, intending to go all the way to California, that beguiling new state to which thousands of gold-seekers had preceded them in recent years. Elias learned of a California-bound wagon train passing nearby, with a wagonmaster named Sutton.[27] The chance to travel the long, dangerous route with the train was an advantage not to be missed.

The hardships of their westward trek across Texas and New

Mexico in the spring of 1857 can be inferred from their own recollections and those of other travelers of that time. As the oxen lumbered slowly across Texas, Larcena sometimes rode horseback or walked beside creaking wagons. Some days the train made ten miles or less—fifteen on a good day. When they camped by a stream, she and her sisters scrubbed the family's dusty clothes. The younger boys, Green and Will, gathered wood and buffalo chips for the cooking fires over which the older girls prepared meals at dawn and dusk.

To Amanda Jane Pennington, then eleven years old, the daily routine of life on the move became monotonous as weeks jolted by in a wagon bed. There was little for her to do there except keep her little sisters contented. When the train paused at noon or camped at night she and thirteen-year-old Margaret could climb down and search for edible wild plants to vary the family's diet. The boys fished or hunted small game. The family never went hungry, but Jane remembered once suffering from thirst.[28]

Between Keechi and the Colorado River of Texas, the land they traversed had been wooded, watered by little streams. They gradually entered upon dry plains that stretched ahead flatly as far as they could see, where nothing grew but grass and weeds. It was criss-crossed with well-worn buffalo trails and, in places, winds had shaped shifting sand hills. This was part of the Llano Estacado, and it may have been here that the wagon train ran short of water.

On these plains prairie dogs and buzzards watched many a thirsty, footsore traveler leading his exhausted horse toward shimmering mirages, phantom lakes always out of reach. After a hundred miles or more on the Llano, such persons would rejoice dementedly when their animals, sniffing the breeze, quickened their steps, and real water finally became visible between the steep, treeless banks of the Pecos River.[29]

The Pecos which confronted Larcena and her family was not the refreshing stream in which other travelers had enjoyed a swim. Distant rains had sent a flood roaring down to fill the deep channel. The Penningtons waited a long time for the torrent to subside, but eventually the wagon train attempted the crossing. Men on horses drove their cattle ahead of them into the swirling brown waters. Larcena saw many of the poor animals swept away to drown in the swift current. When it was time for the Pennington wagons to cross, Jim rode into the flood, his horse swimming beside the lead oxen. He had an uncanny ability to control the huge beasts by voice alone, and he guided them safely to the far bank.[30]

Once across, Larcena and Ellen loosened their grip on the smallest children and investigated the damage done to their belongings. To their dismay they found the precious family Bible and school books wet. Around them other travelers were unloading their wagons and spreading water-soaked articles out to dry. When all had rested and repacked, the train resumed its westward journey toward distant blue mountains on the horizon.[31]

Across from El Paso del Norte on the Rio Grande was a fast-growing young village, Franklin, where they could at long last replenish some supplies. Here they turned north, following the Rio Grande to La Mesilla, formerly a Mexican settlement, and a nearby American post, Fort Fillmore. Near this point they forded the river and headed west again. Ahead, water would be very scarce, obtainable only at a few springs and intermittent streams which were traditional water sources for Mimbreño and Warm Springs Apaches.[32]

The most hazardous section of the Penningtons' route lay before them. Their way ran through three different canyons where hostile Indians might easily ambush them — Cooke's Canyon, Doubtful Canyon, and Apache Pass. Early settlers reported that another wagon train on this path was "entirely destroyed" by Apaches during this period, "the men . . . all killed and the women ravished to death!"[33]

The next water was fifty miles away at Cooke's Spring. It had become a regular stop for travelers on the new El Paso-Fort Yuma wagon road. A few hundred yards southwest of the spring began the dry wash known as Cooke's Canyon, which wound four or five miles through foothills. Hundreds of travelers died in ambush in this narrow gap from the 1850s through the 1880s.[34] Alertly threading the rocky hills, Larcena's sixteen-year-old brother Jack may have imagined Indians hiding behind every boulder. Four years later he would see real Apaches there, hear their cries, smell their gunsmoke, and fight desperately for his life. Now he proceeded safely.[35]

A few days later, Larcena and her family rode nervously through the second ambush site, Doubtful Canyon, near Stein's Peak. Bloody Doubtful Canyon it has been called, described by one man who rode through it as a deep, narrow mountain gorge extending over a mile between almost perpendicular walls.[36] Chiricahua Apaches led by that fearsome chief, Cochise, were known to gather here, their lookouts constantly watching from the heights. Wagonmaster Sutton would have avoided this canyon but for the many extra days of travel required for the alternate route around the mountains. Any unseen Indian sentries were apparently discouraged by the size of the emigrant party, for again it passed without incident.

The Penningtons could not relax their guard, however, for the whole region was Apache country, and Apache Pass, the third critical site, was not far ahead. It held a small spring long used by Cochise's Indians. The uphill trail was rocky and winding, slow going for the oxen. Riders and wagon drivers made excellent targets for any enemies lurking behind brush and boulders. Not long after the Penningtons traveled through the pass, Captain Richard S. Ewell, with two companies of dragoons from Fort Buchanan, chased Apaches who attacked a wagon train there.[37] But this day Larcena's family paused safely at the spring, crossed the flat valley west of it, made a gradual descent to the San Pedro River, and camped by that stream, some fifty miles east of the little village of Tucson. They were now in a desolate, arid region of rolling hills and mountain ranges that had been added three years earlier to the Territory of New Mexico by means of the Gadsden Purchase.

It was about the first of June, when temperatures there frequently exceed one hundred degrees. Larcena was suffering from "mountain fever." She was very ill.[38] Daniel E. Conner, another victim of that disease, described it as "truly horrible," a "most cruel and constant infliction" [sic]. It prostrated him for at least thirty-five days and left him too debilitated to walk for a further week.[39] Daily, high, intermittent fevers led to severe bodily aches and wild delirium, even to unconsciousness. In some cases of mountain fever, death followed.[40]

Fortunately, the only physician within hundreds of miles was relatively close to the San Pedro River. He was Lewis Kennon, an army contract surgeon stationed at Fort Buchanan, a small new military post southeast of Tucson then commanded by Major Enoch Steen.[41] In another four or five days trek, the wagon train reached this haven. Captain Ewell and Company G of the First Dragoons were temporarily away, chasing Apaches in the upper reaches of the Gila River.[42]

Larcena was alarmingly ill by this time. Elias decided that, before continuing to California, his family would wait near the post until Larcena had recovered and was fit to travel. When the wagon train moved on, the Penningtons stayed behind.[43]

The fort itself was hardly the place for them to remain. The soldiers had just arrived and were living in tents. In June, 1857, most of the Buchanan buildings were as yet unconstructed. The garrison was busy making adobe bricks and erecting temporary "picket houses." The Penningtons watched the men place log poles vertically in the ground, then chink the walls and roofs with mud. Dried and thatched, such roofs were still vulnerable to heavy summer rains, when muddy drips spattered anyone and anything inside.

Buchanan lacked the uniform ground plan common in army posts. Lieutenant B. J. D. Irwin, the contract surgeon who replaced Kennon later that year, described the post's layout. "Stables, corrals, pig-pens, root-houses, open latrines, and dwellings" were haphazardly situated as the camp developed. All were surrounded on three sides by swampy areas where the springs arose that fed Sonoita Creek. It was not an ideal location, as the high incidence of malaria among the soldiers soon indicated.[44]

When the Pennington men explored the vicinity, they found that immigrants had begun to settle along Sonoita Creek below the fort. Most of them were single men. However, the Penning-tons met three Anglo-American farming families — the Akes, Thompsons, and Wadsworths — with whom they, especially young Jack, later became involved.

Elias and James Pennington found an available patch of bot-tomland beside Sonoita Creek, probably downstream from the Akes, where their family could camp until Larcena got well.[45] Leaving Fort Buchanan, the Pennington wagons rumbled down-hill along the narrow, rocky road between the post and Calabasas. The little creek, which at first ran underground, suddenly surfaced beside the road four or five miles below the fort and glided on through the Wadsworth, Thompson, and Ake farms.

The Pennington girls stared curiously, no doubt, as they jolted on past Sarah Bowman's adobe establishment. Forty-four-year-old Sarah and some of her Mexican girls might have waved cheerily at the Penningtons as they passed. Pioneer merchant Solomon Warner called her place a "resort." Butcher Samuel Hughes referred to it as "eating house and madame."[46] Mrs. Bow-man did a lively business with the soldiers at the fort and the bachelors in the valley.

Sarah was better known to the soldiers as "the Great West-ern." She had recently come from Fort Yuma on the Colorado River, where she cooked for the army officers. She was a living legend, red-haired, six feet tall, and a battlefield heroine of the Mexican War.[47] Grundy Ake told his son Jeff she was "the greatest whore in the West."[48]

Larcena, wrapped in the delirium of her fever, must have been oblivious to these sights and to the beautiful countryside that intrigued her sisters as they bounced along. As Lieutenant B. J. D. Irwin observed, "The general aspect of the country is wild, pic-turesque and bold; broken into the most fantastic shapes."[49] The road generally followed Sonoita Creek, which trickled southwest-erly, widening twenty miles downstream where it curled around the southern end of the Santa Ritas to join the Santa Cruz River. Here and there erosion had carved meandering side-canyons into the rolling, grassy, oak-sprinkled hills that hemmed in the brook.

They were deceptively dry most of the time, but drained torrents of muddy water into Sonoita Creek after prolonged rains.

Now and then a bend in the road revealed a crumbling adobe ruin whose ancient owner, holder of a land-grant from the king of Spain, had long since abandoned it to hostile Apaches.[50] Rocky outcrops held unseen riches, notably silver. Live oak, cottonwood, sycamore, black walnut, and mesquite trees shaded the creek and formed a habitat for a large variety of wild animals and birds.

The Penningtons reached the site that Elias had selected and began to set up their camp near the stream. In the days that followed, Larcena's father and brothers cut cottonwood branches and erected a picket house like those they had seen at the fort. It sheltered Larcena and her family despite its shortcomings in the rainy season, which was soon upon them. They dug an irrigation ditch and planted a patch of corn, pumpkins, squash, and beans to supplement the dwindling store of provisions they had brought from Texas. Apparently they realized that it might be quite some time before they could safely continue to California.[51]

Larcena's mountain fever changed the lives of all thirteen Penningtons. Only one, Amanda Jane, ever lived in that golden California of which they dreamed. Five Penningtons found early graves in this part of the Gadsden Purchase, which later became Arizona Territory. And here Larcena met bold John Hempstead Page, her future husband.

THREE: WOMAN OF COURAGE

It was close to midnight on March 16, 1860, the day of Larcena's capture, when Bill Kirkland's messenger galloped into Fort Buchanan on a sweat-lathered horse. He had ridden from Canoa ranch over the mountain pass to the small military post. The sentries awoke the commanding officer, Captain Richard Stoddard Ewell. Before daylight Ewell had his men armed, mounted, and ready to ride to the rescue. He planned to extend a line of soldiers across the Tontos' escape route and hoped, with the help of civilian searchers, to encircle the Indians and their captives.[1]

Under Ewell's command at this time were G troop of the First U.S. Dragoons (cavalry) and Company B of the Eighth Infantry, a combined force of perhaps 140 soldiers and officers.[2] He chose the dragoons for the present mission. The infantry would remain to protect the fort, which was often the target of Apache raids.

Ewell sent the messenger back with instructions for John Page's party, trailing the Tontos, to signal its location. He ordered Lieutenant John R. Cooke to ride out at once with one platoon. Ewell himself followed with reinforcements. He was bitterly disappointed when they saw no signal. He had to conclude, at the end of a hard day's riding, that the Indians had evaded his net.[3]

Returning that evening, the weary cavalrymen trotted up the grassy slope to the fort's scattered log cabins and adobe buildings.

They attracted an excited following of infantrymen who had stayed behind. The troopers answered a babble of eager questions as they dismounted, pulled off saddles, rubbed down their horses and led them into the corral. Captain Ewell strode into his quarters where he prepared a report of the incident for department headquarters at Fort Thorn.[4]

As is customary with soldiers, the cavalrymen had private nicknames for their officers; Ewell was "Baldy" or "Old Bald Head." He had bright, bulging eyes, a prominent nose projecting over a full beard, and an unimpressive physique. His appearance, squeaky voice, and mannerisms belied his considerable courage and competence as an officer. In spite of his eccentricities, soldiers and settlers alike had learned to respect him.[5]

He doubted that the Indians and their captives were still hiding in the snowcapped peaks or rugged foothills of the Santa Ritas. They were probably Pinals, he guessed, taking hostages to exchange for twenty braves and their families whom he had confined at the fort as punishment for previous depredations.[6] Various Apache bands constantly stole livestock from the settlers in this vicinity. But, since American occupation in the region, they had not—until yesterday—taken women and children.[7] There would be fear and outrage among the settlers, and probably renewed accusations of military ineptitude.[8] He would have to mount another scout in the morning to find the trail and, if possible, rescue the captives before the Indians took them much farther.

Ewell knew from recent experience that it was expensive and usually futile to pursue marauding Apaches into their own domain. North of Fort Buchanan, the rugged two hundred miles between the White Mountains and the Gila River held an estimated seven thousand Apaches dispersed into separately led groups in various locations widely spread from east to west. For the most part, they survived by warfare, raiding villages of more sedentary Indians as well as non-Indian settlements far into Mexico. Among the various Apache bands were the Chiricahuas, who

Ewell in pursuit of Apaches (from Samuel W. Cozzens, *The Marvelous Country,* 1873).

Confederate General Richard Stoddard Ewell, captain at Fort Buchanan, New Mexico Territory, 1857–1860 (Arizona Historical Society).

Gen. Ewell, Confederate Army Officer.

ranged from southwestern New Mexico down into the upper San Pedro River Valley. The Pinals, or Pinaleños, ranged along the middle Gila and San Carlos Rivers, some of them living at Arivaipa Canyon where it emptied into the lower San Pedro. Northwest of the Pinals were the Tontos, scattered through the Tonto Basin and beyond to the present town of Flagstaff, Arizona.[9] Only six weeks earlier Ewell and a sizeable party of soldiers and citizens seeking to retrieve a stolen cattle herd had returned empty-handed from a chase into the Tontos' remote haunts.[10]

After some deliberation, the frustrated captain at last decided to send two of his Pinal prisoners back to their people to negotiate an exchange for Mrs. Page and the child. He finished his report to the Department of New Mexico and went outside to greet officials of the St. Louis Silver Mining Company who had just arrived on the mail stage. Ewell had a personal stake in a local silver mine and welcomed a chance to discuss the subject.[11]

• •

On the day that Larcena and Mercedes were captured, John Page followed the shoeprints that led him farther and farther beyond his wounded bride. Page and his companions had set out after the captives in frantic haste as soon as he returned from Kirkland's. Now chilly evening shadows filled the mountain canyons. Before long, darkness obscured further signs of the Tontos' trail, and Page was forced to stop. He reluctantly agreed that they must go back to the pinery and equip themselves for an extended search, starting again at daylight. As he trudged back in the cold night, Larcena's distraught young husband once again unknowingly passed her still form lying in the ravine below his path.

John Page's dramatic arrival at Canoa at noon that day had put rancher Bill Kirkland on the road to Tucson, riding hard and fast. Kirkland reached there that night with the electrifying news that Apaches had taken his little ward, Mercedes, and Mrs. Page. A dozen men—a good percentage of the Anglo-Americans then in the village—agreed to help him hunt for the captives. They rousted a blacksmith from his bed and he shod their horses by lamplight. By dawn the men were well on their way to Cienega, some thirty-five miles east of Tucson. Kirkland was sure, he said, that they would "cut the trail of the relentless savages" at this point. He felt certain that the captors were Pinal Apaches who would return to their camp at Arivaipa Creek.[12] Another search party, described by pioneer Edward F. Radcliff as composed of volunteer Mexicans "commanded by [Juan] Elías, a renowned Indian fighter," left Tucson the next morning.[13]

The villagers of Tucson were aroused by the capture of the woman and child. They rounded up members of a small unidentified band of Apaches which had entered Tucson a few days earlier to sue for peace, their aged chief insisting that the whites, not his people, had broken the treaty made the previous year. "Exasperated" citizens sent forth one of these natives, according to a bulletin published in the St. Louis *Missouri Republican,* "with instructions to effect the release of the captives and produce them within fifteen days, under penalty of certain death to their comrades."[14]

Forty-eight hours after her capture, Larcena's lacerated body still lay motionless and undisturbed in the snow of the ravine. An express rider had reached Tubac on March 17 with news of her abduction. Thompson Turner, local correspondent to the St. Louis *Missouri Republican,* included the sensational item in a bulletin he was preparing for that newspaper. "The town is alive with excitement," he wrote. "'What family will be next?' is asked; and some of our sturdy farmers have made arrangements for bringing their women and children into town for the present."[15]

On Sunday, March 18, Edward F. Radcliff, an accountant for the Sonora Exploring and Mining Company, arrived at Tubac from the Arivaca mine with silver bullion for the company treasurer. He found the company's director, Solon H. Lathrop, in front of the hotel, listening to Elias Pennington. As Radcliff recalled later, Larcena's father, "with tears coursing down his cheeks, was beseeching the director to render what help he could to recover his daughter Mrs. Page from the Indians."[16]

Lathrop summoned Tubac's predominantly Mexican populace to the plaza. He urged every man to join a search for the
woman and child, offering to provision the party and reward each
member of it. Over twenty, including Radcliff, volunteered.[17]

While the men equipped themselves for a lengthy ride through
the wilderness, they waited "in anxious suspense" for word that
Page's wife and Kirkland's ward had been rescued. It did not come.
Instead, more alarming news arrived, filling Tubac residents with
fear for the town and neighboring ranches. Apaches had stolen
thirty head of cattle from the Arivaca mine and viciously killed two
Mexican woodchoppers, stripping them, almost severing their
heads with axes, and riddling their bodies with bullets and arrows.
Mine workers were hot on the renegades' trail.[18]

On the morning of Monday, the nineteenth, Solon Lathrop
received a message from Lieutenant Horace Randal, who was in
charge at Fort Buchanan while Captain Ewell and Lieutenant
Cooke roamed the countryside looking for the Tontos' trail.
Ewell had sent word to Randal that the Apaches and their
captives were probably still in the Santa Ritas, stealing animals
from settlers in order to make their getaway. Randal asked Lathrop if fifty or a hundred Papago Indians—traditional enemies of
the Apaches—could be sent immediately to "surround the mountain." He promised to pay them well and give them all the beef
they could eat.[19]

Lathrop sent for the Papago chief, who offered his entire
available force of seventeen warriors. Don Antonio Gándara, son
of a former governor of Sonora, took command of Tubac's
twenty-eight Mexican volunteers. Lathrop responded to Lieutenant Randal that he would arrive at Fort Buchanan at daylight with
at least sixty men—Americans, Mexicans and Papagos. The Mexicans would need arms.[20]

By sundown these various units were ready at Tubac. The
Papagos and Mexicans started for the fort, followed by Lathrop
and Gándara with eight American men. The combined group
totaled about fifty-seven. Larcena's worried father was probably
among them. The party pushed on all night along the mountain

trail and reported at the fort at seven-thirty the next morning, March 20. Lieutenant Randal had six pack mules ready with a week's provisions and ammunition for the searchers.[21]

As the men rested before commencing their expedition, another message from Captain Ewell arrived at the post. He had discovered signs of the Indians he was seeking. They had left the mountain and separated. Those with Mercedes had crossed the Butterfield Mail route thirty miles east of Tucson near Cienega, as Bill Kirkland had surmised. The little girl had left bits of her clothing to guide pursuers, and here and there, in the dark, she had taken long steps sideways onto soft ground, leaving footprints which her captors had not seen and erased. The rest of the Apaches had presumably taken Mrs. Page, but Ewell feared they had already killed her. Nothing indicated Larcena's presence with either group.[22]

A soldier scouting south of Fort Buchanan found a trail leading from the Santa Ritas, crossing Sonoita Creek only four miles below the fort. It appeared to have been made by Indians with eleven animals. Solon Lathrop directed the forty Americans and Mexicans from Tubac to follow this trail until they could determine if there was a female in the party.[23] Lieutenant Randal sent the Papagos off to search in another direction. "After laying in a supply of medicines, such as spiritus frumenti and vino gallici," recalled Radcliff, the rest of the Tubac contingent proceeded toward the San Pedro Valley. James H. Tevis, a pioneer visiting at the fort, joined them.[24]

The Tubac miners, the Papagos, the soldiers from Fort Buchanan, the two parties from Tucson, and the lumbermen in the mountains made at least six groups simultaneously scouring the region for signs of Larcena Page and Mercedes Sais Quiroz. For the small number of settlers and military troops then on the Arizona frontier, the combined search effort was intensive. Keen-eyed, high-flying hawks would have seen the dust of these determined men spreading out over the basin between the Santa Rita, Rincon, and Santa Catalina Mountains, and the Santa Cruz and San Pedro Rivers.

• •

Larcena Page awoke on the third day after her capture to find herself at the foot of a pine tree in the ravine where the Apaches had left her. The snow in which she lay may have saved her life, slowing the flow of blood from the eleven spear wounds her captors had inflicted in her back and arms. Her battered head throbbed and her limbs felt heavy, sore, and stiff. She was cold and terribly thirsty. With effort she cradled a handful of snow and swallowed it, then another.

As the sun gradually warmed her, Larcena was able to sit up and rub snow on her bloodstained arms. Her back ached and she knew that it, too, was gashed, but she could do nothing about that. She could not stand, much less scramble up to the trail above her. She looked around her and saw that at some distance downhill the slope leveled off. She later said that "she ate some more snow and began to crawl down the mountainside. . . . After getting on the level ground at the foot of the ridge she . . . slept until morning."[25]

Sunrise aroused Larcena. She struggled slowly and painfully to her feet. She could see below her the broad valley of the Santa Cruz. A cone-shaped hill stood isolated on the plain. She had often seen that hill, "Huerfano" (orphan), northeast of Canoa ranch. It and the rising sun helped her get her bearings. She realized she was many miles from the lumber camp. It was not likely, injured as she was, that she could make her way back. If she remained where she was, however, no one would ever find her alive. She would starve.

Remembering the direction in which the Tontos had brought her from Madera Canyon, Larcena took a few cautious steps. She staggered barefooted among the rocks and brush. Each slight twist of her body pulled at her aching, blood-encrusted wounds.[26]

• •

After leaving Larcena for dead in the ravine, the Tontos had not gone much farther along the trail in the darkness. They

Huerfano Butte, a landmark that helped guide Larcena to salvation. Right, the forbidding but beautiful Madera Canyon— landscape which Larcena traversed with great difficulty.

camped for the night, and Mercedes thought she could occasionally hear Larcena crying for help. The Indians separated the next
day, and those with Mercedes passed undetected within sight of
Tucson as they skirted the western and northern sides of the Santa
Catalina range. They treated the child kindly and took turns carrying her. They gave her almost nothing to eat, however, having
little to give. Once they offered her the head of a rat, and at other
times roots or herbs. They traveled swiftly during the day and at
night they slept under bushes. Mercedes was soon famished and
exhausted. In a few more days, her Tonto captors brought her into
the camp of the Pinal Apache band near the juncture of Arivaipa
Creek with the San Pedro River.[27]

John Page had resumed his pursuit of the Tontos the day
following Larcena's capture, but many long miles northward he
lost the trail and was forced to return empty-handed a second time
to the pinery, seeing no sign of her along the way. Unwilling to
quit trying to rescue her, he rode to Tucson to muster up still
another search party.

The *Arizonian* of March 22nd published a progress report of
the search for the captives which was reprinted in the San Francisco *Daily Alta California:*

> Of the many outrages committed by the Apaches in the last
> few weeks, none has produced so startling a sensation or
> caused such a general feeling of sorrow and indignation, as the
> report . . . of a woman and child being surprised and taken
> prisoner by a party of Pinal Apaches. . . . Thus far pursuit has
> been fruitless; being on foot their trail is very indistinct, and is
> lost in many places. Most of the parties have returned unsuc-
> cessful, and it is supposed ere this, they are far in the Pinal
> country. Every effort is being made to secure their liberation.
> A large number of Apache prisoners are held in captivity at the
> fort and at [Tucson] who will be given for them. Word has
> been sent to the Pinals, to that effect, and it is hoped their
> return may be early looked for.[28]

Captain Ewell and his scouts had returned to Fort Buchanan.
"Supposing [the Apaches] to be Pinals and their object to be the

liberation of their families," whom he had confined at the fort, he dispatched two of his Pinal prisoners to the Arivaipa camp to negotiate an exchange of captives. The two Indians returned a few days later to say that the Pinals knew nothing of the missing woman and child but would attempt to find them. Before long they informed Ewell that Tontos were holding the little girl, but had killed Mrs. Page in the mountains. The Pinals offered to buy Mercedes from them and meet Ewell at Arivaipa Canyon to exchange her for their families. The captain agreed.[29]

• •

Larcena Page began each morning with the agony of forcing herself over one rocky ridge after another. She welcomed each patch of snow because it eased her thirst. Her eyes roamed as she inched along, seeking edible grass or the familiar leaves of wild onion, which she laboriously dug up with sticks or sharp rocks. She found little food, however, and day by day she grew thinner. Her feet became "filled with small stones," her arms and legs scratched by thorns. The midday sun blistered her face, her bare arms, and shoulders. Once she found a large matted heap of dried brush and grass. It looked soft, and she wanted to collapse there and sleep, but she knew it was a bear's nest. She crawled on.[30] She described the terrible ordeal shortly after it ended:

> My feet gave out the first day and I was compelled to crawl the most of the distance. Did not dare to go down to the foot of the mountain for I could find no water, and was therefore compelled to keep on the steep and rocky mountain. Sometimes after crawling up a steep ledge, laboring hard for half a day, I would lose my footing and slide down lower than the place from which I started. As I had no fire and no clothing, I suffered very much from the cold. I was at a point said to be six thousand feet above the sea, and only wonder that I did not freeze. I scratched holes in the sand at night in which to sleep, and before I could travel was obliged every day to wait for the sun to warm me up.[31]

Larcena was steadily weakening, but each nightfall found her one or two miles closer to the pinery. About twelve days after her capture Larcena strained feebly over a high ridge and, as she remembered later, "saw some men down in the valley with an ox team. She called to them and waved her petticoat, but could not make them hear and they did not look up. They hitched up and drove off, but left their fire burning."[32] Imagine her despair as they moved farther away; but the sight of those men had renewed her strength. She knew now that she was close to help.

Larcena spent two more days making her way down off the ridge. She found coals still glowing in the ashes of the men's campfire by the creek, near the site of her capture. She held a stick in the embers until it blazed, then built up the fire. She could see small heaps of flour and coffee still lying on the ground where the Apaches had dumped them. She tore off a piece of her chemise and piled flour on it. She crawled to the creek where she mixed water with the flour and patted out a small round of dough. She cooked and devoured it and slept soundly.[33] As morning sunshine wakened and warmed her, the sounds of lumbermen toiling drifted down from the canyon above.

"I could hear the men at work," she recalled, "and sometimes saw them, but could not attract their attention. At length I crawled along to the road over which [the workers] must pass."[34]

There are conflicting identifications of the man who strolled a short distance down that road from the pinery on Saturday, March 30th. Years later, Larcena herself referred to him as a superstitious person named Smith. Bill Kirkland said he was "a notorious Texas negro known as 'Nigger' Brown," who, with "his white woman known as 'Virgin Mary,'" was cooking for the lumbermen.[35] It was two full weeks since Larcena had been captured. The man must have blinked in the bright sun and stared at the apparition laboriously approaching him on all fours. A tattered, once-white cloth was draped on its gaunt frame, and a tangled, blood-clotted mass of light-colored hair hung around its head. Unnerved at the ghostly sight, the man ran back to camp for his gun.

He returned with it at once, accompanied by several curious

workmen, and aimed it. Larcena lifted her head and croaked out her name. One of the workmen ran forward and picked her up. She was hardly a burden. He carried her into camp, and laid her on a bed. She later remembered how the man who had first seen her kept declaring that she must be a spirit. The woman, Virgin Mary, brought her food and bathed her lacerated feet. She brought in her own clean clothes and put them on Larcena.[36]

Tom Childs, one of the lumbermen, rode rapidly to Canoa, where he changed horses, then continued to Tucson, carrying the unbelievable news to John Page. At Canoa, Childs had found Bill Kirkland preparing to join Captain Ewell at Arivaipa Canyon for the exchange of the Pinal prisoners for Mercedes. Childs returned with Page before Kirkland got underway the next morning. Childs had ridden about seventy miles in twenty-four hours on Kirkland's horse, which was ready to drop.[37]

Trotting on the heels of the two men came Dr. C. B. Hughes of Tucson on his excellent horse. Edward Radcliff, riding a mule, lagged behind. Radcliff and the Tubac search party had spent several days patrolling the San Pedro River without finding a trace of the Tontos or their captives. Kirkland proceeded toward Arivaipa Canyon as Page, Hughes, and Radcliff rode the last thirteen miles to the lumber camp where Larcena lay, more dead than alive. "What a sight," recalled Radcliff in later years:

> . . . emaciated beyond description, her hands and knees and legs and arms a mass of raw flesh almost exposing the bones, caused by crawling over the cruel rocks, up hill and down hill for nine [sic] days, she being unable to stand on her feet. Sixteen miles in nine [sic] days. You can imagine what she must have suffered.[38]

Dr. Hughes had little hope of saving Larcena, according to Radcliff, but John Page put her in a wagon the next day and drove her to Tucson, where she could have the doctor's constant attention.

Thompson Turner of the *Weekly Arizonian* interviewed Larcena and posted the joyful news of her return to distant newspapers. The *New York Times* received and printed the story three weeks later, describing the whole account as incredible:

> How Mrs. Page, a feeble young woman with quotidian fever and ague, with several lance wounds in her body, left for dead on a high, bleak mountain, far from home, how she should, unassisted, bind her own wounds, seek her own food and summon to her aid the energy requisite to gain her home, is a mystery that can only be explained by attributing it to Providential causes.[39]

Larcena must have spent the next few days in the doctor's rooms. It was almost impossible, when the Pages arrived, to find an empty bed in Tucson. Almost every private home and inn was bursting with delegates who had journeyed there from settlements scattered from the Colorado River to the Rio Grande. They were convening to consider creating a provisional government for Arizona until such time as Congress saw fit to make it a separate territory or, at least, a judicial district of New Mexico Territory. Congress had ignored their petitions and pleas too long.

On April 2nd, as Larcena Page clung precariously to life in an adobe-walled room not far from their meeting place, Samuel W. Cozzens, a Mesilla lawyer who had once retrieved John Page from a squalid county jail and cleared him of a murder charge, opened the convention as temporary chairman. Rafael Ruelas, the justice of the peace who had discharged Page and his fellow vigilantes on the same occasion, was another delegate from Mesilla. William Wadsworth, a lawyer-farmer who employed Larcena's brother Jack, represented Sonoita Valley.[40]

The idea of a provisional government was not universally popular among the settlers. Mesilla and Arizona City (now Yuma) supported it enthusiastically. Tubac, concerned about constitutionality and taxes, had resoundingly rejected it at a village meeting, and their delegates were there to argue against it. Tucson was split on the issue. But harmony and cooperation prevailed. The delegates formulated a government and wrote its constitution. They elected a governor and other territorial officials, provided for a militia, and put William Wadsworth at the head of it with the rank of major general.[41]

Bill Kirkland, who had stopped in Tucson, left for Arivaipa Canyon as the convention began. Captain Ewell was already there, with his Pinal prisoners in boarded-up wagons. He allowed them to show their heads to the waiting Indians, and announced that he would free them when Mercedes was safely in his hands. The Pinals let the little girl run to him and he ordered the boards removed from the wagons.[42] Kirkland, Mercedes' guardian, arrived at that moment. He was struck by the sight of the "file of soldiers drawn up with their backs to the bluff, every surrounding eminence . . . literally swarming with Indians." The first thing Mercedes said to him was that she was hungry.[43]

The Pinals, reunited with their kinsmen, quickly disappeared into the surrounding hills. The troops, with Kirkland and Mercedes, lost no time leaving the hazardous area. As they drew near Tucson two days later, on April 5, Captain Ewell offered to let Kirkland ride his handsome pinto horse into town. The rancher mounted the spirited animal and lifted the child up in front of him.

When Kirkland and Mercedes entered the village at the head of the column of blue-coated dragoons, joyful residents immediately swarmed around them, exclaiming, singing, and offering thankful prayers. One of Mercedes' aunts, who insisted that Kirkland hand the child down to her, took hold of the bridle, and the horse nervously began to buck. The crowd fell back at that, and Kirkland took Mercedes on to her mother.[44] The bell of the little church signaled the devout Mexicans, who gathered in the plaza. As the St. Louis *Missouri Republican* informed its readers who had followed the story of the capture, "The little girl, now a heroine indeed, passed from one to another to receive their embraces, congratulations and welcome. Such a scene of hugging and kissing!"[45]

The man of the hour was modest Captain Richard Stoddard Ewell. Amid all the excitement in the streets outside, Samuel Cozzens moved that the delegates seat the captain in the convention hall, and the motion carried with cheers. The delegates finished their work, defining the boundaries of "Arizona Territory," dividing it into four counties, and giving the name "Ewell County" to the one in which Tucson, Tubac, and Sonoita Valley were located. "It was too much for the captain," reported the *Missouri Republican*, "and he was compelled to beat a retreat, something he was never known to do when facing an enemy."[46]

The happy day ended with a "grand military ball," hastily organized in honor of "Baldy" Ewell and the safe return of Larcena and Mercedes. The little girl made a brief appearance. Back at Fort Buchanan later, Ewell mentioned these honors, which he did not take too seriously, in a letter to his niece Elizabeth.[47]

Larcena continued to improve, making a slow but constant recovery during the spring and summer of 1860. Edward Radcliff reported that she was "entirely cured" when he saw her several months later. "If I had not known the lady," he said, "I would not have recognized . . . the blooming woman before me. . . ."[48] But Assistant Marshal D. Miller, who saw her on September 1, while listing residents for the 1860 Census, wrote down after her name, "Mrs. Page has recently returned from Indian captivity. She bears dreadful wounds upon her person."[49]

FOUR: ROUGH TIMES ON THE BORDER

Exactly when and how Larcena Pennington had met John Hempstead Page will probably never be known. It is quite likely that her brother Jack brought him into the Pennington's camp on Sonoita Creek when they first arrived in June, 1857, or to one of their later homes. Jack, an adventurous and gregarious sixteen-year-old, soon became a frequent and welcome visitor at the nearby farm of Grundy Ake, for whom Page worked as a teamster. The boisterous Ake family enjoyed Jack. Annie Ake, who was about his age, thought of him as a "nice orphan boy." According to her, he lived at the Ake farm much of the time he was in the valley.[1]

The Akes appear to have settled very close to the site of present-day Patagonia. Felix Grundy Ake was a Tennessean by birth. He and his black-haired, blue-eyed, Scottish-Irish wife, Mary, had five children ranging in age from sixteen to infancy still at home. Mary's twenty-seven-year-old niece, America, also lived with them. Grundy was forty-seven the summer that the Penningtons came to the valley. Fun-loving Mary was ten years younger. She enjoyed singing the songs of her youth and telling her children about the night she had danced with Andrew Jackson in Tennessee.[2]

Ake had been a moderately prosperous farmer in Arkansas, but a venture to California had convinced him to move his family there. By early 1857, they had gotten as far as Calabasas on the

Santa Cruz River near the Mexican border. There they had found a camp of dragoons—the first United States troops stationed in the Gadsden Purchase.[3] Realizing the economic potential of taking government contracts to supply the military camp, Ake and his fellow travelers William Wadsworth and Thomas Thompson halted their westward journey. They followed when the troops moved to the head of Sonoita Creek in June and established Fort Buchanan, shortly before the Penningtons' arrival. Grundy Ake supplied the fort with lumber from the Santa Rita Mountains and wild hay from the hills. Thompson, husband of Ake's oldest daughter, planted vegetables, and Wadsworth got a beef contract from the post quartermaster.[4] Cheap Mexican labor was readily available to tend their farms and livestock and do housework.

At the Akes' farm, Jack Pennington became acquainted with two young men destined to become notorious in the valley and lead him into serious trouble. One was twenty-three-year-old John H. Page; the other was Grundy's nephew William W. (Bill) Ake, a wild and dangerous youth of nineteen. These two had come together from California in April, 1857, with a group referred to in the Sonoita Valley as the "filibusters."[5] Jack, hanging on their eye-widening tales of gold and adventure, must have considered his two older companions experienced and daring.

No one has left a picture or physical description of Page, but his actions show him to have been strong, passionate, and daring. He was born in Maryland about 1834.[6] Little is known about him before he came to Sonoita Valley, but he was in California some time before 1857. He may have migrated west with his family or ventured on his own, smitten with gold fever. Somewhere in California he met Bill Ake, who was there as early as 1850. Bill was thirteen that year. He lived with a grazier in San Diego County and probably earned his keep tending cattle.[7]

Before Bill Ake was twenty he had killed several men. By the time Jack Pennington met him in Sonoita Valley, Bill limped from an old gunshot wound. Even Grundy Ake's son Jeff, who seems to have liked his cousin and found excuses for some of his murderous acts, conceded that he was "a ring-tail tooter."[8] Within four years of his arrival in southern Arizona, Bill earned a reputation as the worst outlaw in those parts.

Acquaintance with "hard-living, hard-fighting" Bill Ake undoubtedly influenced John Page. They were apparently together at Bill Ake's mining claim on California's Kern River, where a gold rush had started in 1855. Anti-Chinese feeling was then running high in the mines, as it was everywhere in California. The state had imposed an intentionally discouraging foreign miner's tax on those hard-working competitors for the earth's riches. John Page once described to Grundy Ake's family how a gang of miners at the Kern River placers killed several Chinese mine laborers and their employer, Bob Cloud. Page told the Akes that Bill had struck a match on Cloud's forehead to see if he was dead.[9]

There is no evidence that John Page participated in that massacre, but he was obviously exposed to prejudice, violence and vigilante psychology in California. Such experiences presaged some of his later actions in Arizona.

Bob Cloud's killing may have furnished the impetus for Page's and Ake's departure from California; a sheriff may have made it too hot for them on the Kern River. The two young men and some of their friends decided to join "General" Henry Crabb's 1857 Colonizing Expedition to Sonora. Crabb, an able and ambitious San Francisco lawyer, planned to assemble a thousand American men to colonize an area in that Mexican state. He was recruiting farmers, carpenters, masons, blacksmiths and others who wanted land and a chance to prosper by honest labor. Some who joined him were adventure-seekers, and others, like Bill Ake, were wanted men dodging California law.[10]

Secretly, Henry Crabb had made an agreement with Mexican General Ignacio Pesqueira, who aspired to the governorship of Sonora. Pesqueira had offered Crabb a concession to colonize in exchange for furnishing the arms and money he needed to overthrow Governor Manuel Gándara and assume the office himself. Crabb shipped these items to Pesqueira, then proceeded with ninety men to a rest stop later called Filibuster Camp, forty-five miles east of Yuma Crossing on the Colorado River. He planned to march on south into Mexico with these men. The majority of the colonizers, not yet enlisted, would unite with him later after sailing from California to Port Lobos, Sonora.[11]

John Page, Bill Ake, and about twenty-three companions rode to the camp near Yuma Crossing to join Crabb, only to find that his party had already departed for Sonora. Crabb had sent two of his officers to Tucson, however, to recruit more colonizers. Page's group therefore rode on to that village. Again they arrived too late.[12]

Crabb's advance party had meanwhile reached the Mexican border, where Sonoran officials warned them strongly to go no farther. Crabb retorted that he was within his rights and pushed on with sixty-nine men toward the Mexican town of Caborca. Unfortunately for them, Pesqueira had achieved his aims and was now governor of Sonora. He had no further use for Crabb. In addition, he had second thoughts about his own popularity if he were to allow these Americans to colonize. When informed of Crabb's border-crossing, Pesqueira issued a fervent call for Sonorans to arise and mercilessly to repulse "this accursed horde of pirates."[13]

This they did. They cornered and besieged Crabb and his men at Caborca in April, 1857. The Americans surrendered, expecting leniency, but Mexican soldiers promptly executed them and displayed Crabb's severed head, preserved in vinegar, to an "exulting populace."[14]

Page and his friends learned this when they arrived in Tucson. They heard that a score of Americans recruited there and at Calabasas, being told of the siege at Caborca, had hurried south to reinforce Crabb. But he and his men were already dead when this small party reached the Mexican town. The rescuers had to retreat under fire. They lost one man in their fight to get back across the border. American diplomats filed official protests about the Crabb massacre with the Sonoran government, but Pesqueira ignored them.[15] Crabb's assistant in California never enlisted the nine hundred anticipated colonizers who were to sail to Mexico.

Mexicans generally felt that Caborcans had acted heroically in self-defense. They viewed Crabb's expedition as a filibuster. Given their ignorance of Pesqueira's agreement with Crabb, this was not an unreasonable conclusion. Mexico had ceded hundreds of thousands of square miles of land to the United States at the end of the Mexican War and had subsequently sold the Gadsden Purchase for only $10,000,000. Yet several American filibuster groups had attempted to seize more Mexican territory by force in the nine years since the war ended.[16]

John Page, Bill Ake, and their tough companions were infuriated by the "Crabb Massacre." Like many other Americans, they saw it as a clear case of betrayal and murder. They galloped angrily toward Sonora, bent on retaliation. They killed a few Mexicans and Indians unlucky enough to be in their path, but found the border strongly defended by Sonorans. Turning up Sonoita Creek, they chased some peaceful Mexican laborers cutting hay for Grundy Ake. Grundy confronted the rampaging Californians and ordered them to desist. Bill Ake called off his companions in the face of his uncle's unyielding opposition, but their violence earned them a reputation as trouble-makers among the area's American settlers, who referred to them as the "filibusters."[17]

According to historian Edward S. Wallace, that term was used in those days "in its most masculine sense, meaning free-booters." He stated that "the officers and hard core of these adventurers must have been a magnificent lot of men, the pick of the frontiersmen of the time."[18] One would like to think that John Hempstead Page, whom Larcena Pennington learned to love, was such a man. Certainly, as later events were to prove, he confronted the hazards of the frontier boldly.

Grundy Ake hired Page to drive the ox and mule teams that in the next two years hauled many a contract-load of lumber to the fort and developing mines and villages. Grundy's two young sons, Will and Jeff, often accompanied Page on these trips.[19] Grundy Ake may not have considered Sonoita Valley improved by the presence of his hell-raising nephew or some of his nephew's belligerent gang, but Bill was family and the Akes tolerated him in the troubled months ahead.

Filibuster Robert Phillips soon married Mary Ake's niece, America. He took her to Tucson where they opened "the Astor House of the place," a crude hotel which, according to occasional patron Samuel Heintzelman, was redeemed only by America's superb "chicken fixin's."[20] Other men who had come with John Page also took advantage of work opportunities in the vicinity. Some, however, remained footloose and nursed an unsatiated desire to avenge the killing of Crabb and his party.[21]

Distrust and resentment seethed on both sides of the border long after the Crabb affair. This posed a problem for Americans settling in the beautiful Sonoita and Santa Cruz valleys, inasmuch as the bulk of their labor force and the majority of the several hundred non-Indian inhabitants of the Gadsden Purchase were Mexican by birth and culture. Frequent harrassment by hostile Apaches added to the continuing unrest and kept settlers apprehensive. Charles D. Poston, manager of the Tubac-based Sonora Exploring & Mining Company, described the region in 1857 as "little better than a field of guerrilla warfare, robbery and plunder . . . a state of anarchy [where] . . . every man goes armed to the teeth."[22]

The Penningtons, newly arrived in 1857, saw an example of this almost at once. A Mexican pack train of about forty-five mules clopped southward past their camp on June 27 after delivering a contract of flour or corn to Fort Buchanan. It belonged to Francisco Padrés, a Magdalena merchant who occasionally sent supplies for sale to American mines or the fort.[23] Following the returning train several minutes later, and keeping well behind it, came five rough-looking filibusters. At least two of them, men named Davis and Ward, had come from California with John Page and Bill Ake.[24]

The Mexicans crossed the international boundary at a large grove of black walnut trees near the present town of Nogales. The filibusters caught up to them within the next mile, shot and killed some of the packers, raced off with all Padrés' mules and leather packsaddles, and herded their booty north to a hiding place near Tucson.

Alarmed and irate settlers discovered the hideout and informed Major Enoch Steen, then commanding Fort Buchanan. These citizens, with an escort of soldiers dispatched by Steen, arrested Davis and Ward, but the other filibusters escaped. One or two of them made off toward California with some of the mules. Davis also escaped, but the posse jailed Ward in the fort guardhouse and returned most of the stolen property to Padrés. Such civil matters were strictly outside military jurisdiction. Since at this early date there were no authorized law officers within three hundred miles to whom he could take the prisoner, Steen soon released Ward.[25]

Outrage erupted at the commanding officer's act. Mine manager Charles D. Poston protested vehemently. The "robbers," he complained, "have again been turned loose upon the community . . . . We have no remedy but to follow the example so wide spread in the Union, and form a *Vigilance Committee* — contrary to all good morals, law, order and society." The more stable residents of the area, Poston continued, beseeched Congress to establish civil authority and "avert this unhappy alternative."[26] However, territorial law was still seven years in Arizona's future. In the long violence-filled interim, many a settler felt obliged to deal with intolerable situations himself. John Page undoubtedly felt that way two years later when he participated in the vigilante actions that became known as the "Sonoita Murders."

Larcena's slow convalescence from mountain fever continued as the furor over the pack-train incident gradually subsided. While he waited for an opportunity to continue to California, Elias Pennington obtained a contract from Fort Buchanan's quartermaster to furnish hay for the army horse herd. He and Larcena's older brothers cut the tall wild grass that flourished on the hillsides and mesas near the valley, loaded it into their ox-drawn wagons, and hauled it to the fort. Unfortunately, however, the quartermaster did not pay them. He was temporarily out of funds. The long, hot days of summer passed, cooler breezes signaled the approach of fall, but each time Elias rode to Fort Buchanan, he came away empty-handed from the quartermaster's office.[27]

As the Penningtons lingered by Sonoita Creek, waiting for the money, disaster suddenly struck them and their neighbors. In early October, 1857, a large band of Apaches approached boldly within eight hundred yards of Fort Buchanan. They stayed there for some time, then swept suddenly and rapidly through Sonoita Valley, stealing all the livestock within eight miles of the post. The Penningtons and other settlers were left afoot, virtually unable to get about and earn a living, and wondering fearfully when the Indians would strike again.[28]

Hard times and great distress plagued the Penningtons and other Sonoita Valley settlers after the theft of their livestock. It became evident that being near Fort Buchanan was worse than having no military protection at all. The post itself was a magnet for Apaches. They raided that vicinity as persistently as vultures flock to carrion. They were said to have stolen an incalculable amount of property during this period, and they grew bolder. In December, a large party of them clashed with twenty of the army's mounted riflemen close to the fort.[29]

The desperate circumstances that had fallen upon Larcena and her family sorely tried her natural optimism and religious faith. The settlers themselves described their grim situation:

> . . . the citizens generally have lost the greater portion of their stock; some of them all. Many lives have been lost. It is unsafe to leave familes [sic] without able bodied men to protect them, unsafe to herd cattle, unsafe to work in the field, unsafe to travel. Up to this time, the military have not followed and captured or killed a single indian [sic], or recovered a stolen animal. The Apaches have entire control, especially in the vicinity of Fort Buchanan, such a perfect contempt have they for U.S. Dragoons, and so exceedingly favorable is the locality for the indians [sic] peculiar mode of robbery and murder. That neighborhood is in fact entirely abandoned by citizens & of late the onslaught of the savages throughout this entire region has been so bold and apparently in such numbers, that those having families and living isolated, are in terror respecting

Hills and cultivated fields of Sonoita Valley below old Fort Buchanan. Below, Sonoita Creek watered the farms of William Wadsworth and Felix Grundy near the present-day town of Patagonia (both photos by author).

their safety, & would leave the country provided they had the means.[30]

It was this sort of adversity, however, that strengthened the resolve of the tiny band of white settlers and may have brought John Page and the Penningtons together. The plight of these devastated people also evoked the compassion of the fort's military personnel, who used army wagons and mules to transport "citizens living near Fort Buchanan and rendered helpless" by Apache theft of their livestock "to other points within the Territory where they thought themselves more secure."[31]

The Penningtons chose a new site where the Santa Cruz River flowed north across the Mexican border, about twenty-five miles south of Buchanan and a few miles east of the present town of Nogales. It was on a fertile, open plain of rich virgin soil and abundant grama grass,[32] but it was far removed from neighbors. "Never in all my wandering life have I seen a cabin erected in such a desolate place as the Pennington cabin on the upper Santa Cruz," wrote their fellow pioneer Charles D. Poston.[33]

Here the Penningtons laid up a house of adobe blocks, roofed in the usual fashion with branches, mud, and grass. Jack Pennington and a young farmer, D. A. Spencer, constructed a small stone dwelling close by. Both structures were fortress-like. Instead of windows in the walls, small holes provided for ventilation and for shooting at any attackers outside.[34] The new home was near a road which ran between Calabasas, a few miles northwest of it, and the Mexican town of Santa Cruz, a day's ride to the southeast.[35] Occasionally a passing traveler, Spanish-speaking more often than not, may have interrupted the Penningtons' seclusion.

Even in this area of relatively mild climate, freezing nights were common in winter. Frosts could be expected in November, cold rains in December, and snow in January. It was late for fall planting by the time the Penningtons made their move, and in any case, Elias had no horses, mules, or oxen to pull the plow. With

The Pennington stone house on the Santa Cruz River near the Mexican border.
Photo by Robert H. Forbes, 1913, taken from the southeast, showing defensive portholes (Arizona Historical Society).

the money for his hay contract Elias could have replaced some of his stolen animals, if he could have found any for sale, but Lieutenant David H. Hastings, the quartermaster at Fort Buchanan, still postponed payment.

It must have been a time of bare subsistence for Larcena and her family. Fortunately, they had ample water and firewood and a roof over their heads. They may have had a sack of Mexican beans and a little dried corn or squash harvested from their former camp on Sonoita Creek. But there were thirteen mouths to feed. Elias, James, and Jack hiked over the plain hunting game. Guajalote [Turkey] Wash lay a short distance north of their home.[36] The name suggests that those delicious wild birds were plentiful there. Deer, rabbits, and squirrel abounded, if they could be caught. There was little the Penningtons could do until spring but eke out an existence and try to keep up their spirits.

Elias was not the only settler waiting for payment from the quartermaster. At least fifty-four others met with him and his son James at Tubac late in February, 1858, to discuss what might be done about their grievances. The group was largely Anglo-American, although a few Mexican-Americans joined them. Charles D. Poston and trader Edward Dunbar were its leaders. The assembly drew up a petition to Congress, and designated Dunbar to take it to Washington.

Even if these settlers phrased their complaints for utmost effect, it can hardly be doubted that most of them were experiencing severe hardship as well as anxiety for their dependents. Larcena's father made this point, as he signed the petition, by adding after his name, " . . . and twelve children." The following statements from the petition illustrate the injustice and desperation that he and the other petitioners felt:

> Harrassed [sic] without by fiendish indians [sic], poverty stares your memorialists in the face from within. Robbed of their animals to an extent that renders it difficult to move from place to place, many of them destitute [sic] of arms, crippled in means to carry on their farms or other occupations, the nec-

essaries of life scarce and high and not to be obtained on credit, they are totally prostrated. . . .[37]

These worried, angry men castigated Lieutenant Hastings and the New Mexico military system in general. They pointed out that most local residents had worked one way or another for the quartermaster, often paying expenses out of their own slim purses in anticipation of fair reimbursement. "Furnishing supplies and laboring for the government was in fact, the [immigrants'] first & only resource," they asserted in their petition.[38] They had waited months for their money and still no payment was in sight.

They accused Hastings of willful, self-serving procrastination at their expense. They said they had asked him, since he could not pay them cash, to give receipts for work done or supplies delivered, but he had refused to do so. Now he was preparing to move to Santa Fe, and the settlers had been informed that his debts to them were those of a private individual rather than direct obligations of the government. In that case, they faced the "tedious, *ruinous* [sic] process" of filing claims at Washington or of following the quartermaster to Santa Fe and pressing civil suits before he left New Mexico. Hastings had caused them more grief, the settlers asserted, than had the thefts and murders of the Indians.[39]

To be fair to Hastings, it should be mentioned that cash was then scarce in the Gadsden Purchase. Quartermasters at remote posts did have difficulties with money supply, and no currency had reached Fort Buchanan from army department headquarters in Santa Fe for a long while. Any number of factors could have delayed its arrival; payment in the Department of New Mexico was irregular at best. Lieutenant Hastings apparently had even tried to obtain American money in Sonora, but without success. Gold coin, the usual medium of exchange, was what the settlers expected and wanted. Treasury or bank drafts were, for all practical purposes, useless to them. Such drafts could be cashed only at the issuing institution, located in some faraway large city and virtually impossible for these stricken contractors to reach.[40]

The quartermaster was in bad shape physically as well as financially. His horse had fallen on him during a pursuit of Apaches on October 7, perhaps immediately after their sweeping theft of all Sonoita Valley livestock. One of his legs had been badly hurt at that time and he never afterward returned to active duty.[41]

The suffering petitioners had little sympathy for Hastings' problems, however, and they were even less charitable about the military system in New Mexico, which they called a "degrading, disgraceful . . . despotism," ineffective, corrupt, imbecile, and marked by "drunkenness and debauchery." They asked Congress to remove the totally useless troops at Fort Buchanan and instead establish volunteer ranger companies paid by the government.[42]

Whether or not the petition influenced their departure, Major Enoch Steen left Fort Buchanan on leave in April, 1858, and in May, two companies of the garrison were transferred to California. No militia took their place, which left Captain Richard S. Ewell in command of the post with its manpower cut in half.[43]

Elias Pennington finally received the money for his hay contract at some unspecified date after he had signed the petition to Congress.[44] It helped relieve the extreme stringency of his family's situation. He replaced his stolen oxen and milk cow, plowed his farmland, planted, and prayed. Three of the acres that he put into cultivation apparently extended across the line into Mexico. Corn was his principal crop and it thrived in the rich soil.[45]

His wagons mobile once again, Elias—in partnership with his older son, James—commenced freighting as he had done in Texas. Freighters were in demand in the Gadsden Purchase. Frontier mines and sprouting settlements needed supplies, many of which had to be hauled in from distant places. In the next few years, Elias drove as far as the Yuma Crossing on the Colorado River to pick up goods which had arrived by riverboat. He delivered consignments to Tucson, Tubac, the Heintzelman Mine at Cerro Colorado—wherever they were destined.[46]

It may have been on a trip to the Colorado with his father and Jim in the summer of 1858 that Elias' second son, Jack, heard of Arizona's first gold discovery. Prospectors were rushing to the hilly site where flecks and nuggets of gold had been found near the Gila River about eighteen miles east of the Yuma Crossing. They called their boomtown "Gila City." Always responsive to the lure of adventure, and perhaps hopeful of contributing toward his family's finances, seventeen-year-old Jack went off to try his luck at the placers. He found, however, that the better ore was some distance from water and that dry-washing for gold required a great deal of effort for slight returns.[47]

While at Gila City, Jack acquired a "chum," Hank Smith, a German immigrant four years older than himself. As the bonanza at Gila City tapered off, the two of them went to work for the Butterfield Overland Mail Company, which that summer was preparing relay stations along its projected route through Arizona. Jack and Hank hauled hay for the horse herd at the "Desert" or "Forty-mile" station near Gila Bend, and each drew wages of eighty dollars a month in glittering gold coin.[48]

Larcena, her sisters, and the two younger boys were left to their own resources at the border farm while the Pennington men were away. It was never easy, but they were capable of looking after themselves. The older girls were continually anxious and aware of danger. They knew how to use guns, but never had occasion to fire their weapons in self-defense, although now and then they sighted a lurking Indian. The younger children seemed confident and unconcerned, and the Apaches did spare the Pennington family at this time. Those flourishing cornfields provided the Indians with grain, to which they helped themselves as they came and went on raids into Mexico.[49]

Larcena was once again strong and full of youthful vitality. Her days were filled with constant chores—preparing food for thirteen or more persons, milking, preserving, washing and mending old clothes, and making new ones. She and the other older sisters sewed all the family's garments by hand. They worked in the fields when their help was needed there. They spent much of their time outside in mild weather. Outdoor cooking was common practice in southern Arizona; it helped keep the houses cool. A pot of beans typically bubbled over the fire while cornbread baked in a Dutch oven topped with coals. Their meat, when they had any, was wild game or, occasionally, mutton. Elias might have obtained the latter by bartering with Grundy Ake, who kept a flock of sheep, or with the herders at the Gándara ranch near Calabasas.[50]

The family needed some way to keep meat, milk, and butter fresh. People in Texas had had springhouses, ingenious shelters in which water diverted from the creek coursed through a small wooden V-channel, filled a large wooden box, and ran out another channel at the other end into a horse trough outside. The shaded flowing water cooled food containers placed in the box. Outside the springhouse, livestock had a convenient place to drink. Here on the Santa Cruz River, however, the family may simply have sunk a weighted box in shallow water, placed their jars and crocks inside, and shaded them with a wet blanket or with branches from the large cottonwoods on the bank.

Every day, for at least a little while, Ellen or Larcena taught the youngsters to read and write. They used the traditional phonics method, to judge from a surviving scrap of handwriting practice painstakingly executed by their brother Green: "Bid him bide with us and dine. Bite a bit. . . . She has a mop. Why then mope?"[51] It was up to those Penningtons who had gone to school in Texas to see that the younger boys and girls did not grow up illiterate in this western wilderness.

There was little social life to relieve Larcena's daily routine, but hers was a strong, blithe spirit that wasted no time brooding over such unavoidable facts. The Penningtons had few English-speaking neighbors, and those lived long distances away.[52] John Page, if ever he came to the border farm to see Larcena, had a full day's ride to get there from Ake's place or the pinery, and another day's ride back. He could not have come often. Unless Larcena's large family was unlike any other, however, they entertained each other. They joked among themselves, teased, laughed, argued, grew excited or angry, sympathized, hugged, and wept together. They had never relied much on the companionship of others.

Once in a long while the whole family piled into a wagon and went visiting. It seems very likely that they journeyed to Tubac for the Fourth of July in 1858. As Phocion R. Way, a young Ohioan working at the Santa Rita Mine in the hills east of Tubac, wrote in his diary, "almost every white settler in the vicinity" was there for that important holiday.[53] Larcena and John Page may well have met there, and perhaps not for the first time.

Phocion Way worried about the outcome of the celebration. At such times, he reported, men tended to become inebriated and quarrelsome, shooting someone and "nearly always" terminating the festivities in tragedy. This time, however, although "a majority of them got a little tight . . . everything went off peaceably," and the settlers had "a merry time."[54]

Enough is known about that celebration and similar ones to reconstruct what must have taken place. Those early pioneers treated the Fourth as a grand occasion. The independence of the Unites States was still young and glorious, proudly cherished in the hearts of most Americans present in Tubac that day. Elias Pennington's generation had listened to firsthand accounts of patriotic sacrifice and were stirred by their parents' patriotic emotion. His own parents lived through the Revolutionary War and the War of 1812.

The Pennington wagon bursting with young women and children would certainly have attracted attention as it reached Tubac. Rarely did the American silver miners, soldiers, farmers, and ranchers who were there for the day see fair-haired, fair-skinned women in this region. Here were five shapely examples — Ellen, Larcena, Caroline, Ann, and Margaret — and three more pretty little sisters. One can picture Elias on the wagon seat, his sons riding alongside on horseback, the excited younger children craning their necks to see unaccustomed sights, and blond Larcena returning John Page's admiring glances with her usual shy dignity, her cheeks colored by the feelings stirring within her.

Some celebrants mingled in the welcome shade of cottonwoods on the broad river bank below the village. Others congregated a short distance uphill in the plaza of the old walled fort built by Spanish *soldados de cuera* a century earlier. The structures were abandoned by Mexican troops after the Gadsden Purchase and fell into decay, but many were now rebuilt and inhabited by employees of the Sonora Exploring & Mining Company.

Manager Charles D. Poston had brought the company's original crew and equipment to the deserted village in the fall of 1856. It was astonishing, Poston remarked, how quickly their mining activities attracted Mexican men and women looking for work, as well as American merchants, saloonkeepers, blacksmiths, and others who now served the community.[55] Phocion Way was impressed by Colonel Poston's very comfortable and convenient house in Tubac. He considered it the nicest dwelling he had seen west of San Antonio.[56]

The largest building in the village was a former barracks with a lookout tower at one corner. The mining company now used it as a storehouse. A dilapidated old church stood nearby. Way estimated Tubac's population that summer at one hundred fifty persons, about three-fourths of them Mexican.[57] These residents and perhaps half that many Fourth of July visitors crowded the village lanes and plaza. Greetings and sounds of celebration rose over the creak of wagons and clop of hooves.

The oppressive summer heat could not wilt the settlers' enthusiasm. They lifted perspiring faces to the occasional breezes that rippled a red, white, and blue flag hung on a tall post. Men inclined to oratory did their best to honor that revered emblem. Hurrahs and laughter followed the more soul-stirring or amusing comments. Some good voice in the crowd led the rest in wholehearted singing of patriotic songs. Smiling, chatting, sunbonneted women set out food they had brought to share, and hungry men heaped their tin plates.

A wildly cheered horse race is sure to have been one of the day's favorite events, with ebullient male spectators eagerly placing wagers on the outcome. Grundy Ake's young sons Will and Jeff may have stood beside Green and Will Pennington, watching the contest, the four of them longing for fast, powerful horses of their

Above, Tubac as it appeared in the early 1860s and probably much as it looked when the Penningtons celebrated the Fourth of July there. Left, Charles D. Poston (both sketches by J. Ross Browne, from *Adventures in the Apache Country*).

own, and heading, after the race was over, to a nearby lane where they could find out which of their common nags was the speediest.

A stir of dismay marred the afternoon's festivities when a dust-covered Mexican messenger from Tucson galloped into the village on an urgent errand. He was making a hundred-mile circuit to find and fetch Fort Buchanan's doctor, Lieutenant B. J. D. Irwin. A Mexican manservant had shot Tucson storekeeper Edward Miles twice in the breast, and Miles would soon die without expert surgery. The messenger did not find Irwin racing his renowned horse "Rascal" at Tubac that day, as might have been expected, and he soon rode on to Buchanan on the other side of the Santa Rita Mountains.[58]

The assorted Anglo-Americans at Tubac doubtless discussed this news with varying degrees of anger. They viewed such an assault by one of their kind upon another, which occurred with altogether too much frequency in Tucson, as a serious threat to peaceful settlement; but that a Mexican servant had attempted to kill the inoffensive Miles revived their barely suppressed resentments and prejudices. The incident was probably one more link in the chain of events that later landed John Page in jail.

FIVE: MURDERS
AND MARRIAGES

Not long after the 1858 Fourth of July celebration, Larcena's family moved into the old Gándara hacienda at Calabasas, a few miles distant from their farm.[1] It was the third of several places where the Penningtons dwelt between 1857 and 1870. They moved when danger from Apaches threatened seriously or when a particular location offered an economic advantage. Presumably Calabasas was a more convenient base than the remote farm for Elias Pennington's freighting. Elias worked other fields from time to time, but he retained his claim to the border farm, lived there again with his family in 1860, and in 1865 filed a homestead notice on it.[2]

The adobe Gándara ranch house — originally constructed in the 1770s as a small Jesuit church — was situated on a moderate bluff on the east side of the Santa Cruz River. A series of tenants preceded the Penningtons. Sonora's former governor Manuel Gándara, present owner of the building, had rented it a few years earlier to two Germans who tended his vast herds of goats and sheep. The Germans built an adobe addition to the old church, but Apaches drove them and their Mexican laborers away. Major Enoch Steen used the empty hacienda as a temporary residence when he established Camp Moore at Calabasas in November, 1856, but he vacated it when he moved the post to the head of Sonoita Creek in June, 1857, and renamed it Fort Buchanan. A U.S. Customs officer had occupied the hacienda since then and kept a small store there. He collected duties on Mexican merchandise coming across the border.[3]

The Penningtons shared the hacienda buildings with the Customs collector. They had to carry water up a steep path from the river, as there was no well on the bluff. Larcena's sister Jane described the house they lived in as built around a courtyard containing an *arrastra,* or grinding device long used by Mexican millers and miners. It consisted of a sunken, stone-paved circle enclosing a large flat boulder drilled through the center. A burro walking round and round outside the circle dragged the stone over kernels of corn or wheat, grinding them into meal or, at a mine, reducing ore.[4]

While the family stayed at the hacienda, Larcena's brother Jack returned to them, and his new friend, Hank Smith, arrived about the same time. One can imagine the many Penningtons sitting around in the courtyard overlooking the river, listening to the youths tell of their recent escape from Indians. Larcena must have been as round-eyed as her little brothers and sisters at the adventure the two friends related.

He and Jack, Hank said, were working at the Overland Mail station near present-day Gila Bend, when they learned that wild cattle were roaming to the east beside the Gila River. On foot, since they had no horses, they set out to find the herd and bring back fresh beef. Jesse Sutton, the station keeper, allowed his fourteen-year-old son, Abe, to go with them. After following the river about twenty miles, the boys found the cattle and shot four of them. They made a raft, loaded the beef, and started floating it back to the station, Jack and young Sutton riding the raft while Hank Smith walked along the brushy bank. Indians suddenly attacked, sending an arrow through Abe's left wrist. He and Jack dived into the river. A blast from Hank's gun surprised and frightened their assailants, who had not noticed anyone in the bushes. Leaving the boys, the Indians dashed after the meat-laden raft drifting downstream. They packed off all of its cargo they could carry, but the three young hunters made it back to the station with four quarters of beef.[5]

Jack's friend Hank soon accepted the enticing pay of five dollars a day from the Calabasas customs house officer to work a risky job: endangered by roving Apaches and some of his more desperate countrymen, Hank rode the line—the international boundary—on the lookout for smugglers trying to dodge the high duties that United States Customs agents collected on goods coming in from Mexico.[6] Sonora was often the only source of supplies for impoverished Americans struggling to survive, and the prohibitive tax created an additional hardship for them. Outspoken Charles Poston criticized the tariff and the Customs officials at Calabasas. "God send that we had been left alone with the Apaches," he declared bitterly. "We should have been a thousand times better off in every respect."[7]

What Jack Pennington did while Hank Smith rode the line that winter can be surmised. He probably helped his father. He undoubtedly spent a good deal of time at Grundy Ake's farm, renewing his acquaintance with John Page and with Grundy's wild and worthless nephew Bill Ake. That association later led Larcena's young brother into serious trouble.

Page, meanwhile, was hauling consignments of lumber for Grundy, who had contracted to deliver several loads to the Arivaca mines that fall.[8] Samuel P. Heintzelman, president of the Sonora Exploring & Mining Company and director of operations at Arivaca and nearby Cerro Colorado, noted in his diary the coming and going of Ake's teams. On November 28, 1858, he wrote that three of Ake's wagons arrived with "very fine vigas."[9] The vigas were tree trunks, smoothed and sawed into appropriate lengths for roof beams. John Page is likely to have driven one of the wagons that Heintzelman mentioned. He may even have cut the vigas, for he had entered a partnership, at some undetermined time before the spring of 1859, in a sawmill at the Santa Rita Mountains pinery.[10]

Page's partners in the enterprise were Alf Scott, Joe Ashworth, Jim Cotton, George Fulton and William Randall. Some or all of these men had come with him from California. Grundy Ake's boy Jeff knew them all. Jeff visited the sawmill and later described

John Parker "Jack" Pennington (Marshall L. Pennington).

Hank Smith (Panhandle-Plains Historical Museum).

how they operated the sawpit: two men, one in the pit and another on top, would saw tree trunks into boards, leaving a few inches at one end joined as a tie.[11] The work was hard and heavy, but there was ample demand for their products.

• •

In addition to the 1858 Fourth of July at Tubac, there were other well-attended events which may have brought John Page and Larcena Pennington together. Two of these were mentioned briefly in the first issues of the *Weekly Arizonian,* Arizona's earliest newspaper, which began publishing from Tubac on March 3, 1859.

The first was the wedding of Grundy and Mary Ake's eighteen-year-old daughter, Annie, to farmer George P. Davis. The marriage was one of the earliest between Anglo-Americans in Arizona. A justice of the peace performed the ceremony in Tucson about the first of March.[12] Three or four days later, wagons full of guests from near and far poured in to the "Ake mansion" on Sonoita Creek for the wedding feast. Larcena and her family may have been among them. John Page and Jack Pennington, both friends of the Akes, are very likely to have been there. Grundy's brash nephew Bill certainly made his presence remembered.

It was a night for hard-working, weary settlers to forget their problems and have some fun and good food. Charles Poston, one of the guests, described it. The outdoor tables held "all the sumptuous dishes of the Castilian menu," many of them spiced with red or green chiles. Civilian men and soldiers stashed their demijohns of whiskey on opposite sides of the woodpile and generally hung around those areas. Women crowded into the house to admire Annie's wedding finery, which included a new-fangled corset she had sent for. Tipsy Bill Ake caught a glimpse of his Aunt Mary out on the back porch, Poston said, putting her foot on Annie's torso and pulling hard on the corset strings. Bill shouted out for all to hear, "That's right, marm cinch her till she sneezes, and then trot her out to be married."[13]

Still another opportunity for Larcena and John Page to see each other occurred when the Akes held a community worship service six weeks later at their farm.[14] Elias Pennington, a devout believer, still clung to his membership certificate from the little Honey Grove Baptist Church in the hope of someday joining another congregation. It is unlikely that he and his family had attended a religious service in the four years since they had left Texas. They may well have undertaken the two- or three-day trip required to get to the Ake farm and back, joining other settlers who camped out there the night before the meeting.

Like Elias, Mary Ake was Baptist. Grundy was Catholic, but he was willing to host a spiritual gathering and hear a sermon.[15] The itinerant preacher who conducted the service was Methodist, the Reverend Mr. Tuthill, the first protestant missionary known to have ventured into the Gadsden Purchase.[16] The day dawned unusually cold and frosty but the religion-hungry pioneers shivering in the farmyard must have endured it gratefully.

The infant newspaper that announced these happenings, Tubac's *Weekly Arizonian,* soon had more than a normal significance to the Pennington family. It was, of course, a Godsend to such settlers, virtually isolated on the frontier and out of touch with news of the nation and the world. Before its publication, they had heard only infrequent, outdated accounts from letters or from travelers' tales. Literate immigrants were constantly hungry for fresh reading material. Larcena and her family had doubtless re-read their old school books and their Bible until they knew each word by heart. It was a great day, therefore, when the March 3, 1859, issue rolled off the little hand-operated press at Tubac.

The *Arizonian* — its name reflecting the settlers' increasing use of the name "Arizona" for the region — consisted of four pages of advertisements, humor and news. The Penningtons, if Elias brought home a copy of that first issue for them to read, learned a good deal of what had been going on around them in the Sonoita and Santa Cruz Valleys. Military control of Indian depredations was of paramount interest. Lieutenant Colonel Isaac Reeve would soon assume command at Fort Buchanan; Apaches had driven off all of Grundy Ake's cattle, but Ake and his new son-in-law had recovered them by immediate pursuit; Apaches

The Gándara hacienda at Calabasas, used in 1858 as a U.S. Customs house and also the temporary home of the thirteen Penningtons. Photo by Robert H. Forbes, 1913 (Arizona Historical Society).

had killed a cow belonging to William Wadsworth; two Pinal Apache chiefs had come into the post under a flag of truce to arrange a peace meeting with Captain Ewell.[17]

Then, to their undoubted dismay, Larcena and her family read their own brother Jack's name in the May 19th issue. The *Arizonian* had recently reported a vicious murder that occurred near Calabasas. As a consequence of the killing, seven "lawless men" committed what editor Edward Cross termed "cruel and unjustifiable reprisals." Cross, fresh from Ohio, rejected the notion that vigilantes or "regulators" were necessary in the absence of law officers on this remote, sparsely populated frontier.[18] He dubbed the seven men "the Sonoita Murderers." Among them were Jack Pennington, Bill Ake, and John Page. Influential citizens demanded their arrest. A furious manhunt began.[19]

The first link in the chain of events that made fugitives of Larcena's eighteen-year-old brother and her future husband was forged on May 6, 1859, when two Sonoran farm laborers swung an ax blade into rancher Greenbury Byrd's skull as he slept in his house near Calabasas. Leaving Byrd to die, the killers fled to Mexico with the victim's horses. The *Arizonian* portrayed Byrd as "a quiet, good-natured, respectable young man" who had immigrated a year and a half earlier from Texas and had treated his employees kindly. "It was a cold-blooded murder," raged the little newspaper, "and if the perpetrators could be found, they would receive no mercy from the people of this neighborhood."[20]

It was not the first killing of that sort in troubled southern Arizona, nor would it be the last. The previous fall, a similar but even more horrible tale of mayhem and murder had shocked every settlement in Arizona. The Butterfield Overland Mail Company had nearly completed building the relay stations on its southern route. Silas St. John and three other American employees, assisted by three Mexican laborers, were finishing a rock-walled house and corral at Dragoon Springs. At midnight on September 8, 1858, while the Americans slept, the laborers attacked them with axes. St. John, alone in one of the small rooms, awakened to terrifying sounds outside just before the Mexicans entered to kill him. Horribly wounded, he still fought them off, and they fled. With his injured right hand he somehow managed to rig a tourniquet to stop the blood gushing from his severed left arm and bound other deep gashes on his body.[21]

Four days later, American travelers found Silas St. John still alive, his companions all frightfully killed. The lone survivor was half crazed with pain and thirst, unable to speak. His rescuers gave him water and first aid and sent a man galloping to Fort Buchanan for Dr. Irwin. Although the surgeon came with all possible speed, it was the ninth day after the attack when he arrived at Dragoon Station. Irwin amputated what was left of St. John's putrifying left arm, and took him by wagon to Fort Buchanan, where he recuperated.[22] That sickening story undoubtedly aggravated the anti-Mexican sentiment that had smoldered within Bill Ake, John Page, and their filibuster friends ever since Sonorans massacred Henry Crabb's party at Caborca. It is not surprising, therefore, that Ake, Page, and company took a personal interest in Greenbury Byrd's murder.

The motive for the slaying appeared to be revenge. A few days earlier, the two killers and other Sonorans were working for manager George D. Mercer at Reventon ranch north of Tubac. These laborers did something—reports were not specific about what they did—that Mercer felt deserved punishment. He ordered them whipped and their hair cropped. As Colonel Reeve at Fort Buchanan later wrote, "in the latter ceremony some slight mutilation or cutting of the scalp *happened* [sic]."[23] Mercer denied rumors of scalping, and offered satisfaction to anyone who disapproved his disciplinary methods.[24]

Greenbury Byrd witnessed the punishment, whether or not he participated in it. In addition, he was said to have owed wages to the two laborers who hacked him to death while his partner was away in Tucson getting money to pay them.[25] Byrd's gory killing was a fresh jolt for the residents of the Sonoita and Santa Cruz Valleys. "Much feeling has been caused among the Americans against the native residents on account of this wanton murder," the *Sacramento Union* reported.[26]

Even had the killers not escaped to Sonora, there were no lawmen on hand to bring them to justice. Therefore, while other settlers verbalized their frustration, six angry men and a boy took swift action: hot-headed Bill Ake, John Page, Page's sawmill partner Alf Scott, one Sam Anderson, two others named Bolt and Brown, and young Jack Pennington. Reports point to Bill Ake as the prime instigator among the seven. Exactly what part John Page played as the drama unfolded is unknown. Jack Pennington was guilty of little, apparently, except being with the vigilante group.

The "self-constituted regulators," said the Arizonian, rode through Sonoita Valley with the purpose of compelling "every Mexican employed upon the different ranches to leave, under penalty of extermination for disobedience."[27] Their acts of retribution for Byrd's murder brought down on them the immediate condemnation of the newspaper's vocal editor, Edward Cross, and the very citizens who earlier predicted with despair the necessity for a vigilance committee.

Seven farms and ranches were, by May, 1859, laid out in the wild and lovely little valley of Sonoita Creek. John Page and his companions had taken the narrow road from Calabasas toward Fort Buchanan, through a wide gap in the Santa Rita foothills, past an ancient peach orchard of Spanish origin. They came first to the farm of William Finley and then to fields that Elias Pennington cultivated while his family lived at the Gándara hacienda. If they found and harassed Mexican laborers at either place, it was not reported. At the third farm—160 acres of good land and timber belonging to B. C. Marshall—Mexican laborers tended some of the best crops in the region. Here the regulators' scare tactics sent workers scurrying toward the border and aroused farmer Marshall's wrath.[28]

The seven determined Americans continued upstream, chasing panic-stricken Mexicans wherever they found them. Joe Ashworth's place lay beyond Marshall's. Ashworth had come from California with the filibusters and was another of John Page's sawmill partners.[29] Above his farm was Johnny Ward's ranch and beyond that were Grundy Ake's fields, tilled by Sonoran farmhands.

Thomas Thompson's house and vegetable plots adjoined Ake's farm, and a short distance up the creek, only four miles from Fort Buchanan, lay William Wadsworth's well-watered, productive acres. Wadsworth had reaped a $5000 barley crop the previous year. He also kept a cattle herd, tended by Mexican vaqueros, and furnished the fort with beef.[30] Dozens of terrified farm laborers fled these farms and ranches in the wake of the seven rampaging men.

The climax came on Sunday, May 9th, when the vigilantes charged into a mescal distillery near Grundy Ake's ranch where a number of Mexicans and Yaqui Indians were peacefully working. For the first time, the vigilantes encountered resistance. According to one of the Mexicans, these workers ran when they saw the vigilantes coming, but the Americans fired on them, and they fought back to defend themselves. The foreman or owner of the *destilería,* Manuel Carea, escaped harm by crawling into an oven ordinarily used for roasting mescal. In the ensuing skirmish, one or more of the angry avengers shot and killed three Mexicans and one Yaqui and mortally wounded another Mexican. One of the regulators was "slightly injured with a lance thrust."[31]

Reventon ranch manager George Mercer was at the distillery when the shootings occurred. His presence implicated him as one of the "gang," but he hastened to explain it otherwise. He said that someone, foreseeing violence, asked him to precede the vigilantes to the distillery to save the life of a Mexican boy there. Mercer swore he had not left his wagon or fired a gun. Instead, he said, he begged the vigilantes "to desist until the voice of the people should decide what punishment was due to the Mexican offenders in our country."[32]

Which of the seven regulators fired the deadly shots will probably never be known. Circumstantial evidence and past record point to Bill Ake and the man named Brown. The entire avenging gang, however, sobered by the killings, realized they had gone too far. They decided to scatter and hide out until any furor of community disapproval had dissipated. Southern Arizona citizens determined to have law and order, especially those who had lost their laborers, were predictably outraged by the affair.

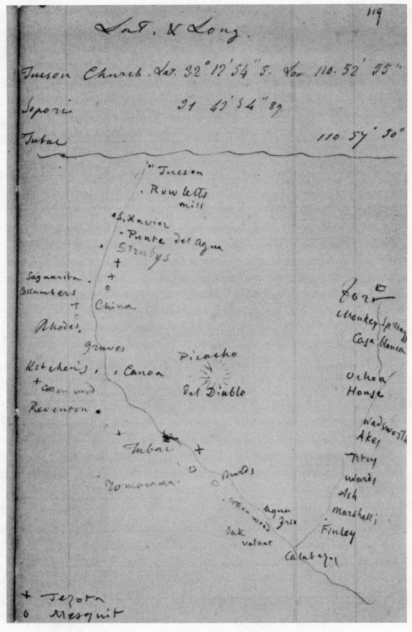

A map of the Sonoita and Santa Cruz river valleys drawn by mining engineer F. Biertu in 1861 (Henry E. Huntington Library, San Marino, California).

Colonel Isaac Reeve's first inkling of the event was when William Wadsworth sent a message to Fort Buchanan that some "difficulty" had occurred between Americans and Mexicans a few miles below the post. Laborers tending Wadsworth's beef herd had been driven off and the cattle were scattering through the hills. Reeve sent four mounted men to help round them up. An hour or two later, as he reported to headquarters, he learned that the difficulty "consisted in nothing less than the brutal attack, without provocation, upon some Mexicans, by a band of American Murderers [sic], who had sworn to drive all the Mexicans out of . . . Arizona."[33]

Reeve recalled Lieutenant Cooke from a trip he had begun to Sonora, fearing that reaction there might cause him injury. The Colonel also sent Captain Ewell galloping down the valley with thirty dragoons to restore peace. A large delegation of citizens descended on Fort Buchanan the next day. The Colonel promised them he would hold any of the outlaws they might deliver to him until such time as the culprits could be taken to court at Mesilla.[34]

In his report to Department of New Mexico headquarters, Colonel Reeve described John H. Page, William Ake, and Samuel Anderson as leaders of the group, "considered much the worst men." Ake, Reeve wrote, was "the most notorious and worst of all." Citizens quickly cornered two of the regulators, but sent word to the fort that they needed assistance to bring them in. Reeve dispatched six soldiers, who accomplished the mission. Another of the fugitives was hauled in the next day. Reeve had these three vigilantes — John Page, Alf Scott, and Bolt — chained and locked up at the fort. Still at large were Bill Ake, Sam Anderson, Brown, and Jack Pennington.[35]

Editor Edward Cross at Tubac agreed with Reeve's assessment of Ake. "Bill Ake is a young man, but has committed several murders," he wrote.[36] Cross filled a whole page of the May 19, 1859, *Weekly Arizonian* with news of the "cowardly, cruel and totally unwarranted" attack on peaceful workers and sent bulletins to out-of-state newspapers. An endorsement with the names of sixty-four local settlers who had met to protest the vigilantes' acts appeared after his editorial.[37]

Americans felt just indignation, Cross declared, that "a band of men claiming ordinary decency, should constitute themselves outlaws, under pretence of avenging the murder of an American citizen."[38] His account was printed both in English and Spanish, for he felt economic as well as moral pressure to reassure Mexicans on both sides of the border that Americans would not tolerate such lawless conduct. Producers were worried. Since the attack on the distillery, a hundred workers had left the Cerro Colorado mines west of Tubac; the Patagonia mine, southeast of the fort, was deserted; peon labor had abandoned employers on farms and ranches — all translating into lost income. There was also the fear of Mexican retaliation on Americans traveling in Sonora.[39]

The New York *Daily Tribune* published an embellished report which reflected Edward Cross' sentiments. It described the vigilantes as a "gang of lawless characters, mostly refugees from California." It told of the consternation and flight of the Mexican population and the "intense excitement" generated in northern Sonora. Men in Mexican frontier towns had armed themselves and prepared to repel an invasion, "every fugitive from the American side bringing some horrid version of the murderous intention of the Americans, who it was declared intended to invade Sonora and exterminate the people."[40]

These weeks were undoubtedly disturbing and painful for the Penningtons, especially for Larcena, if she and John Page already loved each other. Elias and James Pennington and Grundy Ake were steady, peace-loving men, but their names were not among the sixty-four that followed Cross' protest in the *Arizonian*. It is not likely that they approved the vigilantes' conduct, but, as Cross admitted, there were some settlers sympathetic toward the gang.[41]

A citizens' committee asked Colonel Reeve to turn the arrested vigilantes over to them, but, fearing a mock trial, the commanding officer declined.[42] His firm refusal may have saved John Page from a lynching.

Jack Pennington was still a fugitive from the manhunt comb-
ing the Sonoita and Santa Cruz valleys when his sister Caroline
married on May 12, 1859. She was the first of the Pennington
girls to do so.[43] Caroline was eighteen, two years younger than
Larcena. Her bridegroom was farmer Charles Burr, thirty-five, a
native of Virginia who had been in Arizona since 1857.[44] Only
three weeks before the marriage he fought a duel with Sonoita
Valley saloonkeeper Paddy Graydon over some unknown "difficulty." Graydon, a discharged soldier, had opened his "International Boundary Hotel" between Wadsworth's farm and the fort
within the past year. It was a popular place with military and
civilian men alike. Wadsworth and Grundy Ake frequently met
there for drinks and cards, and the former California filibusters, of
whom Burr may have been one, made it their headquarters.
Rough and tough as many of his customers were, Graydon was
capable of controlling them.[45] He and Burr exchanged shots without harming each other, according to the *Arizonian,* and friends
"satisfactorily adjusted" their disagreement afterward.[46]

Anxiety about her brother, and perhaps about John Page as
well, must have hung like a dark cloud over Caroline's wedding.
Jack may have been hiding out at the pinery where Page's sawpit
was located. Colonel Reeve learned on the night of May 16 that
two of the regulators had taken refuge there, and he sent sixteen
dragoons into the Santa Rita Mountains to apprehend them. The
soldiers brought back only one — Sam Anderson, whom Edward
Cross described as "a cowardly, sneaking fellow, a great liar, a
carpenter by trade, [with] a bad scar across his face."[47] The ever-
energetic Paddy Graydon and two other civilians, accompanied by
soldiers from the fort, continued to hunt for Ake, Pennington, and
Brown.[48]

Just how long Larcena's brother eluded the searchers is unknown. He was still at large on May 19 when an article in the
Arizonian showed some softening of attitude toward him. Jack
was very young, editor Cross stated, "evidently led into the affair
by his older associates, and as he did not take an active part in the
affray, he will probably only be required to give his evidence."[49]

Apparently John Page, the other vigilantes already arrested, and witnesses questioned by Reeve cleared Jack of serious wrongdoing. Community respect and sympathy for the Pennington family may also have worked in Jack's favor.

Bill Ake still roamed loose despite the hundred dollars offered for bringing him in. There were rumors that he and his two fine horses had been seen in the vicinity since the arrest of Page, Scott, and Bolt. "Ake may yet be in the country, harbored and assisted by some of his few sympathisers [sic]," Cross reported to his readers. "If he appears any where in the settlements he should be taken if possible."[50] Farmer B. C. Marshall joined Paddy Graydon and others in pursuing Bill Ake as far as Tucson, but they did not catch him. Someone saw him shortly afterward near Fort Yuma, heading west. That news brought sighs of relief throughout Sonoita Valley, but the manhunt continued.

The *Arizonian* of May 26 reported under the headline "The Sonoita Murderers" that in addition to Ake, two vigilantes, "one of whom is said to have shot the wounded Mexican now at Fort Buchanan," had not yet been arrested.[51] The reference was to Jack Pennington and Brown. It had already been determined that Jack had done no shooting. That left Brown, and possibly Bill Ake, as the men likely to have fired the fatal shots at the distillery.

As if symbolic of the recent violence and emotional upheaval, "great fires" raged in the Santa Rita Mountains during the last of May, flaring at times even on the highest peaks. Lumbermen in timber areas saw several grizzly bears, driven from their usual haunts. Larcena and her family marveled at the sight, which Edward Cross described:

> At night the scene was grand—a vast illumination of the mighty hills—the fire in circles, in long lines, in scattered patches, and glowing in the distant horizon like the watch-fires of a great army. The entire western slope of the mountains has been burned over, and the fires are now working over and around to the eastern side, making at night a strange and beautiful spectacle.[52]

Meanwhile, Page, Scott, Bolt, and Anderson languished "in irons" at the fort, waiting to be taken three hundred miles to the Rio Grande to Mesilla, county seat of New Mexico's Dona Ana County. Colonel Isaac Reeve published a request for witnesses to their misdeeds.[53] Early in June the *Arizonian* announced that there was sufficient evidence to convict the four of murder. They would be sent to Mesilla for trial immediately, under heavy guard. "We are well rid of a desperate and dangerous gang of men who, if they do not escape, and they receive due justice, will trouble this country nor any other, but a short time longer," predicted the newspaper.[54]

"Nor any other" had the sound of doom, a hanging, but those hoping for a quick and permanent end to the four prisoners were soon disappointed to learn that Judge Boone at Albuquerque had decided not to hold court at Mesilla until November. The *Arizonian* complained that the judge's decision, while convenient for him, was improper and unjust. Judge Boone should at least try the "Sonoita Murderers," claimed editor Cross, in order to sustain the efforts of the law-abiding citizens of Arizona.[55]

Preparations for the murder trial moved ahead in spite of the judge's announcement. A deputy sheriff from Tucson came to Sonoita Valley about June 20th to summon witnesses, including Jack Pennington, B. C. Marshall, Paddy Graydon, George Mercer, and "many Mexicans . . . that were present at the massacre." "The trial ought to take place as soon as possible," Cross told his readers, "so that the witnesses from this [section] will not be obliged to make but one journey."[56]

Some or all of these witnesses may have accompanied the contingent of guards and vigilantes which Colonel Reeve sent to Mesilla, ignoring advice that the county jail there was small, dirty, "crammed full of murderers, horse thieves, common thieves, and vagabonds," and incapable of safely keeping the four "assassins."[57] If John Page, Alf Scott, Sam Anderson, and Bolt were put in that miniature hell, they avoided weeks or months of incarceration there by hiring a clever Mesilla lawyer, Samuel W. Cozzens.

"Good name that for a lawyer," quipped Cozzens' friend Ned McGowan, adding, "Sam is a great stickler for that writ of right, the habeas corpus—always has one at hand—carries it in his hat."[58] The attorney was an intelligent and imaginative man who later became renowned as an author.[59] He filed his writ of habeas corpus, which forced an inquiry into sufficient cause. Probate Judge Raphael Ruelas of Mesilla held the preliminary hearing on July 6. After Cozzens' arguments and questioning of witnesses, the judge discharged the vigilantes. There was no trial, no conviction for murder. Ruelas, however, fined the four an aggregate sum of $900. The prisoners scraped up $100 on account and were free to leave.[60]

The law-abiding citizens of the Sonoita and Santa Cruz Valleys had to admit that due process had been followed in the case of the "Sonoita Murderers," however little they may have liked Judge Ruelas' decision. With Bill Ake temporarily out of the country, things quieted down for a while. Editor Edward Cross, who had relentlessly hounded the vigilantes in the columns of his newspaper, sold the *Arizonian* to Sylvester Mowry and turned his attention to mining.[61] Jack Pennington and his friend Hank Smith hired on as cowboys for William Wadsworth.[62] John Page and Alf Scott resumed work at their sawmill, whatever was left of it after the forest fires.

Larcena and the Pennington family remained at Calabasas through September, 1859. Samuel Hughes, a Tucson butcher substituting as stagecoach driver for one trip that month, stopped on his way to Fort Buchanan and got a drink of milk from them. In his opinion, Pennington had excellent cows.[63]

The summer had been a good one for Larcena's father and other Sonoita Valley farmers even though they had lost their Mexican farmhands for a time. Their laborers slowly came back from Sonora. In August the farmers harvested wheat and barley. They replanted with corn, hoping to reap an excellent crop before winter. Water was plentiful; there were heavy rains, and the Santa Cruz River and Sonoita Creek were running bank to bank. Several other farming families were en route to the valley, it was rumored. Various mines, also, were developing well. The future looked bright, and the steady growth of population in southern Arizona seemed assured.[64]

Thievery and violence, however, continued to threaten the settlers' peace and security. In late June, a band of Mexicans had attacked and mortally wounded Santa Cruz Valley rancher John Ware, injuring his partner as well. Incensed once again by this latest incident, the citizens of Tubac and representatives from the Santa Rita and Sópori mines, Reventon ranch, and Sonoita Valley met and elected James Caruthers justice of the peace and N. Van Alstine constable. They tried a thief and sentenced him to fifteen lashes, which the new constable laid on in "prompt and effective manner."[65]

When Ware died of his wounds despite a doctor's care, the citizens held another meeting on September 5 and passed a resolution: ". . . in future, until establishment of law and courts among us, we will organize temporary courts, and administer justice to murderers, horse thieves, and other criminals, ourselves."[66] At that meeting, they elected Edward G. Page constable, instead of or in addition to Van Alstine.

Edward Page had worked at the Salero Mine a year earlier and in August, 1859, had become the proprietor of the "Arizona House" in Tubac.[67] The presence of two men with the same surname in the same small place at the same time suggests a possible relationship between them. The new constable may have been a brother or cousin of John H. Page.

In October, a month after his election, Constable Page was put to work after another gruesome ax murder. Jack Pennington's friend Hank Smith and rancher Sam Rogers discovered the body of Sam's brother at the Rogers' house between Tubac and Calabasas. According to the *Weekly Arizonian* of October 20, the Rogers brothers had come to Arizona from Texas with Greenbury Byrd, who had been killed in the same fashion.[68] John Rogers was "lying on his bunk with his head split open with an ax, the ax still lying on his body," Hank Smith said.[69] The killers had also stolen horses and mules.

Following telltale tracks, Hank and Sam determined that two Mexicans known around Tubac were guilty of these crimes.[70] An enraged Sam Rogers went to Constable Edward Page. Page and Rogers then sought out another Tubac Mexican who was a known associate of the murderers and induced him to go with them by telling him that his friends wanted to see him. A few miles out of town, the man must have grown suspicious, for he refused to lead them further.

Rogers and Page then put nine bullets in the Mexican, according to one account, and cut off his ears. These trophies Rogers carried back to Tubac. In addition, claimed an indignant citizen, they took everything valuable they found on the Mexican's body.[71] "Sam Rogers nearly went crazy," Hank Smith recalled, "and swore that he would kill a Mexican for every hair on John's head." The last time Smith saw him, "he had a big sombrero full of Mexican ears and he said he was not done yet."[72]

The unhappy citizens of Tubac met again and ruled that future horse thieves would be hung by the neck.[73] When they attempted to indict Edward G. Page and Sam Rogers for murdering the Mexican, the two "suddenly decamped for California."[74]

As the turbulent year of 1859 drew to an end, the Pennington family left the Gándara hacienda and moved back to their border farm. Jim Pennington staked out his own claim of 160 acres on the Santa Cruz River on December 1.[75] And some, if not all, of the Penningtons probably accompanied Larcena to Tucson for her marriage to John Page on Christmas Eve.[76]

Whatever inner turmoil, anguish, and doubts the violence of that year had caused Larcena, she had resolved them in Page's favor and put them behind her. The marriage suggests that Page, rugged though he may have been, was not the utter villain his critics portrayed. Larcena, a respectable young woman of strong religious faith, would not have married such a man, nor would Elias Pennington have consented. As it turned out, Page lived less than fourteen months after the wedding.

Part II: Lean and Hard and Hungry

Why were they able to maintain it, decade after decade? Because the pioneer fringe, the cutting edge, remained lean and hard and hungry. Because they were able to work for themselves and their families without interference or restriction. Because they were proud of the independence they had won (consider how they celebrated the Fourth of July!), and jealous of it, and determined that it should not be lost or whittled away again.

Norman Vincent Peale
Sin, Sex, and Self-Control
(New York: Doubleday & Co., 1965)

SIX: LONELY GRAVES

The wild frontier had only begun to try Larcena's fortitude. The worst of times were just ahead for the embryonic Arizona territory, with death and destruction everywhere. Later generations of Americans can hardly imagine what dreadful experiences its pioneer settlers endured and how dearly they paid for their foothold in the Gadsden Purchase. Will Oury on April 6, 1885, reminded a sympathetic audience of pioneers assembled in Tucson that in the 1860s the Indians "had held a carnival of murder and plunder in all our settlements while our people were appalled and almost paralyzed."[1] Ten days later another speaker assured the pioneers that "There is no one among you who has not seen a friend or a relative fall beneath the murderous attack of the Apache. On every hill are to be seen the graves of those who have died in defense of these, our homes."[2]

"The abduction of the woman and child," Thompson Turner wrote to the St. Louis *Missouri Republican* on March 30, 1860, "was a fearful warning to those living in exposed situations, and it is well for them that they profit by it."[3] Some isolated settlers, thoroughly shaken by the incident, fled from the perilous frontier; others moved their families into the relative safety of Tubac or Calabasas. The Penningtons, for the time being, stayed at their stone house farm on the border.

The beginning of summer gave few clues to the disasters that were to come, except for Indian thefts of settlers' animals, which resumed after a brief lull following the prisoner exchange that ransomed Mercedes. Tonto attacks north along the Gila River in late April caused employees to desert two Overland Mail stations there. Apaches stole the entire horse herd from the Santa Rita Mine on May 28, made off with stock from a ranch near Fort Buchanan on May 29, and did the same at Sylvester Mowry's Patagonia Mine, southeast of the fort, on June 7.[4]

Spurred by the unchecked lawlessness and violence of the previous year, settlers moved purposefully toward civil order. They held county elections and convened the first session of county court in May, 1860. They scheduled the first legislature of the Provisional Government to assemble the following spring. They prayed fervently that Congress would soon grant them separate territorial status, but some knowledgeable citizens feared that that would be delayed by the determination of Congressional Republicans and their presidential candidate, Abraham Lincoln, to exclude slavery from new territories.[5] This pessimism proved well-founded.

Larcena was well enough by summer to move into the cabin John Page built near the mouth of Madera Canyon. Her wounds healed, leaving scars on her body, and the mental trauma of her ordeal slowly faded. She became something of a celebrity; her contemporaries marveled at her courage. A dozen or more pioneers, in the memoirs they later wrote, described her incredible feat of survival.[6]

Larcena's home was ten or twelve miles from Canoa ranch, within visiting distance of it. She acquired a new English-speaking neighbor close to her own age when Bill Kirkland married and brought his bride to Canoa a few weeks after Mercedes was ransomed. Missouri Ann Kirkland was a petite young woman with luxuriant long hair, a daughter of William Bacon, a Presbyterian preacher from Missouri. The Bacons, a large family, had stopped in Tucson the preceding year and operated a restaurant there before completing their journey to California. The daughters had waited on customers, of which Kirkland, on his occasional trips to town, was one.[7] Living almost entirely among men in a largely

Hispanic region, Larcena and Missouri Ann must each have welcomed the proximity of another female who could share her thoughts and feelings.

Deceptive indications of peace and prosperity encouraged the Pages, Kirklands, and Penningtons for a little while. There were between eight hundred and a thousand inhabitants in Tucson, twice as many as four years earlier, Tubac was flourishing, and about thirty separate small communities now dotted the Gadsden Purchase.[8] Communication and transportation to and within the territory were improving. The Tucson to Fort Buchanan Stage Lines made scheduled stops at Canoa ranch and, in spite of recent troubles with Apaches, the Butterfield Overland Mail Company was heavily patronized. Stages coming from the west coast were packed, and east-bound Arizonans could hardly find an empty seat.[9]

In addition, there were rumors that Tucson would have telegraph service within another year. It looked as if freight rates might drop, reducing the high cost of goods, all of which had to be expensively imported over long distances. Farmers were happy: hay was growing tall and B. C. Marshall of Sonoita Valley confidently expected to harvest six hundred bushels of peaches. Mines, too, were producing well. The discovery of a new mine — the San Pedro — excited everyone.[10]

Improved security for settlers seemed assured when the army began constructing another post — Fort Breckenridge — about the first of May. It was located at the mouth of Arivaipa Canyon on the San Pedro River near the home grounds of the Pinal Apaches in order to protect the soon-to-be-improved El Paso-Fort Yuma wagon road. A number of farmers hurried to claim land near Breckenridge. Among them were men whom John and Larcena Page knew: "Colonel" Nathaniel Sharpe, who had arrived in Arizona with the Akes, William Redding, one of the filibusters who had attacked Padrés' flour train in 1857, and the mulatto, Hampton Brown, who had cooked at the pinery.[11]

Indian raids soon made things hot near Breckenridge, however. It proved no more impervious to depredations than Fort

Mrs. and Mrs. William Hudson Kirkland in their later years (Arizona Historical Society).

Buchanan, and no more effective in countering them. In August Apaches "made a thorough cleaning out of the farming district" near Breckenridge. They killed a farmer and forced Sharpe, Redding, Brown and the other settlers to hole up in one farmhouse for collective defense. An American renegade named Gray was suspected of having sold arms and ammunition to the Apaches, making them bolder and their raids more deadly. Some irate pioneers expressed their conclusions that the army should place Apaches on reservations controlled by military posts and shoot them off limits.[12]

To help control hostile Indians, citizens looked to the militia authorized by the provisional government. A group of "Provisional Rangers" enlisted in Mesilla was expected to report for duty at Tucson in June and the newspaper announced that Major General William Wadsworth of Sonoita Valley would personally lead them on a campaign against the Apaches.[13] But an important event in which Jack Pennington and Hank Smith participated distracted the ranger unit and disrupted these plans.

Wadsworth had sent Jack and Hank to El Paso with a beef herd consigned to the Fort Bliss quartermaster. As the cattle drive progressed, a number of starving Apaches of Mangas Coloradas' band approached it. The apprehensive cowboys avoided a conflict by giving several beeves to the Indians, who accompanied them a good part of the way, and by this strategy they reached El Paso safely.

There, after delivering the rest of the cattle, Jack and Hank joined up with two California miners, Jacob Snively and Henry Burch, who wanted to prospect in the Pinos Altos Mountains of New Mexico. The site lay within the boundaries of "Arizona Territory," as the provisional government had defined it. Their party struck gold on Bear Creek, about two hundred miles east of Tucson.[14] A newspaper bulletin to St. Louis from Tucson on June 4 reported "great excitement" everywhere and published the following letter from an unidentified writer "to a leading citizen." It may well have been from Jack Pennington to William Wadsworth.

We have found mines of gold and silver. The gulch in which we struck the gold is very rich, paying on the average twenty cents per pan, some of the dirt paying even as high as a dollar. The section of gold-bearing country is extensive and thousands of poor men can find employment.[15]

As soon as this became known, eager, hopeful men, including most of the militiamen destined for Tucson, beat a trail to Pinos Altos.[16] Employees at nearby Butterfield Overland Mail stations left their posts and hurried to stake claims near Bear Creek, where log cabins were sprouting like mushrooms. Several mail stations were left with only one man to operate them. Thompson Turner, at Tubac, predicted the company would have to offer high wages to get replacements.[17]

It may have been the gold strike, or the job opportunity with Butterfield that followed it, that caused Charles Burr, husband of Larcena's sister Caroline, to leave his wife. A census taker that summer showed Charles Burr as an employee at a Butterfield station near Pinos Altos only ten days after another enumerator had listed him with Caroline at Elias Pennington's farm.[18] Burr never returned to Caroline, apparently, and nothing more is known of him. He may have been one of those unfortunate nameless miners who died near Pinos Altos during the following year at the hands of Mangas Coloradas' Apache band.

In the meantime, another murder by Mexican laborers agitated the American settlers in southern Arizona. Eleven Mexican workmen at the new San Pedro Mine, thirty-five miles east of Sonoita Valley, surprised and slew three American employees of the St. Louis Mining Company, which owned and operated the diggings. They also stole as much property as they could carry off. Grundy Ake's adolescent sons, Will and Jeff, discovered the gory scene of death and mutilation when they arrived at midnight on July 23 with the mine superintendent. Their father had sent them from Fort Buchanan with a wagon of provisions for the miners.[19] Such brutal incidents caused Captain Ewell to comment that Americans and Mexicans murdered each other on both sides of the border "without the slightest remorse, and as if they wanted to see which was the most atrocious."[20]

By August Larcena was cooking for three men who shared the Page cabin—Thomas Hutton, William Dennison, and John B. [sic] Pennington. Dennison and Pennington may have been related to Larcena.[21] It is likely that they worked with her husband. William Dennison was a very likeable young man with a beautiful singing voice. He played the banjo and guitar, and one imagines there were happy times that summer and fall in Larcena's little home.[22]

John Page and these friends must have relished and retold the newspaper story that circulated through their neighborhood in September about General Wadsworth's runaway horses. The four-horse team had raced uncontrollably down into Sonoita Valley from Fort Buchanan one day as their owner drove several acquaintances toward Paddy Graydon's saloon. His passengers, according to the story, each "looked out for No. 1" and jumped out of the wildly swaying vehicle. All were injured to some extent. "Brown of Tucson" (probably Charles O. Brown, owner of the Congress Hall Saloon) was said to have been badly hurt. But three miles down the road, the storyteller continued, the wild-eyed animals "brought up at a tavern called the Boundary Hotel [Graydon's]—the usual stopping place of the General. The horses knowing his failing, stopped of their own accord—being, like their master, very dry."[23]

Then, as 1860 drew to a close, began a series of dire events that, in retrospect, seemed ill-omened for Larcena and John Page. On September 13th Indians killed Page's sawmill partner Joe Ashworth. Ashworth and two other men had been driving cattle near General Wadsworth's ranch not far from Fort Buchanan when eight armed Apaches emerged from a clump of trees, making signs of friendship. Ashworth had a pistol with him; his companions had no weapons. As the Indians began a conversation, three of them "elevated their rifles and fired at Mr. Ashworth, probably on account of his being armed," guessed Thompson Turner, who reported the incident.[24] Joe was hit twice and mortally wounded.

The Apaches quickly drove off fifteen head of cattle. Ashworth's comrades dismissed any thought of pursuit. They got the dying man to Wadsworth's house but he lived only a short while longer.

It was only two weeks later that approximately a hundred fifty Apaches struck a surprise blow at Fort Breckenridge, driving off most of the fort's animals. The one small company of infantry then manning the new post looked on, "powerless to offer resistance."[25] It was the same old story of inadequacy. The citizens could only hope that these incidents would awaken the War Department to the need for increased military protection and control of the Indians.

Settlers lost the officer they most respected as an Indian fighter, however, when "Baldy" Ewell left Fort Buchanan in September to attend a court martial at Fort Bliss.[26] As it turned out, he never came back to Sonoita Valley. He did not mind being relieved of the responsibility of pursuing depredating Apaches. "I would prefer," he had earlier written his mother, "the less romantic but hardly less inhuman business of raising potatoes and cabbages. . . ."[27]

The bright outlook immigrants had so recently held for Arizona had darkened by the end of the year. A "general blight" lay over the land. Wages had decreased, money was scarce and necessities were high-priced. The number of Indian depredations and killings rose. Citizens felt widespread dissatisfaction with the infantry now at Fort Buchanan: they seemed unable to thwart or catch the fleet, cunning Apaches. The Provisional Rangers from Mesilla had never reached Tucson. The government discontinued the post office at Tubac, which served the Pages, Penningtons, and other settlers along the Santa Cruz. Life and property were more insecure than ever, and investors were spurning Arizona mines.[28]

As this discouraging situation developed in the Gadsden Purchase, Abraham Lincoln won the presidential election in November, 1860, and in December South Carolina seceded from the Union. When six other states soon followed its example, the federal government was threatened with disintegration, an alarming thought to most of the settlers. Arizona's provisional government, planned the previous April, had never been implemented and was virtually useless. Some Arizonans seriously considered a proposal, which originated in Mesilla, to form a state constitution and apply for admission into the Confederacy that was rapidly taking shape. The new South, they argued, might offer their struggling region more consideration than Congress had given.[29]

At the mines in Pinos Altos, as in every Arizona settlement, people hotly discussed secession. The miners there were split on the issue, but most of them, including Jack Pennington and Hank Smith, supported southern rights.[30] "The crisis excites the most intense interest" in Tucson, reported Thompson Turner. In his opinion, however, the majority of the town's residents were loyal to the Union.[31]

"Everyone here is on the tenter hooks of impatience to know what the Southern States will do," wrote Captain R. S. Ewell from Albuquerque in January, 1861.[32] Persistently ill, he returned to Virginia shortly afterward. The faithful soldier was torn between his love for his southern home state and his oath to the United States Army. He had friendships with officers from the north as well as the south and he opposed Civil War and disunion. But he and several other officers serving in New Mexico Territory eventually made the painful decision to resign their commissions and join Confederate forces.[33] In that service Ewell later lost a leg in battle but rose to the rank of lieutenant general.

Larcena and John Page and the three young men living with them could momentarily forget the troubles of Arizona and the nation when an unusually heavy snowfall blanketed the Santa Rita Mountains in January, 1861, working its magical transformations on the landscape around their snug cabin. Mesquite and creosote branches arched under its weight, cacti and tall grass clumps stood up like snowmen, and the ordinarily dry brown earth sparkled pristinely white. Each fencepost by the Page cabin wore a fluffy, glistening cap. American settlers could not remember having seen a more severe storm in the vicinity, and they huddled close to their fires.[34]

Calamitous events, however, were quickly multiplying. The

secession of Texas on February 1st doubtless stirred the hearts of many settlers who, like the Penningtons, had once lived there. The union was drawing closer to separation. To make matters worse for Larcena and John Page and their neighbors, "at least a dozen" incidents of Apaches killing settlers and stealing livestock occurred in their vicinity. The Indians, observed newspaper correspondent Thompson Turner, seemed fully to "appreciate the uselessness of infantry troops and, having less fear of pursuit than formerly, [became] bolder and more daring." [35] People who were forced to travel hesitated, "as never before, to start out alone."[36]

Apaches raided John Ward's ranch, eleven miles south of Fort Buchanan, late in January, taking his twelve-year-old stepson as well as cattle.[37] Soldiers from the fort trailed the band to Apache Pass. There, on February 5th, Lieutenant George N. Bascom conferred with the head Chiricahua chief, Cochise, and demanded the return of the boy. Cochise denied stealing the child, but promised to get him from the Coyotero band while the troops waited at Apache Pass. Bascom, however, outraged the chief by taking four of the Chiricahuas hostage, and Cochise reacted swiftly. In the next few days his Indians attacked stagecoaches and a wagon train pulling into Apache Pass, took some hostages of their own, and killed stage drivers, passengers, and would-be peacemakers. Bascom hung some of his prisoners in reprisal.[38]

Readers shuddered at the headlines in the *Arizonian* of February 9th:

OVERLAND STAGE ATTACKED BY INDIANS!
. THE STAGE DRIVER AND TWO MULES SHOT
ONE STATIONKEEPER KILLED—ONE WOUNDED
DRIVER CARRIED INTO CAPTIVITY
EIGHT DEAD BODIES ON THE ROAD
THE STAGE ROAD BARRICADED FOR TWO MILES
AN EXPRESS RIDER ARRIVES AT TUCSON[39]

Disastrous incidents occurred in ever faster succession. The driver of the Fort Buchanan stage returned to Tucson about this time with news that Indians had burned down General Wadsworth's house in Sonoita Valley. It was a narrow escape for the

Wadsworth family; they had left their home some days earlier "on account of their isolated position" and were staying at the Ake farm. Apaches also prowled near the Overland Mail Company's Cienega station and pursued men working at a hay camp a few miles from Tucson.[40]

Cochise's angry band next attacked a wagon train heading eastward into Apache Pass. A stagecoach stopped at the site of the massacre a few hours later, and its nine passengers climbed out and buried eleven of the train's emigrants who had apparently been chained to their wagon wheels and "roasted alive." The Indians fired upon the stagecoach passengers and injured the driver, but the whites managed to reach the mail station. At about the same time Apaches also ran off all the relay horses from other stations east of Apache Pass. Tucson citizens, reduced almost to panic by all these developments, pledged money for the support of a "ranging company." Fort Breckenridge sent reinforcements to Apache Pass.[41]

With such destruction raining all around, William Wadsworth may have had some trouble finding experienced men willing to escort a wagon load of provisions he had to send to Fort Breckenridge at this time, but John Page and two of his sawmill partners, Alf Scott and Jim Cotton, agreed to go. Scott was another of Page's California friends, one of the "Sonoita Murderers" arrested with him a year and a half earlier.

Larcena knew it was no time to be out on the roads. If she had learned of the atrocities at Apache Pass before her husband left home, she may have tried to dissuade him from making the trip. John Page—strong, bold, and self-confident—would have laughed at her fears. The fort needed the provisions, and it was an opportunity for him to make some money, a scarce commodity. He had a growing family to support: Larcena was in the early stage of pregnancy.

Page and his friends, guarding Wadsworth's wagon, were in La Cañada del Oro thirty miles north of Tucson on the evening of February 20th.[42] Three Mexican men and a Mexican woman rode in the wagon. Cañada del Oro in its upper reaches, where the party now plodded along a narrow road, is a gorge that winds southward through the northwestern foothills of the Santa Catalina Mountains, whose pine-clad shoulders and granite heights rise impressively above it. Water runs most of the year in that part of the canyon, but disappears underground closer to Tucson where the gully becomes a broad, shallow, dry wash, except after heavy rains. The road from Tucson north to Fort Breckenridge crossed the wash, traversed lower foothills, and descended to the stream. This it followed for a mile or two to a point later known as Samaniego's Ranch, where it ascended a ridge and exited the canyon near the present town of Oracle.[43]

Page's party stopped for a while by the water in late afternoon, and as they rested, Jim Cotton said he thought he saw Indians on the hill above them, where the wagon would have to pass. Apparently John Page could not see them nor could the others. They prepared to push on farther before nightfall although Cotton nervously insisted that he had seen Indians. Page derisively replied that his partner "had a very fertile imagination and would see an Indian behind every bush on the road."[44]

The party moved on out of the wash, uphill and along a ridge that fell away on both sides, with Page, Scott, and Cotton riding some distance ahead of the wagon. Cotton pointed to a spot they were approaching, saying that he had seen the Indians right there. John Page retorted that Cotton "would have a lance in his back before he went twenty steps." His friend, perhaps offended as well as apprehensive, turned back, saying that in that case he would go to the wagon for his blanket. He did so, dismounted, tied his horse to the tailgate, and climbed into the wagon.[45]

It was just turning dark. Cotton was pulling his blanket loose when he heard shots. He jumped to the ground and tried unsuccessfully to unhitch his jittery horse. He saw in the fading light that up ahead John Page and Alf Scott, both apparently wounded, were running their mounts off the road to the left. They were bent over, leaning on their horses' necks. Just then Indians came dashing toward the wagon. Cotton fired at them with his "little revolving rifle" and the attackers scattered. The frightened oxen pulled the wagon off to the left of the trail, however, and ran it rapidly down the steep hillside, where it overturned in a ravine. The assailants followed the wagon, intent on plunder.[46]

Cotton, the woman, and the three Mexican men—one with an arrow wound in his shoulder—fled on foot toward Tucson, leaving Page and Scott hurt and alone in the hills with the Indians. As Cotton swiftly made his way in the protective cover of the boulders and bushes alongside the road, one of the Mexicans suddenly appeared dimly beside him. Cotton, thoroughly spooked, mistook the ally for an enemy and struck him alongside the head with his pistol butt, sending him toppling into the weeds. Then Cotton hurried on.[47]

The refugees hardly paused for rest until they reached Tucson about noon the next day, the man who had unluckily sought Cotton's companionship arriving somewhat later than the others. They told their story and learned that other violence had occurred the day before: near the Overland Mail's Cienega station thirty miles east of Tucson Pinals had raided the ranch of Asa McKenzie and burned his house to the ground.[48]

Saloonkeeper Charles O. Brown, a leading citizen of Tucson, tried to find enough men to ride at once to the assistance of Page and Scott, but only one, Tom Smith, would go. The accumulation of recent Apaches hostilities was enough to put fear and caution into almost anyone. Brown and Smith waited, knowing the futility of going by themselves to find John Page and Alf Scott.[49]

Late that day William S. Oury, Tucson agent for the Butterfield line, returned to Tucson from Apache Pass. His was only the second stage to make it through since the confrontation with Cochise had taken place. Charles Brown told him about the ambush of the Wadsworth wagon and the plight of Page and Scott. Oury was tough.[50] He had just experienced "twelve days and nights of continuous uneasiness and mental excitement" and was hoping for rest, but he was aware that "something must be speedily done to try and relieve" the missing men. He went downtown with Brown and Smith and they finally succeeded in recruiting two more men to accompany them. They all slept a few hours, rose early, and started for the Cañada. Tom Smith brought along his black servant and Jim Cotton guided the party.[51]

It was nightfall when they arrived and they could see nothing, so they slept on the ground by the stream until daylight. After sending Cotton and the black man back to Tucson, the remaining five men scouted the scene. The rising sun revealed camouflaged holes dug in the ground where the Apaches had lain concealed beside the road on the ridge. The searchers estimated there had been at least eighteen or twenty Indians. Two had apparently hidden under a small mesquite tree, rested their rifles on its limbs and commenced the attack by shooting at the lead escorts, Page and Scott.

Down in a deep ravine the rescue party could see the over-turned wagon. They followed the tracks of Page and Scott in a long semicircle to the head of the ravine and back on its opposite side to a point only about three hundred yards from where the wagon now rested. There, in a thicket of mesquite trees filled with black crows, Oury and the others found the body of John Page. Page's horse, its throat cut, was stretched out beside him. Alf Scott was nowhere in sight, but the saddles of both horses were on the ground. Near Page were blankets and a knife and pistol belonging to Scott.[52]

The five Tucson men looked at the evidence around them and tried to reconstruct what had happened. They guessed that the two wounded friends lost their bearings and thought themselves farther from the Apaches than their half-circle had actually brought them. Page must have been mortally wounded and un-able to stay in the saddle any longer. The unmounted Apaches, probably seeing little sense in chasing horsemen, had concentrated on looting the wagon, but John Page and Alf Scott must have spent a long, painful, anxious night.[53]

It appeared that Page might not have died until one or two days after the attack. In the meantime, Scott tried to make him comfortable, moving him into morning sunshine and afternoon shade. The Tucson men hypothesized that Scott "remained with him till the last agonies of death were over when he, almost per-

Charles O. Brown, proprietor of Tucson's Congress Hall Saloon, who was with Oury and performed the impromptu autopsy on Page (Arizona Historical Society).

William Sanders Oury, early Tucson resident who found and buried John H. Page in 1861 (Arizona Historical Society).

ishing from thirst, cut the horse's throat in order to imbibe a draught of its blood."[54] Then, they reasoned, Scott set off on foot to find water, but was taken by the Indians or died on the way.

The five men debated as they dug a grave for John Page. They wondered if Page's wound actually was fatal or if he died of thirst. Could his life have been saved if help had reached him sooner? Oury and Brown, critical of the many frightened men back in Tucson who had refused to go immediately to the rescue, maintained that the wound had probably not been mortal. The others disagreed. Charles O. Brown took out his Bowie knife and split Page's torso open for examination. Tom Smith turned away in horror and disgust, which amused Will Oury. Brown's impromptu autopsy convinced them that John Page had had a good chance for survival with timely aid. They buried Page and searched further for Alf Scott, but they could not pick up his trail. Late that evening they started back to Tucson. Two weeks later someone found Scott's body in Cañada del Oro.[55]

"John Page leaves a wife to lament his untimely loss," reported the Sacramento *Union* on March 14, 1861. Larcena later stated that all she ever saw of her dead husband was "his handkerchief, a lock of his hair and his pocketbook," which one of the five men carried back to her.[56]

SEVEN: THE GREAT EXODUS

After John Page's death Elias Pen-
nington brought Larcena back to his border farm, where there
were sisters and brothers to comfort her. She must often have
thought sorrowfully of the husband who had loved her, of his
vigorous life suddenly and brutally ended, of his once warm,
strong body now cold and forever still on some remote hillside.
She must have wondered what this grim frontier held in store for
her and for the child growing within her. The religious faith she
had learned at her father's knee now sustained her. "Hardships like
these might easily have embittered a less courageous person," observed Robert H. Forbes, Larcena's son-in-law, in later years, "but
I have heard her exclaim that God is good, and knows best!"[1]

Meanwhile, the terrifying violence continued. Department
headquarters ordered soldiers guarding the critical sites of Apache
Pass and Stein's Peak back to their forts to prepare for a general
campaign. This left the Butterfield mail route totally unprotected.
As Apaches continued to attack scheduled stagecoaches, Congress
voted to change the route, bypassing troubled Arizona altogether.
Arizonans were stunned. They felt that the permanent loss of the
Overland Mail would be a "death-blow" to their region. There
would no longer be passenger service in and out of Arizona, no
letters or newspapers brought in or taken out except by private
enterprise or the courtesy of travelers. "'What will we do — where
will we go?' is in every man's mouth," reported Thompson Turner

from Tucson.[2] Many settlers prepared to move away to a less deprived and dangerous land. Others grimly chose to dig in and hold on in hopes that Congress would soon restore the southern route of the mail company.[3]

The secession of Confederate states gave rise to rumors that all military troops would soon be withdrawn from Arizona. That possibility intensified the general consternation and caused Turner to declare, "If it is done, the citizens must abandon their investments and make their escape with the troops."[4]

Apaches struck close to the Pennington farm on March 2, 1861, and again on the 3rd, raiding B. C. Marshall's place in Sonoita Valley. Lieutenant A. W. Evans marched out of Fort Buchanan with thirty-one infantrymen and twelve pack mules to scout for the Indians. By following "narrow trails and direct routes over the hills," he reported, he "arrived at Pennington's, on the upper Santa Cruz," on the 6th. Larcena's father guided the soldiers through the surrounding countryside, but they found no Apaches. For two more days Evans continued a futile search along Sonoita Creek, where he saw Marshall's burnt houses still smoking.[5]

The soldiers then cut across the rugged hills to the Santa Rita Mine. Evans thought that the Indians who had attacked Marshall's were probably the band, armed with guns and bows, which had stolen horses from the mine's brush-and-pole corral on the same day. Horace Grosvenor, one of the mine managers, helped Evans search in the mountains to the south. This time scouts found fresh signs of the Apaches. It appeared that the marauders were still lurking in the vicinity.[6]

They were indeed. Samuel Robinson, accountant for the mine, heard them late one night pulling apart the corral, and at other moments nearly every day the following week. "We are always prepared for them, but do not really fear them," Robinson wrote on March 17 to his brother.[7] The miners may have been overconfident of their personal safety, for seven weeks later at the mine, when Horace Grosvenor walked out in the dark on the road to Tubac to check on an overdue wagon load of supplies, Apaches killed him.[8]

Apaches continued to strike here and there near the Pennington farm. In May they stole seventy-five head of cattle from Peter Kitchen's ranch south of Calabasas and took sixteen mules belonging to a freighter, Nathan Appel, as he hauled lumber to the Santa Rita Mine. Early in June they ran off 250 head of William Wadsworth's cattle which were grazing near the border. Soldiers, fearing an attack on Fort Buchanan itself at any moment, refused to leave the post to chase the raiders. Workers at the Santa Rita Mine moved into Tubac on June 15th, hoping to return when things quieted down.

The situation grew steadily worse, however. Before June 1861 was over, a band of Indians killed an American who was chasing them, attempting to retrieve sixteen mules they had stolen from the Arivaca Mine. About the same time another Apache party ran off seventy-five head of cattle from William Roods' ranch near Canoa and raided the Fort Buchanan herd. Others harassed Fort Breckenridge and drove miners away from their diggings at Pinos Altos.[9]

On June 17th, Grundy Ake's ruthless nephew Bill Ake added to the general turmoil by shooting and killing a Sonoita Valley farmer named Davis. Bill had come back from California after the judge at Mesilla released the other "Sonoita Murderers" and anger over that incident cooled somewhat. He had married seventeen-year-old Lizzie Bacon, who may have been a sister of William Kirkland's wife.[10] For several days after the murder Bill evaded irate citizens determined to kill him or run him out of the country. Six or eight men who saw him at Calabasas shot at him, but missed, and he outran them on his speedy horse.

All the American men at Tubac signed a resolution condemning Bill and pledging assistance in his arrest. Members of a citizens' posse stationed themselves at different points waiting for him to appear. William Dennison, who had lived with Larcena and John Page, was one of them. Someone sighted Bill Ake on the

20th and fired at him, but managed only to wound his horse slightly.[11]

Grundy Ake put his nephew's pregnant young wife in a wagon and sent her to Tubac, where she arrived on June 21st. Five or six posse members patrolled the town and the roads in case Bill Ake tried to communicate with her, but they saw no sign of him. They roamed from Tumacacori to Arivaca in the next few days in response to reports that the outlaw had been seen in those places, but always he eluded them. Tubac residents now began to view the posse's unsuccessful efforts as "a farce." Grundy Ake himself came to Tubac on the 24th. The posse was elsewhere that day.[12] Grundy and some of Bill Ake's friends started Lizzie out toward Tucson at night and her hunted husband met her secretly along the way. A few days later the couple left Tucson for California on a flight path now familiar to the hard young desperado, and Bill Ake plagued Arizona no more.[13]

Settlers, divided by differing political sentiments, did not hold their usual patriotic celebration in Tubac on the Fourth of July. Samuel Robinson, who had moved there from the Santa Rita Mine, made a diary entry that day: "On rising this morning, I got out the Stars and Stripes and hung them up in the house. The only flag in town. Although we are nearly all Union men in Tubac it was thought best not to make any public display."[14] That month Robinson saw a brilliant comet about forty-five degrees above the western horizon, streaking across the night sky like a torchbearer beckoning beleaguered settlers out of the troubled territory.

Meanwhile, Civil War hostilities had begun in the east in April, just as some Tucsonans were saying that the latest news from "the States" gave hope "for an amicable adjustment of national affairs."[15] The more remote, isolated settlers like the Penningtons did not know of the war for some time, and it was May 27, 1861, before men at the Santa Rita Mine heard the news.[16] Then reverberations of the worrisome national crisis, which had seemed far removed, shook Apache-tormented Arizona with earthquake force.

Department headquarters summoned all military troops

from Forts Breckenridge and Buchanan, as well as from Fort McLane near Pinos Altos, in July. It ordered these units to assemble near the Rio Grande to repel an imminent invasion of New Mexico by Confederate Texans. Arizonans were aghast at this confirmation of their worst fears, although in the past they had considered the posts ineffective except as an economic benefit.[17] Now there would be no semblance of military protection. Nor would there be the government contracts which had provided an income for many of them.

These had been stressful months for the residents of the Sonoita and Santa Cruz valleys. Ranchers and farmers with families had already begun moving into Calabasas, Tubac, or the fort. Many of them now flocked to Tucson to form wagon trains for common safety en route to destinations west or east. Some went south, seeking refuge in Santa Cruz and other Mexican towns.

The ever-watchful Apaches were quick to observe that the whites were leaving their settlements, and the presence of hostile Indians in the area increased. Almost a hundred of them laid waste the Canoa and Sópori ranches on July 14th. At Canoa they attacked William Roods, who escaped with an arrow in his arm. They killed three less fortunate Americans and a Papago.[18] Bill Kirkland, his wife, and their newborn daughter were in Tucson at the time, preparing to move to California.[19] Kirkland had sold or leased the Canoa ranch to William S. Grant, who had spruced up the old stage station there, renamed it the "Canoa Hotel," and opened it under the supervision of Edwin Tarbox, "a young gentleman well qualified" for the job.[20] Tarbox was among the dead the Apaches left strewn around Canoa, as was his guest, Richmond Jones, manager of the Sópori ranch. At Sópori the Indians drove off an estimated three hundred head of livestock, and the remaining employees there fled for their lives.[21]

In the sweep of the great exodus, the Ake and Wadsworth families, "bringing all the cattle on the Sonoita with them," reached Tubac on July 20th, and moved on toward Tucson the next day.[22] With them was "The Great Western," the big redheaded madam, who returned to Fort Yuma. They and other

Sonoita Valley residents were bitter because officers at Fort Buchanan refused to sell them the fort's abandoned stores at reduced prices, preferring to burn or destroy supplies left behind. The officers even placed a night guard over civilians at the post, and finally ordered them immediately off the premises.[23] Soldiers razed Buchanan on the 23rd, and marched off toward the Rio Grande.[24] Paddy Graydon, Sonoita Valley's saloonkeeper, followed them, rejoined the Union army, and was soon fighting with his usual energy against the Rebels.[25]

Once the garrison had gone, Samuel Robinson noted on July 24th, Sonorans arrived, "put out the fire, and carried off the provisions to the amount of twelve wagons and eight or ten cart loads."[26] One can hardly blame needy people for such a practical act, but it showed that Mexicans as well as Indians were ready to take advantage of the American settlers' misfortune.

A messenger reached Tubac on July 24th with news that five Sonoran bandits had murdered the only three Americans still at the Cerro Colorado Mine near Arivaca and had stolen all the valuables they could find there.[27] One of those slain was Charles D. Poston's brother John, the mine superintendent. The next day Samuel Robinson wrote in his diary that all persons on ranches "above here," a designation which included the Penningtons, had arrived in Tubac, leaving the countryside "completely depopulated."

When "Randal" (presumably John Page's former partner William Randall) brought word to Tubac on the 28th that Sonorans were coming to "clean out the Americans," most settlers, especially those with families, promptly headed for Tucson. Larcena and her family may have already gone there, but if not, they did so now.[28] Charles Poston and a few companions rode into Mexico.[29] Tubac was left empty except for half a dozen of the principal Mexican landowners and about twenty die-hard American men.[30]

These few remnants of the once thriving, industrious population were in the village when an estimated two hundred Apaches invaded it on August 4th. All that the residents could do was shoot from behind their adobe walls. Samuel Robinson, weak and suffering from malaria, hid in his house as the Indians swept through town, killing a Mexican and taking almost all the livestock that was still there.[31] The Apaches, said Robinson, "retired to a distance of a few hundred yards, killed a beef and encamped for the night."[32]

The Tubac men sent a messenger to Tucson that evening, and some thirty Mexican- and Anglo-Americans promptly came to reinforce them.[33] The defenders in the village were a mixed lot. Some of the Americans were more to be feared than Sonoran bandits, in Robinson's estimation. "There are a few men here we would like to get rid of," he declared. Two of the "rough set" spent precious bullets shooting at each other as the rest awaited another attack by the Apaches.[34]

After daylight on August 7th some seventy-five Sonorans, all armed and mounted, were discovered close to the southern edge of Tubac and to Robinson, "their intentions seemed to be anything but good."[35] The fifty defenders, heavily outnumbered by Apaches on one hand and Mexican bandits on the other, made a hasty retreat to Tucson the next morning, leaving Tubac absolutely deserted and at the mercy of those who waited to plunder it.[36]

In Tucson, a "few Americans whom circumstances . . . compelled to remain in Arizona, and to accept the fortunes of the country" published an issue of the *Arizonian* on August 10th. The newspaper's young editor, Thompson Turner, had left town in May, and no editions had come out since then.[37] The August 10th edition included a letter signed by Herman Ehrenberg, surveyor and cartographer for the Sonora Exploring & Mining Company, and Charles D. Poston, the company's manager. It contained an enumeration of the killings and other unnatural deaths of Americans and Mexicans in "Western Arizona"—that is, from Stein's Peak on the east to Fort Yuma on the west—between 1857 and August 1, 1861, so far as the two men were aware. The total, 172, amounted to almost a fourth of the non-Indian population which Ehrenberg estimated the region to have averaged during that time.

He guessed that whites had killed about 265 Apaches. "Every mine has been babtised [sic] in blood," the writers continued. "What country and business can prosper under such monstrous adversity? And what man would settle his family in these blood-drenched valleys?"[38]

By mid-August most of the settlers waiting in Tucson with a burning desire to join the great exodus had found a way to safer places. The *Arizonian* stated that all outlying settlements were now abandoned and that only sixty-eight American men, some with their women and children, were still in town on August 10th. This number was reduced when Bill and Missouri Ann Kirkland, a sickly Samuel Robinson, down to 120 pounds, William Roods, and others left for California on August 14.[39] It would be even less when the Ake-Wadsworth wagon train departed for the Rio Grande.

The Akes and Wadsworths had lived on neighboring farms beside Sonoita Creek.[40] Now they were leaving it together. William W. Wadsworth had captained the wagon train in which he and his wife, Esther, traveled with the Ake family to the Gadsden Purchase in 1856–1857.[41] The Tucson convention of April 1860 had made Wadsworth a major general of the proposed militia. The general, who described himself in the 1860 census as a lawyer, was also a successful farmer and beef contractor, somewhat more prosperous than many other settlers. In view of all these achievements, one might guess that he now captained the party leaving Tucson for the Rio Grande, although Grundy Ake seems to have shared that honor.

General and Mrs. Wadsworth hid a scandalous past known only to the Akes, to whom Esther had once tearfully confessed. Annie Ake later disparaged Esther's position as Wadsworth's wife, but in Sonoita Valley the Akes had kept the secret.[42]

Before coming to Arizona, Wadsworth had soldiered in the Mexican War, then taught school and served as clerk of court in Jefferson, Orange County, Texas. There he had married and fathered five children. He subsequently met seventeen-year-old Esther Saxon, mother of a baby girl and wife of a boorish, unfaithful

man. Saxon returned home unexpectedly one evening and caught
Wadsworth consoling Esther. In the face of Saxon's dire threats,
the pair hastily left Jefferson together, abandoning their spouses
and children. In one of the little towns they traveled through, they
were "married" (prior, of course, to a later divorce action filed by
their mates). Esther believed William when he assured her the
wedding was legal.[43]

Two years later, they were in Fort Smith, Arkansas, where
they boarded with the Akes. Both families joined a California-
bound wagon train. En route to Arizona, Esther and Virginia
Thompson, the Ake's married daughter, became close friends.
They were almost the same age, and an unhappy Esther found it
a relief to confide her troubles to Virginia.[44]

With the Akes and Wadsworths, preparing to leave Tucson
now, were the Thompson family and that of Mary Ake's niece,
America Phillips. America and her husband Robert ran the American House on the south side of Tucson's dusty plaza, and had
recently accumulated a sackful of coins from numerous customers
awaiting their chance to leave town safely. The Phillipses had
recently remodeled and refurbished their modest adobe inn, but
they now prepared to abandon it in order to accompany Grundy
Ake. Ironically, their hotel advertisement still appeared in the August 10th *Arizonian,* offering "to receive all who desire GOOD
LIVING." That gave the hard-pressed settlers something to laugh
about. There was no good living in Arizona now.

Before the Ake-Wadsworth train got underway, Jack Pennington rode into Tucson from Pinos Altos. He fortunately managed to avoid the Apaches harassing the trails. Word of the whole-
sale abandonment of Sonoita Valley had reached him and he had
come to see about his family and friends. He found Larcena swol-
len in the last month of her pregnancy. He was incredulous and
dismayed to learn that Elias planned to keep his family in devastated Arizona.

There is no accounting for Elias Pennington's stubborn decision. Larcena's condition may have influenced him; he may have
rejected the risks of her undertaking a long, uncertain trek to an

unfamiliar destination. Elias is said to have asserted, with considerable justification, that he was as much entitled to the land as the Apaches were.[45] Jack could not change his father's mind. Rebuffed and frustrated, the young man left his father, eight sisters, and three brothers in Tucson and started for the Rio Grande with his friends, the Akes and Wadsworths.

Grundy Ake and William Wadsworth put Jack in charge of the large livestock herds that accompanied the wagon train. The Ake family later claimed that these amounted to 800 head of cattle, 1200 sheep, and 800 goats. They exaggerated, but the herds were sizeable.[46] A number of Tucson men with no other means of leaving the territory gladly availed themselves of Ake's offer of mounts in exchange for their services as drovers. Grundy told them to take their orders from Jack. One of these herders who owned his horse and saddle was Tommy Farrell, a lanky Irishman who had cooked at the Sópori ranch until the recent Apache attack there sent him and the other ranch hands racing to Tucson.

In addition to the mounted men, the Phillipses' light spring wagon, and Wadsworth's two-horse buggy, the train comprised six large, heavy freight wagons loaded with bacon, sugar, coffee, flour, bedding, clothing, and whatever coin or bullion the owners possessed. According to Tommy Farrell, a Santa Cruz Valley rancher named John St. Clair (also spelled Sinclair) had $1000 in silver bullion "sewed up tight in a sack." The Akes later claimed that Grundy had a strongbox containing $2500 in gold and silver coins. Wadsworth undoubtedly carried money and Phillips had his hotel profits squirreled away, but, with conditions as bad as they had been, few of the other travelers are likely to have had much cash.[47]

Mary Ake, Grundy's wife, their sons Will and Jeff, and their four-year-old daughter Emma rode in one of the big wagons. The Akes' married daughters, Annie Davis and Virginia Thompson, their husbands, and the two little Thompson girls shared another. Esther Wadsworth, eight months pregnant, and two-year-old Billy Wadsworth occupied a third. Altogether seven women and about sixteen children traveled in the train.

General Wadsworth drove his buggy, and Grundy Ake often sat beside him as the wagons creaked and clattered slowly eastward in the dusty wake of the livestock and drovers. Among the train's thirty to forty men were also Nathaniel Sharpe, William Redding, and the mulatto Hampton Brown, who had abandoned their farms near Fort Breckenridge, as well as John Page's former partner Jim Cotton and Kit Carson's white-haired brother Mose.[48]

The travelers were justifiably anxious as they headed out of Tucson in mid-August. If they escaped an attack by Cochise, they still had to thread the domain of Mangas Coloradas, head chief of the eastern Chiricahuas in what is now western New Mexico, to reach the Rio Grande. While Cochise and his southern Chiricahuas, along with the Tontos and Pinals, were effectively ravaging the San Pedro, Santa Cruz, and Sonoita valleys, Mangas terrorized the region near Pinos Altos.

The aging Mangas was a Mimbres Indian of outstanding physique and leadership ability. He possessed unusual influence over several tribes, including that of Cochise, to whom one of his daughters was married. An estimated six feet six inches in height, with graying hair that hung to his waist, Mangas towered impressively over Indians and white men alike.[49] One day he had peacefully entered Pinos Altos, where a group of sport-minded miners seized him, bound him to a tree and whipped him. Since that time Mangas and his warriors had been on the warpath. Hunger also motivated them. The onset of the Civil War had disrupted the government's distribution of food to Indians, which had kept Mangas' tribe relatively peaceful. Facing starvation, however, they resumed their traditional practice of raiding. Their angry determination to drive out the whites added murder to these depredations.[50]

Already their furious assaults had forced mining activity near Pinos Altos to a virtual standstill and caused the abandonment of settlements along the Mimbres River, which the Ake-Wadsworth party's route would cross. Many miners, insufficiently armed for self-defense, had deserted the area. As Indians waylaid supply and food shipments, the remaining miners lost weight on scant rations. "It was knick-knocks for breakfast, knock-knicks for dinner, and d — n hard knocking for supper," commented Jack Pennington's skinny pal, Hank Smith, in his memoirs.[51]

To protect themselves and keep supply routes open, Jack, Hank, and other prospectors who had stayed with their claims formed a small volunteer ranger company with Thomas J. Mastin, a twenty-one-year-old miner and storekeeper, as their captain.[52] This courageous, enterprising young leader, as well as a number of miners, had recently supported the South in heated debates at Pinos Altos.[53] Mastin was undoubtedly pleased, therefore, as were many pro-South Mesilla residents, when Colonel John R. Baylor's Texas Confederates invaded and conquered that town on July 25, 1861. Union troops at adjacent Fort Fillmore put up a brief fight before evacuating the post and surrendering shortly afterward.

Baylor almost immediately declared himself head of a Confederate government of "Arizona Territory." He offered to supply and equip Mastin's militiamen if they would continue to protect the roads and settlements near Pinos Altos from Indian attack, according to William Fisher Scott, one of Mastin's men.[54] Others said that Baylor's first act as Arizona's Confederate governor was to publish Jefferson Davis' conscription proclamation and impress the rangers, many of whom were "Northern and Union men," into Rebel service.[55]

Mastin's company debated briefly among themselves, said Scott, then accepted Baylor's offer. Baylor officially mustered them in on August 8 under the name of "Arizona Guards," and German-born Hank Smith found himself a Confederate scout. Mastin made him fourth sergeant. The unit "left on the 14th for Pino Alto [sic] where they will be on constant duty after Indians," the *Mesilla Times* reported.[56]

Jack Pennington was not with his friend Hank at Mesilla on August 8 and is not listed in the Arizona Guards' muster rolls. He had already returned to Tucson to see to the welfare of his family and friends and had headed east with the Ake-Wadsworth party, which halted for the night beside the Mimbres River on or about August 26. In the past ten days or so they had come about two hundred miles and were now some thirty-five miles southeast of the Pinos Altos mines. Their next day's trek would take them through Cooke's Canyon to Cooke's Spring. Barring unforeseen delays, they would reach the Rio Grande in another week. Up to this point they had nervously but uneventfully made their journey eastward along the abandoned Butterfield Mail route. They had detoured south of dreaded Apache Pass after Tommy Farrell pointed out distant Indian fires flickering in the Pinaleños Mountains north of the trail.

On this particular evening, Jack and the cowboys watered the thirsty herds at the shallow, willow-bordered stream. The wagons, fording it, pulled up near an abandoned Butterfield mail station where a lone man known as "Old Dad" was making himself at home. Mary Ake and her daughters began preparing the evening meal.[57] These trail-worn men and women, settling down gratefully for the night, were unaware that a few miles north of them, on the road to Pinos Altos, some of Mangas' Apaches were besieging a small settlement. Even as the travelers sat resting by their campfire, a rider from that settlement was dashing to Pinos Altos to bring back Mastin's Arizona Guards.[58]

About eleven o'clock that evening someone came to fetch Tommy Farrell, who was riding night herd. A stranger had entered the Ake-Wadsworth camp with a disturbing story. He was Eugene Zimmer, a German-born butcher from Pinos Altos. He told them that on the previous day he was driving cattle from Mesilla to the mining town when Apaches attacked him in Cooke's Canyon. They killed two of his herders and took his beeves, but he managed to escape. Zimmer's English was so heavily accented and distorted by excitement that he could hardly be understood. Ake and Wadsworth became highly suspicious of him. Ake mistrusted Zimmer's warning to avoid Cooke's Canyon, suspecting him of being a renegade spy who was trying to decoy them off their route and into a holdup.[59]

Mangas Coloradas' Indians had been spilling much blood in Cooke's Canyon. The destruction of a mail coach and killing of its occupants at that site by a large force of rifle-armed Apaches about six weeks earlier was reported in the *Mesilla Times*. The coach conductor, "Free Thomas," and six other "experienced frontiersmen, picked for the dangerous duty" of escorting the mail from Mesilla to Los Angeles, evidently defended themselves heroically for two days, but the Indians finally slaughtered the last of them. Expressmen from Pinos Altos, passing through the canyon several days later, found their stripped bodies and evidence of the struggle. Three of the dead Americans had been scalped, said the *Times*.[60]

Eugene Zimmer watched the wagon train move out in the early morning, heading eastward as planned across the grassy, yucca-dotted plain toward Cooke's Canyon, contrary to his urgent advice. He shook his head, then trotted north toward Pinos Altos. The sun was high and hot by the time the Ake-Wadsworth party reached the perilous pass. Behind every boulder and bush in the narrowest part of it Mangas' well-armed Apaches clutched their bows and rifles and waited silently for the settlers to enter the trap.

EIGHT: FISHER SCOTT

Eugene Zimmer was well on his way to Pinos Altos when Tom Mastin's Arizona Guards, coming rapidly from that direction, saw him and pulled up in a cloud of dust. They were hurrying to the relief of the Mimbres River settlement which had sent a messenger for help the night before. Zimmer told them of Mangas' attack on him in Cooke's Canyon and of the Ake-Wadsworth train heading obstinately into that favorite Apache ambush site. When Hank Smith, who was riding with the Guards, heard Zimmer mention Wadsworth and Ake, he knew that his former employer was in grave danger, but he could not have known that his close friend Jack Pennington was in their train. Accompanied by Zimmer, the rangers continued to the besieged settlement. Finding that the Apaches had left it, they hastened toward Cooke's Canyon, hoping to prevent the massacre of the foolhardy Sonoita Valley settlers.

With Mastin's company that day was the man destined to become Larcena Pennington Page's second husband, William Fisher Scott. He did not yet know Larcena, but he probably had met her young brother. He was a Pinos Altos prospector who had joined Mastin's volunteers along with Jack and Hank on July 18, 1861.[1]

Fisher, as the Penningtons later called Scott, stood over six feet tall. He had dark hair and his rather plain face was probably then covered by a full, bushy beard such as many frontiersmen wore. He had been born in Lanarkshire, Scotland. Traces of a Scottish lilt still enlivened his speech. At the age of fourteen he had sailed to the United States where, for the next ten years, he lived in New York City with an older brother. He then traveled westward, as so many young men in America were doing, to Chicago, Council Bluffs, and Omaha in turn. In the fall of 1857, while the Penningtons were settling down in southern Arizona, Fisher Scott was marching into Salt Lake City and on to California with Colonel Albert Sidney Johnston's command. There he finished his term of enlistment and began prospecting. In 1859 he tried the placers above the Yuma Crossing, then joined the rush to Pinos Altos after the gold strike.[2]

Seeking to locate rich placer deposits on the San Francisco River west of Pinos Altos, both Fisher Scott and Hank Smith had accompanied George Frazer's exploration party in the fall of 1860. An Apache guide led them across the San Francisco, several miles above the site they were looking for, and on by a circuitous route to the headwaters of the San Carlos. Warily, but without incident, they visited a large Apache camp on Eagle Creek, where one miner traded an Indian his gun and knife for a mule. Scott suspected that gun of firing the shot that put a hole in another miner's hat shortly afterward.

After a disappointing search for minerals along Black River, the Frazer party returned to Pinos Altos via the site of present-day Clifton on the San Francisco River. There Scott and "old Chas. Bob Kirker . . . found copper in quantities up Chase Creek," making them two of the first white men ever to see that copper-rich area.[3]

Now, on August 27, 1861, the day before his thirtieth birthday, Scott and the Arizona Guards galloped after the Ake-Wadsworth party. Meanwhile, the wagon train, having traveled several miles on an almost level plain, reached a chain of hills and started into the narrowing, meandering pass known as Cooke's Canyon. Jack Pennington undoubtedly remembered his California-bound family trekking westward through this gap four years earlier. Larcena's young brother had been a starry-eyed gold-dreamer of sixteen then; now he was twenty, a seasoned frontiersman and miner.

The livestock herds entered the rocky pass first, followed by the cowboys and then the vehicles. There wasn't room for two wagons to move side by side. They formed a single file. Jack was driving one of the Ake wagons in which the rocking motion had lulled young Jeff Ake to sleep. Esther Wadsworth, now twenty-five years old and pregnant again, was sitting in the buggy with her child and a sick man to whom her husband had given his seat. General Wadsworth and Grundy Ake were horseback.[4]

Tommy Farrell, squinting under the glaring sun, suddenly sighted a nude corpse lying near the trail ahead. He shouted and the line of wagons halted. Farrell urged his horse forward a little to a bend in the road and saw another lifeless body. These were Zimmer's herders, killed by Apaches the day before. As Farrell announced this discovery, four or five men riding at the rear of the train turned tail and galloped back toward the Mimbres River. Jack Pennington and the others scrutinized the silent slopes and checked their weapons and ammunition. All was still, and cautiously they urged their oxen on.[5]

When most of the wagons were in the narrowest part of the gap, the quiet hillsides burst thunderously to life, as fifty or sixty Apaches with smoking guns sprang out from behind rocks on the slopes. John St. Clair, leading the train, was killed instantly and fell from his mount. One of the horses pulling the Phillips' spring wagon slumped to the ground. Mariano Madrid, an eighteen-year-old cattle drover, later described the settlers' surprise:

> . . . we weren't expecting it right then, they had a regular ambuscade, walls made of rocks on each side of the road. . . .
> The Indians were all afoot . . . they just turned loose at us; they shot from all sides at us, and the only way of getting out was to go back. It was the hardest place I was ever in in my life.[6]

The Phillips hack, with one horse down, blocked the train's forward movement. Bob and America Phillips deserted the vehicle on the run, clutching their son and their money-sack. The sound of gunfire, reek of burning gunpowder, screams of terrified women and children, and yells of red men and white filled the canyon. The din awakened Jeff Ake. Frightened and bewildered, the thirteen-year-old boy waved his shotgun in one hand and his pistol in the other. His sister Annie's husband, George Davis, seized the shotgun and felled an Indian who was almost upon them.[7]

The sick man riding in the buggy with Esther Wadsworth whined, "What shall I do?"

"Don't ask me what to do!" she cried.[8] Men ran up, lifted her and her little son down, and took them to a wagon with other women and children.

Farmer William Redding rallied the settlers. If he was the same filibuster Redding who had attacked the Mexican flour train at Los Nogales four years earlier, he did much to redeem himself now. Followed by some of the mounted settlers, he charged the Indians in order to divert them while Jack Pennington and the other drivers tried to turn their wagons around. Failing in that, the drivers managed to wedge two wagons and the buggy into a rough triangle, which gave the defenders some protection from the onslaught. The Indians retreated from Redding's charge, but as the settlers on horseback pursued, twice as many Apaches popped out of their hiding places and drove the whites back. There were an estimated two hundred Indians fighting some forty men in the wagon train. A bullet broke Redding's leg, but he stayed in his saddle and led repeated attacks against the enemy until they finally shot him to death.[9]

Behind the triangular barricade, Annie Ake Davis quickly reloaded rifles for her husband and brothers. White-haired Mose Carson, "brave as a lion and quick as a cat," darted about, firing at one target after another with a skill born of years on the frontier.[10] Young Jack Pennington later told his children that this was the only time in his life he felt sure that he himself had killed an Indian. He took careful aim at a rock where a puff of smoke had arisen and fired when an Apache behind it lifted his head.[11]

Sixty-year-old Nathaniel Sharp directed the settlers' defense. An Indian arrow suddenly pierced his neck behind his ears. He reached up and tried unsuccessfully to pull it out. He broke off the shaft and continued to fight with the arrowhead buried in his flesh. Cherokee Brown, a half-breed friend of the Akes, fired at the Apaches with a deadly accuracy that dropped one after another. As Jim Cotton, the lumberman who had escaped to Tucson at the time of John Page's death, tamped gunpowder into his musket, the hammer accidentally fell on the charge, sending the ramrod spear-like into his leg.[12]

William Wadsworth and Grundy Ake rode up the hillside to gain a vantage point. They could see that the Indians who had retreated were driving the cattle herd on through the canyon while the remaining Apaches kept the settlers pinned down. As he surveyed the scene, Wadsworth, struck by a bullet, slid from his saddle. Nathaniel Sharp dashed up the hillside and carried the wounded general to the wagon barricade. Wadsworth was hit again as Sharp brought him down.[13]

Moments later Annie Ake Davis looked up and saw her father unhorsed and wandering in a daze on the hill. She begged Tommy Farrell to go get him. The drover climbed the slope and began leading Grundy. Ake was uninjured, but as they stumbled downhill an Apache bullet thudded into Farrell's back. The two men helped each other down to the wagons where Tommy collapsed.[14]

The battle had started in late morning, and the sun was now high overhead. The embattled settlers carried General Wadsworth to the rear of the train. They lifted him and other wounded men into the crowded wagon with all the women and children. This vehicle, drawn by four strong mules, had not yet entered the narrowest part of the gap when the battle began. The driver finally succeeded in turning it around. When all were ready, he cracked his whip over the mules, and they raced toward the Mimbres River.[15]

By mid-afternoon, the Americans remaining in Cooke's Canyon had gradually withdrawn to more open ground. They had abandoned the ox-wagons at the head of the train. The Indians began to plunder these vehicles. They carried off some of the provisions, bedding, and clothes the travelers had brought with them and ruined the rest. Preoccupied with their looting and intimidated by the defenders' accurate gunfire, few Apaches chose to follow the retreating settlers into the open. Mariano Madrid later declared, "If it hadn't been for the property, none of us would ever have gotten away."[16]

Seeing their chance to escape, the settlers turned two more wagons and placed Jim Cotton and half a dozen other wounded men inside. St. Clair, Redding, and a man named James May lay dead where they had fallen. Tommy Farrell also appeared to have been killed. Farrell opened his eyes just in time to see his companions hastily mounting horses, ready to make a run for it. He never forgot how desperately he called out to them. "I . . . asked if they were going to leave me to be tortured by the Indians. Jack Pennington and Captain Sharp then threatened to shoot anyone who attempted to leave before I was put in the wagon."[17] They quickly carried Farrell to Wadsworth's buggy and lifted him in beside Grundy Ake. Then the settlers dashed away. Young Mariano Madrid turned in his saddle and fired a parting shot that dropped a pursuing Apache.[18]

In the meantime, Fisher Scott and Hank Smith, riding rapidly toward Cooke's Canyon with Mastin's rangers, learned of the fight when they encountered the handful of men who had deserted the train at the first signs of danger. Accompanied by these men, the Arizona Guards rode on for some miles before they spied the careening wagon of women, children, and wounded men approaching on the road. General Wadsworth had just expired in his pregnant wife's arms. After the panic-stricken refugees told of the ambush, their driver whipped the frothing mules on to the Mimbres River station.[19]

The rangers continued quickly on toward Cooke's Canyon, but before they reached it they met the rest of the survivors. Mastin decided to go after Wadsworth's and Ake's livestock. On the spot, he enlisted Eugene Zimmer, Nathaniel Sharp, and other men of the wagon train.[20] Then he led them south, circling south around Cooke's Canyon all night, hoping to intercept the Apaches who were driving the herd away. Shortly before dawn, the captain allowed a rest stop below the concealing banks of a dry wash and posted a guard. At daybreak the sentinel called out, "Indians!" Peering cautiously up over the edge of the draw, Fisher Scott and Hank Smith could see the cattle coming toward them not a mile away.

An examiner later asked Scott what the Indians had when he saw them. "They had a big surprise," Scott answered, "not thinking there were a lot of gringoes in there and not thinking that they would come and take them unawares."[21] Mastin kept his men hidden until the Apaches were almost upon them. Then the rangers charged out of the *arroyo*. The startled Indians held their ground briefly, but after a short skirmish they scattered into the mountains.[22]

Scott and his companions repelled an Apache charge as they drove Wadsworth's rescued cattle to Cooke's Spring and westward through Cooke's Canyon. They saw the debris and dead bodies of the recent battle. In a side-canyon Fisher saw a small flock of Grundy Ake's sheep, cornered and guarded by a still-faithful dog. Several days after the attack on the wagon train, the rangers delivered the remnants of the cattle herd to Grundy Ake at the Mimbres River Station.[23]

Ake and those of his party who had not gone on with Mastin buried William Wadsworth and tended to the injured. Old Dad, who was living at the deserted mail station, shared his meager provisions with the battle-weary settlers. The rangers rested at the station for several days before returning to Pinos Altos.[24]

Mangas Coloradas' Apaches increased their hostilities after the Cooke's Canyon fight. In larger numbers than ever before, Indians attacked white settlements and travelers. Cochise and his Chiricahuas seemed to have joined forces with Mangas. In alarm, the *Mesilla Times* reported, "their tribes [had] gathered in hosts and commenced a war of extermination against the whites, in earnest."[25]

They besieged a freight train belonging to Charles Trumbull

Hayden, who was camped near Pinos Altos. Half of Mastin's company, including Fisher Scott, came to the rescue. The rangers drove off the Indians and accompanied Hayden's train to the Butterfield station on the Mimbres. They found that the survivors of the Ake-Wadsworth party were still there, having sustained a prolonged Apache attack in the meantime. Their benefactor, Old Dad, had been killed in the fighting.[26]

Another troop of Confederate militia, commanded by Captain James Tevis, rode from Mesilla to the Mimbres Station shortly afterward. They paused en route in Cooke's Canyon to pile rocks over the animal-torn corpses of the dead settlers. Escorted by Tevis' company, the remainder of the Ake-Wadsworth and Hayden parties traveled on safely to the Rio Grande.

Passing the site of their recent ambush, the Akes found the charred ruin of Wadsworth's wagon. The women could not bear to see the litter of spilled sugar and flour and torn clothing. They climbed the slopes, salvaging everything they could. Mary Ake and her daughters filled pillowcases with feathers from their slashed bedding while Grundy and his sons-in-law heaped more rocks on the low mounds under which their late companions lay. The widowed and despondent Esther Wadsworth, only a few days away from childbirth, sat quietly and showed little interest in these activities.[27]

The Akes settled in at Las Cruces. Esther and her two-year-old Billy also stayed there, living with Virginia Ake Thompson's family. On September 28th—a month to the day after her husband was killed, Esther said—she gave birth to a second son.[28]

During September, William Fisher Scott, with part of Mastin's Arizona Guards, patrolled along the Mimbres River and near the Santa Rita copper mines east of Pinos Altos. They were again camped at Mimbres Station on September 28 when a breathless messenger reached them with word that a very large force of Indians was attacking Pinos Altos itself. Scott and his fellow rangers "started at once with all possible speed" to reinforce the miners there.[29]

Captain Thomas Mastin had arrived at Pinos Altos with fifteen of his men the evening before the attack. On the 28th an estimated 250 to 500 Apaches, evidently a strong joint force of Cochise's and Mangas Coloradas' bands, commenced a furious assault. The *Mesilla Times*, reporting the battle, stated:

> In such formidable numbers they have never assembled before on the war scout, and never before have they . . . evinced such boldness and daring as to attack a town of two or three hundred houses in open daylight. Nine-twentieths of the Territory of Arizona is under their undisputed control.[30]

Arriving at Pinos Altos, Fisher Scott and the rest of Mastin's company found houses and corrals in flames. Several residents had been killed. Captain Mastin, bleeding uncontrollably from a lacerated artery in a bullet-shattered arm, lay in critical condition.

The Indians might have taken the town at that point, according to Scott, "but for the courage and presence of mind of six women." As the battle raged, he said, these women, knowing that a twelve-pound howitzer and ammunition were kept in one of the stores, hauled it out by themselves and "made stuttering Tom Johnson" load and fire it into a number of Apaches attacking near them. Hank Smith agreed with Scott that the blast of the howitzer demoralized the Indians and saved the day for the defenders of Pinos Altos.[31]

The Apaches, however, continued to surround and attack the town. They also kept the nearby Santa Rita copper mines, several large trains at different points, and a company of forty well-armed Mesilla militiamen "perfectly besieged." An expressman left Pinos Altos for Mesilla to tell Colonel Baylor of the desperate situation. Before he had ridden a mile, the Indians shot his horse out from under him. He made it back to the town, mounted another horse, and ran the gauntlet again. He rode on alone to Mesilla, arriving safely on October 8. Baylor promptly sent a hundred Confederate soldiers to Pinos Altos, where, on October 7, brave young Thomas Mastin had breathed his last.[32]

John W. "Jack" Swilling, Mastin's tall, athletic first lieutenant, took command of the Arizona Guards, which now numbered over fifty members.[33] Fisher Scott and Hank Smith continued to serve under Swilling. Later in October their timely arrival saved a small wagon train faltering under fourteen hours of continuous attack by some hundred and fifty Apaches.[34]

During the next few months the Guards were assigned alternately to the Las Cruces vicinity and to Pinos Altos.[35] Whether or not Jack Pennington rode with them again is uncertain. The only clue is Esther Wadsworth's later statement that Jack remained in New Mexico for quite awhile after the ambush and that she thought he had "enlisted either on one side or the other of the Civil War."[36]

Jack may have continued to work for his friend, Grundy Ake. Ake had recovered three repairable wagons from Cooke's Canyon. He and his sons-in-law were using them to haul forage for the Confederates. Apaches attacked their hay camp north of Las Cruces on December 19. They burned the wagons and took some ninety head of cattle.[37] Jeff Ake recalled both Jack and Fisher Scott visiting occasionally in the Ake home in Las Cruces. When asked later if he had known Jack Pennington, Scott replied, "I knew him well, sir."[38]

A wagon train fortunate enough to reach the Rio Grande safely in December brought letters to a Mesilla resident from someone in Tucson, where Jack had left his family. The *Mesilla Times* printed a report of the despairing news the letters contained. Jack probably read it or heard about it. It would have caused him anguish, although his own circumstances were not much better, and Elias' refusal to leave doubtless still rankled. According to the *Times*,

> The remaining American population was cut off from all communication with the world, and in great fear from all quarters—from an invasion of Abolition troops; from the Apaches, who were becoming bolder and bolder; from the civilized Indians (the Papagos and Pimos), who have assumed a threatening attitude since the withdrawal of the regular troops; and from the Mexicans of Sonora, who were un-

bounded in their insolence. The letters received contain most urgent appeals for assistance of Confederate troops.[39]

The situation in the Gadsden Purchase was grim. Tucsonans seemed to be demoralized. Apaches under Mangas Coloradas and Cochise spread destruction and terror from the Rio Grande Valley to the valley of the Santa Cruz. There were only small militia companies like the Arizona Guards to counteract them. Union troops were holed up in northern New Mexico forts, recruiting volunteers and scrambling to rebuild strength after their ignominious rout by Baylor the previous July. Tension heightened early in January 1862 when three thousand Confederate grays under General Henry H. Sibley arrived in Mesilla and prepared to battle their fellow Americans in Union blue. Their objective was control of the entire region as a pathway to the coveted Pacific coast.[40]

NINE: NOMADS OF WAR

"Our prosperity has departed," reported the Tucson *Arizonian* of August 10, 1861, describing the conditions in which Larcena Page and the Penningtons existed after Jack and their former neighbors started for the Rio Grande:

> The population generally have fled, panic-struck . . . in search of refuge. We think no man ever before saw desolation so widespread. From end to end of the territory, except alone in Tucson and its immediate vicinity, there is not a human habitation. . . . The history of the United States, except, perhaps, in the case of the earliest settlement of Kentucky, cannot furnish a parallel. . . . In this extremity our only reliance is in God and ourselves. Pray, boys! but keep your powder dry!

There was another inhabited site, however, about eighty miles southeast of Tucson: Sylvester Mowry's Patagonia Mine. Curious as it seems, Elias Pennington took his family from Tucson to Mowry's mine soon after Jack's departure and only a short time before Larcena's baby was born. Perhaps he freighted supplies to Mowry and took the family along so as to look after them. He may have considered the mine the safest place for them to stay for the time being, and it was only a few miles from his border farm.

The Patagonia Mine was located in the hills edging the eastern side of Sonoita Valley. It was profitably producing a quantity of rich silver, and Mowry refused to abandon it. The slender black-haired, bearded ex-Army officer fortified it, hired more workers, and stocked a large store of ammunition and provisions. Fifty or more armed guards watched constantly for hostile Apaches.[1]

Sylvester Mowry was a Rhode Islander, an 1852 West Point graduate who invested approximately $200,000 in this mining venture. He shipped lead-silver bars by wagon to Mexico and on to Wales for refining.[2] Elias and Jim Pennington may have freighted some of it for him. Mowry was an enthusiastic promoter of Arizona's resources. Three times the early settlers elected him their delegate to Congress, although Congress did not officially recognize him as such. Historian Benjamin Sacks pictured Mowry as "impressive in his soldierly bearing and his finely tailored garments," good natured, and occasionally hot-tempered.[3] Mowry was also licentious, a lusty womanizer who enjoyed telling friends about his sexual exploits.[4] There is no evidence, however, that he so much as leered at any of Elias' young daughters.

The hills encircling the mine were thickly furred with oaks and junipers. A permanent spring and creek furnished water. When journalist J. Ross Browne visited the mine site in 1864, he described the "beautiful little valley of several hundred acres" as picturesque and cheering. Smoke from the main stack curled over the reduction works, storehouses, and peon quarters. Freight wagons unloaded wood and ore on a broad plaza in front of the works, and a lively hum of machinery filled the air. Around the "little huts of the peons," wrote Browne, "groups of women and children . . . gave a pleasing, domestic interest to the scene."[5]

When Larcena and her family arrived in 1861, however, the lovely site must have had a tense, militant atmosphere, with its many alert, gun-wielding sentries. Otherwise, it was probably much the same as when Browne saw it. It was here on September 4 that Larcena Page, cared for by her sisters, gave birth to a baby girl whom she named Mary Ann.[6]

Larcena would not know Fisher Scott until two years later. In the meantime, each wandered from place to place as circumstances led them. Life was hard and precarious. Apaches roamed uncon-

The hacienda of the Mowry Mine. Below, headquarters of Mowry's Patagonia Mine (both are 1864 sketches by J. Ross Browne, from *Adventures in the Apache Country*).

tested through the San Pedro, Sonoita, and Santa Cruz Valleys. Union and Confederate troops along the Rio Grande vied for control of New Mexico and Arizona, as North and South continued their great Civil War. Larcena and her infant remained for a time at the Patagonia Mine, protected by Sylvester Mowry's rough, unyielding miners, while Fisher scouted near Pinos Altos with the Arizona Guards.

Smallpox, which swept through Sibley's Confederate regiments in Mesilla Valley in December, 1861, and January, 1862, also broke out at the Patagonia Mine. Larcena and little Mary Ann were among those stricken. Mowry did all he could for the afflicted. Jane Pennington later recalled that he fed them "a scanty diet of flour and water, believing that 'no grease' should be fed to those ill of this disease." The smallpox was a comparatively mild variety, and most of Mowry's patients, including Larcena and her baby, survived the disease and the treatment.[7]

Although the major military conflicts of the Civil War occurred far from the Gadsden Purchase, the Penningtons and the few other American settlers who had stayed in Arizona suffered the war's severe effects. It was true that many desperate Tucsonans disillusioned by the lack of attention from Congress viewed Confederate occupation as a potential source of relief. This was demonstrated when the Confederates in New Mexico sent Captain Sherod Hunter and Fisher Scott's ranger lieutenant, Jack Swilling, to Tucson with a small mounted company of "Arizona Scouts." Captain Hunter reported to Colonel Baylor, "My timely arrival [on February 28th, 1862] with my command was hailed by the majority, I may say the entire population, of the town of Tucson."[8]

Hunter exaggerated. Although Tucson residents were grateful for military protection, and some were openly secessionist, there were as many or more who were loyal to the Union. Hunter gave them all the choice of swearing allegiance to the Confederacy or leaving town. Some left.[9]

The Confederate occupation of Tucson was brief. The United States Army's California Column, commanded by Colonel James H. Carleton, had begun to move eastward into Arizona and New

Mexico. Hunter's men bested an advance detachment of this force in a brief skirmish at Picacho Peak, forty miles north of Tucson, on April 15th. In New Mexico, however, General Sibley's inadequately supplied Confederate troops were already retreating to Texas after the decisive Battle of Glorieta. Hunter and his company left Tucson on May 4th to follow them.[10] There was no more Civil War combat in the Gadsden Purchase.

One of Carleton's first acts after he arrived in Tucson early in June, 1862, was to arrest Sylvester Mowry for aiding the Confederate cause. An employee at the Patagonia Mine accused the mine owner of providing Sherod Hunter's men with ammunition. Mowry indicated that he had done so, but only as a measure of defense against Apaches. Nevertheless, a military court arraigned him and several other suspected Southern collaborators in Tucson and sent them to Fort Yuma for trial.[11]

Larcena and Mary Ann Page had probably left the Patagonia Mine before Carleton arrested Mowry and confiscated his property. Some time after she recovered from the smallpox, Elias Pennington took his daughter and her baby to the family's farm on the border. J. Ross Browne reported,

> . . . during the whole time of the abandonment of the country by the Americans, this same Pennington lived with his family in a small cabin a few leagues above Calabasas, surrounded by the most ferocious and hostile of the Apache tribes. . . . Still they continued to live here, utterly alone, seeming rather to enjoy the dangers than otherwise.[12]

One wonders if the Penningtons could have enjoyed the constant vigilance, primitive conditions, hazardous travel, and scarcity of food and supplies that they experienced during that time. Did Larcena, gazing at the tiny babe in her arms, never yearn for better times and wonder how it would all end?

• •

By the first of July, 1862, William Fisher Scott, Hank Smith, Jack Swilling, and other Arizona Guards had a tough decision to make. They were at Fort Fillmore on the Rio Grande, from which the last Confederate unit in New Mexico was about to leave for Fort Davis, Texas. The Guards, as part of this unit, would go with them. Who knew where they might end up? These three were not the only rangers who were far more interested in their mining claims at Pinos Altos than in marching deep into Texas. Only once in the past year had they received any pay from the Confederates, and some had been pressured into Confederate service in the first place.[13]

On July 2, Scott, Smith, and a few comrades rode out of Fort Fillmore carrying their Confederate-issue minie-muskets. They did not return. Several others, including First Lieutenant Jack Swilling, followed their example within the week. Company records list these men as deserters. "Our company broke up and we scattered in various directions," is the way Scott put it.[14] Other Arizona Guards did go on to Camp Davis.[15]

Scott and Smith headed for Pinos Altos. So did Swilling, after working a while in Tucson. Federal troops are said to have captured Hank Smith. They gave him a choice: pledge allegiance to the Union or be jailed. He took the oath and became a military expressman for the Union army in New Mexico. He moved to Texas after the war ended.[16]

Sometime during the winter, Fisher Scott and Jack Swilling fell in with Joseph Reddeford Walker's exploring and prospecting expedition.[17] Walker's party of about thirty-three heavily armed men had traveled from Colorado through Santa Fe to a point about twenty miles southeast of Pinos Altos near the Continental Divide. In the bitter cold of January, 1863, they took shelter at abandoned Fort McLane in roofless log cabins partially burned by Indians.[18]

According to Daniel E. Conner, a member of the group, Walker conceived the notion of capturing an Apache chief to guide them westward across the Divide. Bold Jack Swilling hid a few men at the edge of Mangas Coloradas' own camp near Pinos Altos. Alone, Swilling approached the gigantic old chief as if to parley and succeeded in bringing Mangas, covered by prospectors' rifles, out as his prisoner. Union soldiers just arrived at McLane took charge of Mangas. His guards tormented and finally killed him. After that, Conner said, the Apaches "went to war in earnest."[19]

Walker's company, with Scott and Swilling, left McLane in March, following the San Francisco and Gila Rivers west. Within two months they reached the unexplored region of central Arizona. They followed the Hassayampa River to its head in beautiful wooded uplands near present-day Prescott. There they discovered exciting signs of gold, made camp, and built a stout log corral for their animals. On May 10 they held a miner's meeting to ensure the organized development of claims.[20] Scott recorded claim number 46, on the Oolkilsipava (Hassayampa) River in the Pioneer District, on June 17.[21]

When food supplies ran low, some of the party traveled to the Pima Villages to buy more. Word of their gold strike got out and eager prospectors were soon arriving daily at the site. Among them was Larcena's brother Jack Pennington.[22]

Some prospectors moved to better claims on Lynx Creek before long. Augustus Brichta, an eager gold-seeker destined to become Tucson's first Anglo schoolteacher, described meeting Fisher Scott there:

> I was astonished to see so many Huts and Camps, and in front of each were hanging plenty of fat Deer and ocasionally [sic] a Turkey. We met plenty of Apache Indians going up and down the Creek who were very friendly begging Tobacco. We arrived at the Miller boys Cabin late and cooked supper, there I became acquainted with Col McKinney and the Miller Bros., W. F. Scott, and others who flocked arround [sic] our Camp for News from the other world as they called it.[23]

In the meantime, Congress had separated Arizona Territory from New Mexico. Abraham Lincoln had signed the act on February 24, 1863, as the Walker party wintered at Fort McLane. This achievement, long sought by troubled residents of the Gadsden Purchase, did much to lift their spirits. It also hastened the development of previously unsettled northern Arizona. In the spring of 1863 there was no one north of the Gila River except two or three groups of exploring prospectors, a small garrison of soldiers at Fort Mohave on the Colorado River, and scattered Indian tribes. By the following spring there were a military post, Fort Whipple, and a small but growing territorial capital, Prescott, among the pines and granite dells near the Walker party's claims. Immigrant farming and ranching families soon settled the neighboring valleys.[24]

Fisher Scott went south that autumn with the gold he had gleaned from the Hassayampa River and Lynx Creek. He began sawing lumber in the Santa Rita Mountains — perhaps at John Page's old sawpit — and hauling the boards into Tucson. It was a highly risky occupation. Not only did hostile Apaches frequent the mountains and harass the roads, but also a great many "treacherous and thieving Mexicans" and American desperadoes bent on highway robbery were in the area.[25]

Emotions engendered by the bitter war were slow to fade. Scott later told his son-in-law Robert H. Forbes about one memorable occasion when he was at the Cerro Colorado Mine west of Tubac. It had been abandoned in 1861 but was again operating in 1863. There, "on account of a misunderstanding of his sentiments in connection with the Civil War, [Scott] came near being lynched."[26] The confrontation was undoubtedly tense and dramatic, but no further details are known.

Fisher met Elias Pennington and Larcena Page, the tall young widow with the pretty two-year-old daughter, in Tucson late in 1863.[27] Elias, doubtless enticed by the presence of the California Column there, had moved his family in from the border farm.[28] It is not just coincidence that as the army stationed its soldiers in various locations from 1863 to 1869, the Penningtons followed.[29] Elias benefited economically, as other civilians did, by hauling and freighting for the military.

Few if any other Anglo-American females dwelt in Tucson in 1863. Fair and blue-eyed among the dark Hispanics and Papagos strolling the village streets, Larcena and her seven sisters must have attracted attention. Larcena had turned twenty-six that summer. Caroline, now widowed or deserted, was twenty-four, and the five younger girls ranged from twenty to nine in age. Ellen, still unmarried at twenty-eight, faithfully mothered the family. Josephine, the youngest, was like Ellen's own child.

Elias' daughters were safe from Apaches in Tucson, but rough, unsavory Americans who gave the town a hard time and a bad name were a potential threat. J. Ross Browne, a San Francisco journalist who arrived with a returning Charles D. Poston in January, 1864, reported that the bulk of Tucson's population seemed to be "murderers, thieves, cutthroats and gamblers." Every man went fully armed, Browne observed. Violence and bloodshed occurred daily. Tongue in cheek he added, ". . . volunteer soldiers are stationed all over the town at mescal shops, the monte tables, and houses of ill-fame for the preservation of public order."[30] An unescorted walk to a store in such an environment might have earned the Pennington sisters embarrassing stares and confrontations. However, the appearance and reputation of powerfully built Elias and Jim Pennington undoubtedly discouraged insolence. The respect they showed their womenfolk was obvious.[31]

Browne admired the stalwart, handsome father and family who had refused to surrender their foothold on this perilous frontier. He found the story of Larcena's capture and survival unforgettable and later retold it in his book, *A Tour Through Arizona — 1864*: "For sixteen days," he marveled, "[she] endured the most dreadful tortures of hunger and thirst, subsisting on roots and berries, and suffering indescribable agony from her wounds. . . . She now . . . is an active, hearty woman."[32] Something of Larcena's indomitable spirit is implied in those two final adjectives.

If J. Ross Browne had doubted that there were still hostile Apaches in Arizona in 1864, he was soon convinced. A week or two after he arrived, twelve to fifteen of them attacked a man whom he was supposed to meet — Mr. Butterworth, an executive of the Cerro Colorado Mine. Poston had commissioned Browne to sketch pictures of the mine and to write some articles about it.

The Apaches attacked Butterworth's party near the diggings, killing two of his men. They struck Butterworth again six hours later as he drove toward Calabasas. His seven companions quickly fled, leaving him to face the Indians alone. He prepared to defend himself as well as he could behind a tree. Fortunately, the Apaches only set fire to the grass all around him and departed after ransacking his vehicle. Butterworth escaped the fire, wandered alone for two or three days, and finally made his way back to the mine.

Browne agreed to go with Poston and an escort of thirty soldiers to find the missing members of Butterworth's party. He was aware of the risks he would be taking, however, insisting that Poston should pay him in advance for his services, "something certain in hand to provide for [his large family] in case of misfortune." Poston gave him $5000 in bank drafts "and other assurances," which the journalist promptly mailed to his wife in California. Thus insured, he completed the mission safely.[33]

Browne must have seen Elias and James Pennington working at their sawpit in Tucson, where the army quartermaster paid twenty-five cents a foot for rough pine boards. The Penningtons labored alongside the crumbling south wall of the old Spanish presidio, their muscles swelling across strong backs and arms as they pulled the long two-man saw back and forth through heavy logs.[34] Spanish soldiers and Indian laborers had dug a deep trench there eighty-five years earlier, removing earth and mixing it with straw and water to make adobe bricks for the fort's walls and barracks. The excavation—a ready made spot for Elias' sawpit—ran the length of the south wall and became a narrow thoroughfare known as Calle del Arroyo. Green Pennington, almost sixteen, and Will, fourteen, undoubtedly helped their father and older brother. The only absent member of the clan was Jack Pennington, who was panning and scratching for gold on Lynx Creek.

Elias and Jim felled the raw timber in the Santa Ritas and brought it into town. Fisher Scott, also, may have delivered logs to them. Scott was now thirty-two, still a bachelor. He had been a rover ever since his migration from Scotland, but now he became a miller, a settled Tucson businessman. He acquired a partner, James Lee, and they bought the Silver Lake Flour Mill and subsequently the Tucson Mill, from Charles T. Hayden, the freighter whom Scott had once helped rescue from Apaches near Pinos Altos.[35] Fisher took time off from milling in the spring of 1864 to go to Prescott as an appraiser of town lots that were being laid out. He helped divide them into three classes valued at $7.50, $10.00, or $15.00. These sold at public auction in June.[36]

While Scott was thus engaged, the Penningtons moved again. Elias, anticipating the April transfer of two cavalry companies from Tucson to Tubac, took his family there. The army was closing its Tucson post and establishing Fort Goodwin 120 miles to the northeast. With that accomplished, the military force in Arizona jumped from 223 to 1076 men. Their goal was not to repel Confederates, but to bring marauding Apaches in central and southern Arizona under control—an objective that was not achieved until years later, and then only with still more soldiers and much difficulty.[37]

With the shift of military troops, Pennington considered Tubac a more advantageous place for his base of operations. Not only would the army need lumber for housing, but there was also a demand for freighters like Elias from the mines near Tubac and from citizens gradually resettling southern Arizona. Fisher Scott, also, acquired an adobe house on 160 acres near Tubac that spring, but he probably spent little, if any, time in it and sold it a year later.[38]

Tubac was still deserted when the Penningtons moved into one of the more habitable adobes. It was just north of the old church, facing the Santa Ritas.[39] J. Ross Browne, who had visited Tubac while searching for Mr. Butterworth's missing companions, described the journey there and the appearance of the village at that time. Between San Xavier and Tubac the "roadside was marked" with a number of graves of unfortunate early settlers.

All is silent and death-like; yet strangely calm and beautiful in its desolation. Here were fields with torn-down fences; houses burned or racked to pieces by violence . . . everywhere ruin, grim and ghastly with associations of sudden death.[40]

Browne had not seen a soul at Tubac. The old plaza where the happy Fourth of July celebration had been held in 1858 was overgrown with weeds and grass. Roofs of the houses were falling in, doors and windows were gone, walls were crumbling. Old machinery lay rusting near the former mine company headquarters.[41] Since the terrible summer of 1861, when Apaches and Mexican bandits had sent the last handful of defenders scurrying to Tucson, Tubac had slept, uninhabited.

Work frequently took Elias and James away from Tubac. They cut logs in the pinery and hauled them down to the village, which had a sawmill, or the remains of one. They were often on the road "with their heavy wagons and teams of twelve to fourteen oxen," freighting to and from Tucson and even from the Colorado River.[42]

Elias and James were gone on the April day that a horseman rode into Tubac where he found Larcena Page, her little daughter Mary Ann, her sisters, and two younger brothers in their adobe dwelling. The silent, deteriorating village seemed otherwise devoid of people. The clear-eyed, bearded stranger introduced himself as Charles Genung, a miner from the Prescott area. He was hot on the trail of a friend's murderer.[43]

The tracks had been fairly easy to follow because Genung himself had shod the stolen horse that the killer was alternately riding and leading. He knew the distinctive print that one of the horseshoes left on the ground. Genung—determined to find the Mexican who had repaid the warmth of a night's shelter by Alex Hampton's fireplace by stabbing Alex and escaping on Alex's horse—had persistently trailed his quarry all the way from Peeples Valley near Prescott.[44] The trail had led Genung to a temporary army camp a few miles from Tubac. There the hooves of cavalry horses had obliterated them. The cavalrymen had not seen the killer, but they directed Genung on to Tubac.[45]

Abandoned adobe house at Tubac in which Charles Genung found the Pennington women living in 1864. It is now part of an art gallery. The Penningtons lived in the portion with the thatched roof at the extreme right. Photo by Robert H. Forbes, 1915 (Arizona Historical Society).

The Penningtons must have been excited to discover that the miner knew their brother Jack. They invited him to spend the night, and listened as he told how he had helped pursue Apaches who had stolen Pennington's horse.[46] Jack and his partner, Underwood C. Barnett, had been camped at the time on Groom Creek, about six miles above where Genung, Daniel E. Conner, and others were mining. Genung's party was taking out gold assaying above $300 per ton; Jack and Barnett may have been doing equally as well. "On the thirteenth day of February," recalled Genung, "John Pennington came to our place . . . and found us at breakfast. He wanted help to follow Indians who had taken their last horse . . . only a short time before he left his cabin."[47] Barnett had started after the thieves, and Pennington was to meet him at a certain rocky outcrop on the trail. Genung described Jack as quick, alert, and active. He was hungry as well, and ate while the others made ready to go with him.[48]

When Pennington, Genung, and Conner reached the outcrop they saw Barnett crouched behind it, waving his hat as a signal to be quiet. Peering over the ledge, they saw a small party of Indians camped below in a brushy gulch, roasting parts of the horse which they had butchered. Snow started to fall heavily. Scarcely able to see their targets, the four miners opened fire on the Indians, who vanished, leaving behind an "old butcher knife, a lance, and a bow with a quiver of arrows."[49] Genung and Conner had laughed at Jack as he unconsciously dragged an arrow "which had passed through his pants at the foot and hung by the feathers."[50]

Larcena took a turn at the storytelling that evening. Charlie Genung heard how the Apaches had captured her and Mercedes. He gazed at the scars on her arms and studied the rugged mountains where she had stubbornly and courageously refused to die. Genung, like J. Ross Browne, later related her ordeal as one of the memorable events of frontier Arizona.[51]

In the morning, Genung watched as Green and Will Pennington guarded each side of the path to the spring "with guns as large as they were" while their sisters carried water for the day's use.[52] His sharp eyes detected no traces in Tubac of the killer he hunted. The Pennington women described a road that led from the cavalry camp up Sópori Wash to the Cerro Colorado mine and on to Sonora. They showed him a short cut to the road, and he set out again to find his friend's murderer. The telltale horseshoe prints soon showed up in the sand and before the day was over, Genung bagged his quarry.[53]

The cavalry established themselves in Tubac not long afterward. Early settlers returned with greater confidence in their security, and new immigrants arrived. One of these newcomers was a good-looking, dark-haired young fellow named Abner Jefferson Nichols, who could play a lively tune on the fiddle. It was not long before his blue eyes began to linger on Caroline Pennington Burr. Nichols was an Alabaman who had first come to the Gadsden Purchase as a teamster in 1858 or '59. He had freighted equipment from the Missouri River to the Patagonia Mine and had gone on to California looking for gold.[54] He returned to Tubac for reasons no longer known, and nothing is known of his occupation there. Nichols may have been one of the soldiers in the California Column who remained in the Santa Cruz Valley after discharge from the army. Whatever the circumstances, it had been five years since Caroline had seen or heard from her husband, Charles Burr. Abner courted Caroline and she married him. The date of their wedding can only be approximated, but in April 1866 they were living in Tubac and had a son, James Jefferson.[55]

The Penningtons and their neighbors felt renewed hope as the nation entered the period of reconstruction after the Civil War. Arizona's First Territorial Legislature had made significant strides. It had adopted a code of laws, planned for schools, roads and mail service throughout the territory, and defined counties. One of its highest priorities was to find a solution to Apache depredations and killings. It asked Congress for money to pay volunteer rangers, establish reservations, and induce the Indians to live on them.

Five companies of rangers were enlisted. Most of them were based near or north of the Gila River, far from Tubac. They performed effectively in those areas until disbanded two years later.[56] The attempt to get Indians to stay peacefully on reservations,

Charles B. Genung, who found the Pennington women at deserted Tubac in 1864 while he was on the trail of a murderer. The photo was taken about 1868 (Arizona Historical Society).

however, was unsuccessful until many years later. In the meantime, their hostilities still terrorized southern Arizona's settlers.

A small Apache war party ambushed James Pennington while the family lived at Tubac. He was hauling a heavy iron boiler to the Patagonia Mine at the time. The Indians killed his teamster and made off with the oxen. Jim escaped harm, but it was a close call. It gave the Penningtons a foretaste of the trauma that was about to hammer them.[57]

TEN: A SHATTERED FAMILY

$\qquad$ Larcena and her family, clinging loyally together, had so far survived their misfortunes. With the exception of John Page, they had escaped the fatalities which had overtaken other early Arizona pioneers. Hardship, toil, and danger were always part of the Penningtons' lives. Perhaps they never questioned how long their luck would hold out.

By later standards they were close to poverty, though they were as well off as most of their frontier neighbors and felt no inferiority. They had not established a permanent home since leaving Honey Grove, Texas, but they were not shiftless people — not poor whites in any sense. No skillful farmer equipped with tools, stout wagons, oxen to pull them and horses to ride, would have been considered indigent. These were sturdy, intelligent, handsome men and women — industrious, ambitious, religious, and caring. In one important way, however, they differed from many of their neighbors: they refused to run for cover when the Indians were on the rampage, and they paid dearly for their recklessness — or their courage.

They felt hopeful when the army's General John S. Mason took command of the District of Arizona in March, 1865. Mason immediately began a program designed to pacify and control the Apaches and to provide greater protection for Arizona immigrants. Within the year he doubled the number of military posts and camps from five to ten and requested more manpower. His aim was to drive the Indians onto reservations and make them self-supporting within those boundaries.[1]

One of the new posts, Fort Mason, was at Calabasas. It was manned by three 7th Infantry companies transferred from Tubac, which retained a military hospital and a detachment of soldiers.[2] The San Francisco firm of Garrison & Fish had the concession as post traders at both places. Massachusetts-born Edward Nye Fish employed Elias and James Pennington to freight goods for the stores from the Colorado River steamboat landing.[3]

Tubac began to seem crowded to Elias in 1865 as soldiers and settlers repopulated it, so he made a characteristic decision. He moved his family to the abandoned Sópori ranch, eleven miles northwest of Tubac on the Arivaca road. William S. Oury of Tucson, who had just bought the ranch, gave the Penningtons permission to live there, according to Amanda Jane Pennington.[4] He may have wanted someone there to look after the place. Only traces of the stone foundation remain today, but Robert H. Forbes, researching in 1913, photographed the Pennington dwelling at Sópori before it weathered completely away, and he left a description:

> . . . the house [is] very strongly posted on a rocky point jutting into the creek on the north side. The lower four feet of the structure is stone, the upper portion adobe. The roof is supported by cottonwood logs and thatched with willow, the original building is stated . . . to have been of stone, built about 1801, by one Orosco, manager for the Tumacacori priests. The house was afterward burned by Apaches, and rebuilt as it now stands.[5]

The ranch itself had existed since Spanish times, the de Anza family having held title to it in pre-American days. Colonel James W. Douglas, one of the first American settlers, acquired it in the 1850s and developed it into "one of the most flourishing ranches in the country."[6] After Douglas' death in 1859, it became the Sópori Land & Mining Company.[7] Tommy Farrell worked there as a cook for Richmond Jones, the manager, until Apaches ravaged it and slew Jones in the summer of 1861. Farrell then fled to Tucson with the other ranch employees and joined the Ake-Wadsworth party to the Rio Grande.[8] The ranch was still deserted and desolate when J. Ross Browne saw it in the spring of 1864.[9]

Tubac residents shook their heads at the idea of the Penningtons moving to isolated Sópori. Sópori Creek was a favorite route of raiding Apaches going into and returning from Mexico. Sabino Otero, a Tubac rancher and friend of Jim Pennington, declared that he did "not see how [the Penningtons] managed to live there because of the danger from Indians."[10] The threat was ever present. Larcena and her sisters sometimes heard Indian signals resembling dove and turkey calls. Young Josephine picketed her horse near the creek one morning and walked to the house. "She had not reached the door before an Apache ran out from the bushes, jumped on the horse and made off with him."[11]

For long periods at Sópori, Elias, as usual, left his capable, self-reliant daughters and their youngest brother to shift for themselves while he and his older sons were out earning money with their wagons and ox teams. Besides privacy and a defensive position, the advantage of the new home was the reliable watercourse edged with native walnut trees and cottonwoods. The women cultivated a vegetable garden on a flat area beside Sópori Creek. Although Elias and James brought sacks of beans and flour and other provisions from Tucson or Tubac whenever they returned, there were times when the food supply ran low before the men got back.[12]

Ellen Pennington converted one of the ranch's empty adobe buildings into a schoolroom for the younger children.[13] The older sisters stitched away at the family's clothing, as they always did when the men were gone. They waited out those lonely days with a patience born of long experience, their cheerful talk and laughter veiling a constant apprehension for the safety of their father and brothers.[14]

One of the more encouraging developments in the Territory was the resumption of mail delivery. Once a week now there was postal service to the Cerro Colorado Mine from Tucson and Tu-

Ruins of the fortified house at Sópori, where explorer William Bell found the Pennington women living alone in 1868. Photo by Robert H. Forbes, 1913 (Arizona Historical Society).

bac, and Sópori was a way stop. The Pennington sisters could correspond with Jack, who by 1866 was in Wickenburg, where the rich Vulture Mine was causing a boom.[15] Larcena could send messages to Caroline and Abner in Tubac. She could, if she wished, go on the mail stage to see them or to visit her former student, Mercedes Sais Quiroz, at Punta del Agua near San Xavier Mission. Mercedes, a young woman now, was living there with Bill and Missouri Ann Kirkland, who had returned from California.[16]

Occasionally Fisher Scott stopped at Sópori to see the Penningtons. He and Jimmie Lee were doing well with their flour mills. Elias bought their flour and often camped at their place when his trips took him to or through Tucson.[17]

The isolation of Elias' daughters made their times of trouble particularly difficult. It was at Sópori ranch in 1867 that twenty-four-year-old Ann Pennington sickened with malaria and died. The disease had recently been epidemic along the Santa Cruz Valley; the army had even abandoned Fort Mason at Calabasas the previous fall because malaria was debilitating so many soldiers.[18] Ann was the first of the Penningtons to forfeit their lives to frontier Arizona. Larcena and her sisters undoubtedly tended her with all their abundant love and meager resources. They must have wept as they carried her lifeless, wasted body to a small mesa a few hundred yards north of their house and buried her. One wonders if Elias and James were there to dig the grave.[19]

Malaria affected many settlers and soldiers along southern Arizona's rivers and streams. Samuel Robinson's diary entry at Tubac on July 15, 1861, described the chills and fever in that region as "very severe."[20] It was a major problem at Fort Buchanan in 1860. Most of the Penningtons experienced its effects periodically; the family kept quinine and other remedies on hand.[21] The "ague" that had weakened Larcena shortly before her capture by Apaches was very likely malarial. Years later in Santa Cruz, California, at the age of seventy-three, Amanda Jane also died of malaria, which she may first have contracted in her Arizona days.[22]

Jane and Ellen met their future husbands during the Penning-tons' stay at Sópori. A special census taken in April 1866 suggests that one of these men, William Alexander Crumpton, lived there for a time. Two years earlier he had been blacksmithing at or near Prescott, where he may have known Jack Pennington, with whom he became closely associated.[23] Crumpton, who was thirty-two in 1866, lost his heart to pert and pretty Amanda Jane, then twenty.

It is reasonable to speculate that Crumpton may have traveled from Prescott to Sópori in the spring of 1866 with Jack Penning-ton and Jack's former mining partner, Underwood C. Barnett. Jack was working near Wickenburg then, and his partner had turned rancher at Walnut Grove, near Prescott. Perhaps Jack knew that bachelors Barnett and Crumpton would like to meet all his unmarried sisters. Barnett's visit to Sópori at about this time is a virtual certainty because he married Ellen Pennington on April 28, 1867.[24] Ellen was an "old maid" of thirty-two who had spent her youth caring for her father and his younger children. Barnett was thirty-four.[25]

The younger Pennington children were old enough now that Ellen need not feel she was deserting them when she went north with her husband. The community of Walnut Grove had elected him to represent Yavapai County in the Third Territorial Legis-lature. He attended the session at Prescott in the fall of 1867. By that time, according to Daniel E. Conner, ladies frequently at-tended as spectators. Ellen may have been present when the leg-islators changed the territorial capital from Prescott to Tucson. Thereupon Barnett sold his Walnut Grove ranch and, as the Pres-cott *Arizona Miner* reported on October 12, 1867, "on Tuesday last left with his family, in company with the Pima delegation, for Tucson, where we understand, he intends to reside." Tucsonans elected Barnett to the Fourth Legislature.[26]

One day near the end of 1867, Larcena, four sisters, young Will, and six-year-old Mary Ann Page, were alone again at Sópori, Elias and James having been gone three weeks cutting pine trees. British explorer William A. Bell and his guide left Canoa ranch that morning and proceeded westward on the road that led to Arivaca and on into Mexico. Bell rode a very fine, obedient mule. His companion urged the last efforts out of a miserable grey horse. Their saddlebags bulged with their gear, tin mugs and canteens dangled from their belts, and they carried six-shooters and carbines. Bell, a Fellow of the Royal Geographical and Geological Societies, was now in the Southwest seeking a southern railroad route to the Pacific Ocean. His guide, Van Alstine, was a "tall, wiry old Western man, of at least sixty, but hale and hearty," as Bell described him. He had been "hopelessly drunk" when Bell first found him in Tucson, but he had an active brain and keen senses when sober and proved an excellent guide and congenial companion.[27]

After about eleven miles the two men came at noon to Sópori, "the next inhabited ranche," where they found Larcena and her siblings. Bell's account of the meeting offers an interesting glimpse of the Penningtons. The house was built on upthrust rock, he said, and was "still further strengthened against attack by a wall of stones, which completely surrounded it." He and Van Alstine climbed up and over these obstacles. The Pennington women greeted them warmly, and "chatted away with that perfect ease which strikes a stranger so much." It struck Bell that visitors must be infrequent and welcome. They invited the men to share their humble meal. "Poor people!" recalled the explorer. "It was bad enough, for it consisted of sun-dried Mexican mutton fried in grease, and very badly-made tortillas."[28]

The sisters told Bell of their experiences with Apaches and Larcena explained the scars that he saw on her arms. The family impressed the explorer as "honest, homely people" who would not invent such tales. He thanked them and wished them well. As he and Van Alstine clopped on toward Cerro Colorado they "talked for many a mile" about these surprising women:

> They had plenty of fire-arms, and knew well how to use them behind their stone barricades. But what a life of anxiety and

watching is theirs! and what joy it must be to them when their
father and brother come home safe from the mountains![29]

Jack Pennington decided to leave Arizona that year. He was
tired of dodging Indian arrows, he told his family.[30] Too many
arrows had been finding their mark lately in the Wickenburg vicinity. All the activity related to mining and processing ore had
thoroughly riled the natives. John T. Smith of Tubac, who was
also in Wickenburg at that time, described the way things were.
"The Indians got too thick for us there," he said. "They were
around every day and night," killing or wounding white men.[31]
Jack had been driving ore wagons with an armed guard sitting
beside him. He pointed out the inequity of this situation: he got
less pay than the guard but had to face the same hostile Indians
without a weapon in his hands.[32]

Jack proposed to move to central Texas—to Georgetown, in
Williamson County, where his old friends the Grundy Akes had
lived since leaving New Mexico with the Confederates. No doubt
Jack tried once more to persuade his father and family to give up
on God-forsaken Arizona and go with him. He made only two
converts, however—his sister Caroline and her husband, Abner
Nichols. In 1867 the Nicholses settled in Bell County about
twenty-five miles from the farm that Jack eventually bought outside of Georgetown.[33]

Larcena, her child Mary Ann Page, and the other Penningtons remained at Sópori. Things might have turned out better for
Ellen and Underwood Barnett if they had gone with Jack, but they
unaccountably left Tucson and moved to Tubac. Perhaps Ellen,
expecting their first child, wanted to be near her sisters when her
time came. Her baby girl died there soon after birth in the spring
of 1868.[34]

John A. Spring, a former soldier who tended Wooster's store
in Tubac at that time, described "the small adobe town." No more
than "three hundred souls" resided there, he said, and "two-thirds
of [them] were living in great poverty." Surprisingly, however,
there were also a steam flour-mill and four stores. The store own-

Abner Jefferson Nichols, the second husband of Caroline Pennington (Courtesy of Pearl Deiter and Judith Schuler).

ers profited handsomely from advancing necessary supplies to the twenty or so Anglo-American farmers and a few Mexican-American farmers along the Santa Cruz River, taking in exchange an interest-bearing promissory note payable at harvest time. The storekeepers then bought the farmers' grain at a prearranged price in the neighborhood of "six to seven cents gold coin per pound" and sold it at a higher price in Tucson or at one of the army posts. A crop that Elias Pennington cultivated in Sonoita Valley the following year may have been planted under a similar agreement with one of these merchants.[35]

Elias and his children who chose to stay in Arizona were not ignorant of the hazards surrounding them. Apaches had not ceased harrying settlers in their vicinity. Tom Jeffords achieved a peace treaty in 1867 with Cochise and his Chiricahuas, and most of those Indians left the warpath, but other bands grew even more troublesome as time went on. "I think the Apaches will be worse this year than ever before," John T. Smith predicted in 1868, and he was right.[36] Persistent as angry wasps, they stung central and southern Arizona repeatedly, raiding and murdering despite the increased manpower of the U. S. Cavalry. Apaches roving through Sonoita Valley in July slew one settler and ambushed another who survived. Undeterred by the proximity of a new army post, Camp Crittenden, they next attacked William Morgan's ranch and killed one of four soldiers on guard there.[37]

The following month James Pennington, his brother Green, and two Mexican teamsters left the Santa Ritas with lumber to be delivered in Tucson. Eighteen of Elias' oxen pulled the two heavy wagon loads. Their party halted two or three miles north of San Xavier Mission on a hot August evening, expecting to reach Tucson the next day. The mission's massive walls and high dome, distantly visible through scattered creosote bushes and giant saguaros, glowed amber in the setting sun as they halted. Sweating and tired, the men looked after their animals, fed themselves, and stretched out on their blankets.

They awoke at dawn to find the oxen gone. Moccasin prints in the sand indicated that Apaches had stealthily led them off. Jim and his two teamsters set out at once to trail the thieves through the low hills. They left Green with the wagons because he was suffering from "sore eyes" at the time.[38]

Green was waiting for his brother to return, when Fisher Scott trotted up on his way to Arivaca with a party of workmen. Fisher saw the ox yokes and chains lying on the ground and his young friend alone with the lumber. Green explained, and after a brief conversation Scott continued south on his business, apparently confident of Jim Pennington's ability to handle the problem. In the meantime, however, some of the Apaches who had stolen the oxen circled back, hiding beside their own trail a mile or two beyond the camp. They killed Jim and one of the Mexicans when they passed. The other teamster made it back to Green with the crushing news.[39]

Tall, quiet James Pennington was thirty-five when he died. He was unmarried. To his admiring sisters, he had been a source of protection, good humor, and affection.[40] Elias' partner and right-hand man since his youth, Jim's loss was a serious setback to his father and his diminished family. First Ann and now Jim: the untamed frontier was beginning to exact a heavy toll from these persistent Penningtons.

Larcena had a bit of cheering news in the sad, toilsome months that followed: Mercedes Sais Quiroz married Charles A. Shibell, a Sonoita Valley farmer. The little girl who was captured with Larcena in 1860 was now eighteen. Her bridegroom had been a miner, teamster, and soldier at various times. He passed through Tucson with Carleton's California Column in 1862 and then returned to Arizona to settle. He later served terms as Sheriff and Recorder of Pima County.[41]

The nine remaining members of Elias Pennington's household, including Larcena and Mary Ann Page, returned to Tubac for a short while in 1868. Then once again they loaded their possessions into stout wagons and took to the dusty road. They rumbled through Sonoita Valley to Camp Crittenden, which had been erected close to the ruins of old Fort Buchanan.[42] As usual Elias was seeking an economic advantage. The post required for-

Mercedes Sais Quiroz with her husband, Charles Shibell, about 1868 (Arizona Historical Society).

age for its animals and food for its soldiers. Farmer and freighter that he was, Elias could provide both.

The Penningtons moved into a three-room adobe building next to the sutler's store run by Tucson merchants Hiram Stevens and Sam Hughes. Two big oak trees grew beside the Pennington quarters. Elias hung a swing from a sturdy branch for Mary Ann.[43] As the little girl played, she could watch uniformed soldiers and officers strolling back and forth to the store or performing their mounted drills in an open area between the store and the barracks.

Elias drove his wagons out to the grassy mesas beyond Crittenden, as he had done eleven years earlier, to cut wild hay and deliver it to the camp. He no longer had Jim to help, but Green was now twenty-one and Will nineteen. Tubac storekeeper John Spring remembered one Sunday evening that fall when Apaches attacked "old man Pennington's ox teams" which were hauling hay. They killed a teamster, and drove off the oxen.[44]

Elias and his two sons were not harmed physically, but such periodic losses of working stock kept the family short of cash and strained their credit. In addition to that first disastrous Indian raid in October, 1857, and this most recent theft, Indians had taken two of Elias' horses, two mares and a colt, two mules, and eighteen oxen on various occasions in the last two years. These stolen animals were worth a total of almost $2000 at contemporary prices, a significant sum to most frontier settlers. Replacements were still hard to find, but Elias was able to buy two mules from Fisher Scott.[45]

To earn extra money, Larcena and her sisters put their experienced needles to work. We can imagine them seated in a circle under the two big oak trees, five heads bent over dresses being fashioned for officer's wives.[46] They must have made an attractive picture for lonely, nostalgic soldiers far from their homes and families.

Elias Pennington was a vigorous sixty in the spring of 1869. His handsome face was clean-shaven now, weathered and tan from constant outdoor labor. His clear blue eyes glinted from under a broad-brimmed hat. His body was hardly less lean and muscular than when J. Ross Browne had admired it five years earlier. Elias now decided to plant some crops on Sonoita Creek below William Morgan's farm, twelve to fourteen miles from Crittenden.[47] Passing land once tilled by William Wadsworth and Grundy Ake, Elias and his two sons made frequent trips with their farming tools to prepare these fields. Occasionally, settlers even saw some of the Pennington sisters riding horseback down the valley "with six-shooters strapped about them."[48]

The girls and Will stayed behind at Crittenden, however, on a day in early June, 1869, when Elias and Green started off down the valley. Four miles below the fort, near the site of Paddy Graydon's old saloon, father and son paused at Tom Hughes' farm. They saw the owner plowing near the road and called out a greeting. Hughes walked over. He did his best to dissuade Elias and Green from going farther. He reminded them that "Indians had been raiding [the valley] monthly, killing settlers in that lower portion" and even within ten miles of Crittenden.[49]

Hughes was not exaggerating the danger. Charles Shibell, Mercedes' husband, had farmed in that area and considered it the most hazardous in southern Arizona.[50] Elias probably knew that his son-in-law, Underwood Barnett, and other citizens of Tubac had recently petitioned the government for troops to guard that nearby town from Apaches.[51] He was surely aware of the risks involved, but he told Hughes he thought he would take his chances. As the Penningtons resumed their course, Hughes called after them, "Goodbye Mr. Pennington, I don't expect to see you alive again."[52]

At their fields, Elias and Green met three helpers — Redwood Brown, a man called Pete, and José Andrade. Elias had thirteen mules working the fields, according to Andrade — mules which would have been an almost irresistible temptation to the Apaches.[53]

About eleven on the morning of June 10th, Elias was plowing "with his rifle slung to his plowhandles" when Indians concealed behind thick brush fired at him from close range.[54] Elias slumped to the ground, killed almost instantly, his back full of protruding arrows. Green and Andrade were standing only twenty feet away, irrigating a field already plowed. They heard gunshots and saw Elias fall. Green, not knowing that his father was beyond help, stayed to defend him, but the enemy proved too numerous. There were about twenty-three Apaches, José Andrade estimated. He could never understand how they had gotten so close without detection.

The Indians wounded Green three times before he and Andrade succeeded in reaching the protective walls of the empty farmhouse. Brown and Pete had fled, racing to Camp Crittenden, where they "gave the alarm."[55] Green was still alive when cavalry troops arrived. By then, most of the Indians were well on their way with six of Elias' mules and three of his horses.

The Penningtons at Crittenden waited fearfully for many long hours after learning of the attack. They must have been overwhelmed when they finally saw the troopers carry Elias' body and Green into the small adobe post hospital. Green had always been a great favorite with his sisters. For a week they watched and prayed over him. In spite of all that they and the army doctor could do, he died on the eighth day after the attack. Green was buried beside his father in the post cemetery.[56]

Opinions varied as to which Apaches were to blame for these deaths. José Andrade suspected some of Cochise's Chiricahuas. Fisher Scott, William Morgan, Thomas Hughes, and many other settlers agreed that Eskiminzin's Pinals from Arivaipa Canyon were probably guilty.[57]

The killing of the Pennington men angered eloquent, outspoken Charles D. Poston. Still emotional about it years later, and about the many other struggling Arizona settlers slain by hostile Indians, Poston bitterly reminded the public that these pioneers had received encouragement and assurances of defense from the nation's highest officials. Then he blasted away at Washington:

A government that would permit such a family as the Penningtons to come to the frontier under the sacred obligation of
protection and be butchered and destroyed by Apaches ought
to be ashamed to look [an American] flag in the face on the
Fourth of July.[58]

Elias Pennington's children must heretofore have thought
him almost indestructible, a stalwart, trusted patriarch whose wis-
dom and spirit guided them through the worst of difficulties. Now
they were bereaved and dismayed, wishing that they all had left
this accursed frontier with Jack and Caroline. Larcena and Margaret, the oldest of the doleful group at Crittenden, rallied the
younger ones. It is likely that they raised cash by selling Elias'
valuable tools, wagons and animals, except those they would re-
quire for their own use. Then, doubtless aided by Underwood
Barnett and friends like Fisher Scott and "Uncle Billy" Crumpton,
they moved back to Tucson.[59]

Larcena and Mary Ann Page, Margaret, Amanda Jane, Mary
Frances, Josie, and Will now constituted the Pennington household. The little that is known about William Henry Pennington
leads to the suspicion that he was not up to the role of man of the
family so suddenly and tragically thrust upon his youthful shoulders. Twenty-five-year-old Margaret Pennington, however, had
developed into a clever dressmaker. With her brother and sisters
helping in various ways, her talent and industry became their chief
means of support.[60]

About the first of October, 1869, Larcena received a letter
from Ellen, who was still in Tubac. Ellen praised the fabric samples
and dress sketches that her sisters had sent her. In general, however, she sounded discouraged. "I suppose you have heard by
now," she wrote, "that we have a little boy baby . . . born on the
15 of Sept. [sic] It is small . . . [and] came sooner than we expected
but . . . the Doctor said that it was fully developed."[61] Ellen felt
weak and tired. Underwood had been taking baths for his rheu-
matism; he, too, was very feeble. Josephine had had four or five
fevers. She had not "learned her book any" for three or four weeks,

Mary Frances Pennington Randolph (Marshall L. Pennington).

Amanda Jane Pennington Crumpton, about 1874 (Arizona Historical Society).

but, Ellen reassured her sisters, she must try to make up for it. "Margaret, I am of your opinion," Ellen continued:

> I think that it would be much better to be in a country that a person could make a living in and have good health also. If ever we get able I expect that we [will] try to go to a more healthy place than this. . . .[62]

Obviously, Margaret Pennington had been complaining about conditions in Arizona—the poor economic situation, the ever-present malaria, the irreconcilable Apaches. She had been urging the family to leave the Territory. Another outbreak of smallpox in Tucson that fall reinforced Margaret's arguments.[63]

The event that convinced them all, however, was the death of Underwood Barnett on November 29th, presumably from rheumatic or malarial fever.[64] The Tucson Penningtons needed little more persuasion when Ellen, her baby son, and Josephine arrived at their door early in December with their bad news. Tending her infant and her dying husband had exhausted Ellen. She needed help and rest, but she could not wait to get out of Arizona. California had been the Penningtons' goal twelve years earlier. Now they agreed that they would go on at last to that state which they imagined so much richer, more beautiful, and hospitable than Arizona.

Weary and disheartened even as they started, but longing desperately for a happier future, the six sisters and brother readied a wagon and plodded out of Tucson two days after Christmas.[65] At the end of their first day of travel they halted at Point of Mountain Station, near present-day Rillito, about twenty miles northwest of Tucson. Station keeper William Whelan wrote a December 27th entry in the log he kept, "Pininting Family for San Diago [sic]."[66]

The next day he added, "The family got sick and went back to Tucson."[67] Their hurried return was spurred by anxiety: Ellen had developed pneumonia. Her condition was so obviously critical by the end of that first day that none of the family could consider going on. Ellen died in Tucson two days later at the age of thirty-four. Her little son did not long survive her.[68]

One can picture the downcast sisters and brother gathered around Ellen's grave. In each mind was the memory of the many years she had postponed marriage and a family of her own in order to care for them. They knew only too well the harsh conditions under which Ellen had faithfully persevered and the swift, cruel, successive blows that in these last two years had taken her father, a sister, two brothers, her babies, her husband, and her own life. Larcena, clinging in her despair to her religious faith, must have prayed fervently that Ellen would find a better reward in Heaven.

So a disastrous decade ended. As the 1870s began, the surviving Penningtons, stunned by their additional losses, relinquished their dream of California and wrote to their brother Jack in Texas, asking him to come back and get them.

Fortune seemed to take another malicious slap at them as they waited for Jack's arrival. Tucson's *Weekly Arizonan* of March 12, 1870, told the story. Late on the previous Sunday night, some twenty drunken soldiers from the military camp on the edge of town entered Alexander Levin's saloon. They demanded free drinks. Told that the saloonkeeper had summoned the military police, the frustrated rowdies left and proceeded toward the courthouse, firing pistols with intoxicated abandon as they reeled along.

The Pennington house was situated in the two or three blocks between Levin's Brewery and the courthouse. The family always kept one or more dogs. Many a time these loyal animals alerted them to danger.[69] Now, within the fence surrounding the yard, their dog began to bark as the noisy drunks approached. As casually as one might have swatted a bothersome mosquito, "the whole party fired through the gate, shooting the faithful dog through the head."[70] Inside the darkened house, Larcena and her family must have been startled awake, bewildered and apprehensive at the loud voices and gunshots and the sudden silence of their pet.

The soldiers passed on, "committing fresh outrages at every corner." They killed two men before the night ended. Such things could hardly be tolerated in Arizona Territory's capital city. The irate newspaper editor demanded that military commanders hand the arrested killers over for justice. When this failed to occur, he castigated those responsible for the lack of discipline among the troops: "It is enough," he protested, "that the people are constantly harassed by Indians without being subjected to the outrages of a depraved and drunken soldiery."[71]

In that same month, Pima County Supervisors saw fit to honor citizens who had been killed by Indians. They named Tucson's streets after those unfortunate settlers, giving the name "Pennington Street" to the equally historic and significant "Calle del Arroyo" where Elias and his sons had sawed lumber a few years earlier. Elias' sorrowing daughters may have derived some comfort and pleasure from this act of respect.[72]

Fisher Scott and William Crumpton undoubtedly did their best to dispel the gaunt and gloomy ghosts that haunted the Penningtons while they waited for Jack. Crumpton was now working in Tucson as a carpenter.[73] He may have worked on the new flour mill that Scott and his partner, Jimmie Lee, were building on Main Street. It was going to be "among the largest, and . . . certainly the most expensive building ever erected in Tucson."[74] Hard work and good luck had at last put the tall Scotsman, at the age of thirty-seven, in a financial position to marry and support a family.

Jack Pennington arrived with the summer heat. His sisters and brother Will were ready. They had carefully packed their father's Honey Grove Baptist Church membership certificate among the few family treasures they were taking. "Uncle Billy" Crumpton was going with them.[75] Amanda Jane may not have said "yes" to him yet, but he wasn't going to let her leave him behind.

By now it was possible to travel all the way to San Antonio by stagecoach. The family may have used their own wagons, however. If so, they faced a long and uncertain journey. Ninety days, according to Hall's 1866 travel guide, was required to make the

Early photo of West Pennington Street, Tucson, where drunken soldiers ejected from the Park Brewery (center back) shot and killed the Pennington's dog and two Tucson residents in March, 1870 (Arizona Historical Society).

trip between Tucson and the Missouri River, via Santa Fe, "with ordinary wagons and animals." There would be little danger en route if the travelers had among them twelve or more "determined men."[76] It was something over half that distance to Austin, the Penningtons' destination, and they had but three men and a handful of determined women.

Before leaving Tucson, Jack had his brother James' body transferred to the little cemetery at Sópori, "so that sister Ann would not be out there alone."[77] Five of the original thirteen Penningtons would remain beneath Arizona soil. After thirteen years on the bloody, unyielding Arizona frontier, the chastened survivors were giving up the struggle and going home to Texas.

ELEVEN: NEW LOVE, NEW LIFE

One of the Penningtons — Larcena — did not go to Texas, after all. The *Weekly Arizonan* told why:

"Caught at Last"

Wm. Scott, Esq., of the firm of Lee and Scott of this place, after having withstood the dangers and hardships of about twelve years of frontier life, and reached a standard of prosperity which most men might envy, was last week — not killed by Apaches, as the reader may suppose, but "on the contrary quite otherwise" — united in marriage to a most excellent lady, a daughter of the late Mr. Pennington, a lady who, individually and in connection with her family, has already figured prominently in the history of the early settlers of Arizona.[1]

It is tempting to speculate how it happened — how these two long-time, trusted friends, Larcena and Fisher, finally agreed to spend the rest of their lives together. Fisher may have been quietly sure for a long time that as soon as he had his business going and could provide a suitable home, he would ask her to marry him. It is just as likely that he, a confirmed bachelor it seemed, would have held his peace indefinitely if Larcena's imminent departure had not spurred him.

However and whenever he finally proposed, Larcena had many things to consider before she said yes: the hardships she had suffered in Arizona, the insecurity of the still-bloody frontier, the loved ones she had lost and the future separation from her remaining brothers and sisters. But facing her stood a good strong man offering love, protection, and the prospect of a better life in rough but rapidly improving Tucson. She was now thirty-three, young enough to enjoy a happiness she had not known for many long years — the exciting, comforting warmth of a loving husband's arms. And there was Mary Ann, her daughter. The child, almost nine, would benefit from a kind stepfather like Fisher.

The decision was never seriously in doubt. Larcena told her family they must go back to Texas without her.

Presumably Crumpton and the six Penningtons lingered long enough to help celebrate the wedding, which took place on July 27, 1870.[2] Details are lacking, but since there was no Protestant clergyman in town, it is likely to have been Justice of the Peace "Charley" Meyer who, in his heavy German accent, pronounced them man and wife. The Penningtons then rattled off in their loaded wagons, and Larcena and Mary Ann moved into Scott's new house. He had built it on Main Street beside the innovative Eagle Flour Mill which he and his partner had nearly completed.[3]

For Larcena it was the beginning of her happiest years. Outside Tucson the Apaches still prowled and life was hard and dangerous, but there was comparative safety and plenty in the community. The picket house on the banks of Sonoita Creek, the cramped stone cabin on the border, the dusty adobes of Calabasas and Tubac, the fever-ridden hovel at Sópori, the isolation and grief she had known — all faded into memory as Larcena commenced a new kind of life.

The whole town was excited about the mill, rapidly thrusting like a green young cornstalk above the dusty field of one-story adobes that was Tucson. Together Larcena and Fisher watched its growth. "Before another month shall have passed," reported the *Weekly Arizonan* on August 6th, "the voice of the steam whistle will have awakened the echoes of the adjacent mountains."[4] The mill was in successful operation by October 29 when the *Arizonan*

William Fisher Scott, probably a wedding photograph taken about 1870 (Arizona Historical Society).

praised Lee and Scott's remarkable achievement, adding, "There are still some spirits in Arizona which know not how to yield."[5]

Scott's partner, James Lee, and his family also lived adjacent to the mill. "Jimmie," as Lee was called, was close to Scott's age, a pleasant-looking fellow, full-bearded but rapidly getting bald. Lee had immigrated to the United States from Ireland, and had ended up in Arizona in 1856 or '57. Both men were naturalized citizens of the United States.[6] Lee had been a hostler for the Butterfield Overland Mail Company, and when the company discontinued operations in Arizona he had started freighting and mining. He had married María Ramírez, descendant of two early Tucson families.[7]

María's grandfather, Alvino Ocoboa, born in Spain, had served the King as a *soldado* in the old walled Spanish fort of Tucson before Mexican independence in 1821. He still lived in the town in 1870, at the age of ninety-four.[8] Until the day in 1848 when Apaches killed María's father, Rafael Ramírez, he too had been a soldier at the presidio, which was by then a Mexican outpost.[9] María was very small when she lost her father, but the way he had died was a horror that she had in common with Larcena.

Jimmie and María Lee spent the troubled early years of the Civil War in Sonora, returning to Tucson in 1864 when Lee and Scott jointly bought the Silver Lake Mill. By the time Larcena moved in next door in 1870, the Lee family included four little children and a thirteen-year-old servant girl.[10]

The Scott's way of life probably differed little from that of these partners and neighbors. "We lived like farmers in those days . . . it was a farm town," remembered one of the Lee daughters when she was older. They had cows and chickens, butchered their own meat, canned their fruit. Everyone then, she said, used brick ovens with wide hearths for cooking. Housewives usually had one or more servants.[11] An irrigation ditch known as "the *acequia*" ran from the Santa Cruz River through cultivated fields a short distance west of the Lee and Scott homes at a lower elevation.

Lee and Scott considered themselves prosperous at that time.

Each valued his share of their joint real estate at $5000 when Charles Shibell came around to take the 1870 census. Lee declared $3000 in personal property and Scott $3500.[12] "We lived well," recalled Jimmie Lee's daughter. In 1872 her father imported a "regular stove," a $200 sewing machine for María, and a bulldog to watch his stable of fine horses. All these things came from St. Louis in freight wagons, as did most of their furniture and supplies except what they themselves grew or made.[13]

Mercedes and Charles Shibell also lived near the Scotts. Larcena's former student and fellow captive was now the mother of a year-old daughter. Another neighbor was territorial Governor Anson P. K. Safford, who shared a house across the street from Fisher Scott's with several other prominent men. The governor was forty-one that year, a short, dapper, slim Vermonter.[14] He enlisted Fisher in his energetic fight for public education. That Larcena and Fisher became friends of Safford is indicated by the fact that the governor's second marriage took place in their home in 1878.[15]

There were more than 3000 inhabitants in the village of Tucson when Charles Shibell enumerated them in the summer of 1870. Besides Larcena and her sisters, who had not yet departed when he made his count, Shibell listed only nine other Anglo-American women.[16] One of these was Mrs. Granville Oury, another of Larcena's neighbors. Malvina Oury had arrived from Texas in 1865 and had hopelessly dubbed Tucson "the most forlorn, dreary, desolate, God-forsaken spot of earth ever trodden by the foot of a white man."[17]

Malvina was six years younger than Larcena. She was intelligent, well-educated, and proper, a "lady" who had led a very different life from that of Elias Pennington's daughters. Her husband was then District Attorney of Pima County. He was a brother of Will Oury, who had buried John Page at Cañada del Oro in 1861 and had later allowed the Penningtons to live at Sópori. Malvina considered few if any Tucson women her social equals. She and Larcena had emerged from two different worlds and their contacts were undoubtedly limited to polite, casual greetings. Occasionally when the two met, Malvina inquired about Larcena's sister Margaret, who had probably made some dresses for her. Margaret was pleased when Larcena wrote her that Mrs. Oury had asked. She wrote back, ". . . you know she used to hold her head so high."[18]

The new house Fisher Scott had built may have had such unusual amenities as a wood floor and glass window panes, but no Tucson homes had water piped in as yet. The Scotts lived only a block from the traditional village spring, El Ojito. Larcena saw Papago and Mexican women stroll to and from the spring with earthen jars of water expertly balanced on their cloth-draped heads. Her own long years of carrying buckets from a spring or creek were over. She could now buy water from Malvina Oury's brother, Adam Sanders, co-owner of a water delivery business. Sanders and Joe Phy made their rounds with a two-wheeled water cart pulled by burro or mule, selling water at five cents a bucket. They posted their charges on the door jambs of customers who preferred to settle accounts weekly.[19]

Freight wagons daily rumbled past Larcena's new home on Main Street, as Americans called the centuries-old Camino Real, which had connected the presidio with towns in Mexico. She watched them go by, creaking under their burdens of silver ore or lumber. Other "immense red wagons," pulled by twelve-mule teams, and "clumsy, screeching ox-carts" still brought from Mexico much of the merchandise sold in the stores — flour, corn, jerked beef, chickens, eggs, and occasionally watermelons or stalks of sweet, juicy sugar cane. Mexican laborers in search of jobs often accompanied these freight trains. The women made capable cooks and house servants and worked for low wages in Tucson households like the Lees' and Scotts'.[20]

The Spanish elite of Tucson took pride in their enclosed flagstone-paved courtyards, which were colorful and fragrant with flowers. Constant sprinkling and irrigating kept these small retreats and the adjoining homes cool and fresh. There were few places of that sort, however. "The average Mexican," observed Army wife Josephine Clifford in 1868, "even though his family consist of twenty head, lives in a single dark *adobe* room, without window or fireplace," lying indoors in summer to escape the beating sun and outdoors in winter to soak up its welcome warmth. Papago brush huts fringed the town.[21]

Will Oury's "low, solid, *adobe*" farmhouse beside the Santa Cruz River boasted a scarlet geranium that covered most of the garden wall, a clump of willows shading a large, cool spring, and an adobe spring house full of "rich, sweet milk." Mrs. Clifford described Oury's wife, Inez, as "one of those grand, black-eyed women, with the bearing of a princess, whom we find among the old Spanish families."[22]

The character of the town was gradually changing. John H. Marion, editor of Prescott's *Arizona Miner,* was in Tucson in the autumn of 1870. He admired Lee and Scott's "splendid two-story flouring mill" and observed other signs of progress: the stores were well stocked and nicely finished inside; many built of humble adobe were plastered and painted on the outside to resemble brick or stone. An incongruous sign on one shop—"Ice Cream Saloon"—surprised him.[23] The streets of Tucson, a filthy disgrace in earlier years, were now swept clean. Justice of the Peace Charley Meyer assigned a prisoner chain gang to that task.[24]

Tucson now had several restaurants. Tommy Farrell, whom Jack Pennington had saved at the Cooke's Canyon ambush, ran an eating house on Franklin Street. He advertised that he would "entertain his guests with the choicest viands of the season . . . in the finest style." Apparently excluding ladies, he offered to accommodate gentlemen "with Hot Coffee, Chocolate, Pies, Cakes and Oysters at all hours."[25]

There was even a school for girls in which Larcena enrolled Mary Ann—"The Sisters' Convent and Academy for Females," started by seven Catholic nuns of the order of St. Joseph who arrived in Tucson in the summer of 1870.[26] According to their advertisement in the *Arizona Citizen,* the Sisters of St. Joseph taught "every useful and ornamental branch suitable for young ladies." That meant reading, writing, arithmetic, geography, and (for an extra fee of ten or twelve dollars) music, drawing, painting, and making flowers with "wax, hair, etc." The nuns promised to pay particular attention to plain and ornamental needlework at no extra cost. The school uniform was black dress in winter and white in summer, with a white veil on the head.[27] The native language of most of Mary Ann's classmates was Spanish.

Such evidences of progress and civilization existed only within the town limits of Tucson, Prescott, Yuma, and the infant village of Phoenix, recently founded by Fisher Scott's former lieutenant, Jack Swilling. Between these widely separated settlements, frontier conditions still prevailed and life was at risk. A month after Larcena's wedding Charles Shibell, en route from Camp Goodwin to Tucson, found the mail coach destroyed and four white men with it dead and gruesomely mutilated. In his opinion, the Territory was "now in a defenseless condition."[28]

Eight miles out of Prescott on Hassayampa Creek, less than four months later, Indians put two bullets through William Dennison's chest as they stole his horses and mules. Bill Dennison with the sunny disposition—"a universal favorite wherever he was known"—had shared John and Larcena Page's cabin near Canoa in 1860. Larcena remembered how his ringing voice and banjo had lifted their spirits. Just a few days before his death he had finally received a letter that his father had written to him two years earlier. He had told his Prescott friends that he would soon go home to Tennessee with a fortune in silver if his prospect proved out and "if the Indians didn't get him first."[29]

Fisher Scott and Jimmie Lee had also suffered from Indian depredations. Three times between 1867 and 1870 Apaches had stolen horses and mules from them at the Naguila Mine, another property they owned jointly, ten to twelve miles west of Tucson. It had a rich vein of silver accessed by a shaft 120 feet deep. Will Oury, Sidney De Long, and other interested Tucsonans visited the Naguila in March, 1871, and reported that much ore had been extracted and work was proceeding steadily. Everything they saw confirmed their previous opinion that the mine had great value. They grew euphoric about its potential benefits to the town, and merchant De Long placed a specimen from the mine—"an excellent class of ore"—on exhibit at his store.[30]

Scott and Lee had sent eight good mules out to the Naguila in 1867 to run the arrastras that ground the ore, but Apaches took the animals before they had worked ten hours. A second time, close to town, Indians killed a woodchopper employed by Scott and made off with two horses. More recently they had stolen three horses, one a fine white saddle mare for which a Tucson businessman once offered Fisher ten twenty-dollar gold pieces. On this occasion, Scott and Lee trailed the thieves to the Tortolita Mountains north of Tucson. They found only the carcass of one of the animals, lanced and partly eaten. These losses cost Larcena's husband over $1400 and virtually erased his mining profits.[31]

As such killings and thefts escalated in 1869 and 1870, Governor Safford's consternation grew. He described these occurrences in detail to the Sixth Legislature, which convened in Tucson in January, 1871. That body published a "Memorial" of incidents, complete with affidavits. The importance of preventive action was evident. The additional army personnel and new camps established in Arizona had not yet controlled the ubiquitous, unrelenting Apaches. Indians were not the only cause for concern. As much to blame, stated Governor Safford, at least on the 150-mile road from Gila Bend to Fort Yuma, were roving Mexican bandits who hit their targets, then vanished into Mexico. Anglo-American highwaymen also destroyed mail and took lives.[32]

Fresh Indian depredations and killings near Tucson in March roused the governor and the public further. Most Tucsonans attributed these deeds to Pinal Apaches under Eskiminzin, head of a large band gathered near Camp Grant at Arivaipa Canyon on the San Pedro River.[33] There, under a humane peace policy, the military gave Indians provisions in return for their pledge not to leave their camp without permission. It seemed obvious to southern Arizonans that the Indians were accepting the food while violating their agreement, and that the government was in effect aiding murderers of its own citizens.[34]

"Uncle Billy" Crumpton, who be-
friended the Penningtons and married
Amanda Jane Pennington (Marshall
L. Pennington).

James "Jimmie" Lee, Fisher Scott's
partner from 1864 to 1884 and Camp
Grant Massacre participant (Arizona
Historical Society).

Eighty-two Americans, including Fisher Scott's partner, Jimmie Lee, and possibly Scott himself, reacted by joining a civilian militia company raised by Tucson's new Committee of Public Safety. Will Oury was chairman of the committee and captain of the militia. About March 23, 1871, Oury and two other committee delegates rode to Florence, a budding settlement ninety miles north on the Gila River, to confer with General George Stoneman, the new commander of the army's District of Arizona.[35] Stoneman was making an inspection tour of the Territory. It was the general's opinion that Indian affairs in Arizona were "in as satisfactory a condition as can reasonably be expected."[36] The Tucson men knew otherwise: as increasing American settlement threatened the Apache with loss of domain, freedom, and his way of life, he was reacting more savagely than ever. The three delegates returned from their long, hard ride and bitterly informed their associates that "that august personage" would give them no further military aid and expected Tucson, the largest community in the Territory, to make do with what it had.[37]

Stoneman's attitude, the government's Indian policy and the true state of Arizona's affairs as Safford knew it, were all intolerable. The governor promptly went to Washington, D.C., and conferred with President Ulysses S. Grant, with the result that Stoneman lost his command on May 2nd.[38] But the pot boiled over in southern Arizona before then. Two additional incidents, following all the others, fueled the fire. On April 10 Apaches raided the Papago livestock herd at San Xavier. Three days later four Apaches struck the San Pedro Settlement thirty miles from Camp Grant and killed farmer Alex McKinsey. Five settlers who gave chase ran into a party of about a hundred hostile braves, who killed three of the surprised Americans in the ensuing fight.[39]

Evidence convinced the Tucson Committee of Public Safety that Pinal Apaches from the Camp Grant area had committed these acts. The committee spent the next two weeks in unproductive debate. Then a few members decided it was time for action. Will Oury, Jimmie Lee, Sidney De Long and three or four other Americans, together with forty-eight Mexicans and almost a hundred eager Papagos, rode to the Pinals' camp on Arivaipa Creek, five miles from Camp Grant, arriving at daybreak on April 30.

The Papagos — long the victims of Apache warfare — began a grisly process of extermination with their spears and war clubs while Americans and Mexicans positioned on the bluffs above the creek shot those Pinals who tried to run or climb to safety. Very few Apaches escaped. In half an hour it was over. Between eighty-five and a hundred and twenty lifeless bodies lay on the ground. Most were women and children; few Apache men had been at camp that morning. The Tucson party burned their victims' wiki-ups and returned to town with twenty-seven captive Apache children. Some of these orphans were taken into Tucson households and reluctantly given back to the tribe much later under government orders. Others are said to have been sold into slavery in Mexico.[40]

Across the nation in more populated, sheltered, and secure environments, Americans unfamiliar with events that had prompted the brutal reprisal raised a horrified public outcry. President Grant threatened Arizona with martial law if Governor Safford did not immediately prosecute the participants in the "Camp Grant Massacre." Legal processes take time, however. A Grand Jury convened in Tucson in October and issued 111 indictments, 108 of them for murder. The *Arizona Citizen* retorted that the blood of five hundred fellow citizens killed by Apaches "cries from the ground to the American people for justice — justice to all men!"[41] It took the trial jury only nineteen minutes to acquit Sidney De Long, who was tried on behalf of all the accused.[42] Few Tucsonans thought the verdict anything but just. One pioneer woman still felt that way many years later. She asserted calmly, "It was not until after the citizens took things into their own hands" that they had peace.[43] Considering Larcena and Fisher Scott's past experiences with Apaches, it seems unlikely that either of them would have condemned Jimmie Lee for his part in the affair.

The event of greatest concern to Larcena and Fisher in the fall of 1871 was not the trial that exonerated Fisher's partner, but the

The court and principals of the Camp Grant Massacre trial outside the first Pima County Courthouse, corner of Church and Ott Streets, Tucson, 1871. The white-bearded man framed by the doorway is thought to be William S. Oury. The photo—one of the earliest taken in Tucson—was by itinerant photographer Edward J. Muybridge of San Francisco (Arizona Historical Society).

birth of their son, William Pennington Scott, on September 17th.[44] Fisher apparently wrote a belated letter to inform Larcena's brothers and sisters of this blessing. Margaret Pennington answered, scolding Larcena, "If it was not for Fisher we would not hear from you at all." She was thrilled about the baby, however. "Tell my little nephew if I was there I would cover him with kisses and . . . take him out a bug hunting." She advised Fisher to make his stay-at-home wife get out and visit the neighbors more often, adding, "I know how she is."[45]

The Texas branch of the Penningtons now lived at the Georgetown farm that Jack and "Uncle Billy" Crumpton jointly owned. The men freighted between there and San Antonio. Margaret wrote that she and her sisters had been alone "as usual" for over a month and were "looking for" the men to return soon. Reading that line in the letter, Larcena must have recalled how often she had waited with them for Elias to come home.

There was disturbing news in Margaret's letter, and more to follow. Caroline Pennington Nichols was mentally ill as a result of the recent birth of twins. She was staying at Jack's farm, where her sisters were taking care of her. Neither a clairvoyant whom they had consulted nor the "best doctors" predicted her recovery.[46] To make matters worse, Margaret Pennington died on April 5, 1872, only five weeks after writing to Larcena and Fisher. She was twenty-seven. Jack fenced off a small graveyard on his farm and buried her there.[47]

No doubt Larcena was saddened by these misfortunes of her Texas family, but she was cheerful by nature and too busy with her new life to be depressed for long. She was pregnant again, involved with her little son, and supportive of her husband, who was active in milling, mining, and community affairs. John Capron, pioneer stage-line operator, wrote of Scott in later years, "How I would like to shake him by the hand. We always used to think of him as an honest, hard-working man."[48]

Fisher was enthusiastically promoting Governor Safford's drive for public schools. The Sixth Territorial Legislature in 1871 had enacted a measure to fund public education for Arizona's ever-increasing number of children. When a new school opened in Tucson in March, 1872, the *Arizona Citizen* named W. F. Scott among those who deserved "principal credit in the inauguration of free public schools in Arizona."[49]

The Pima County Supervisors appointed Fisher to the School Board, which rented and furnished a building and hired John A. Spring as the boys' teacher.[50] "Mr. Scott conducted me to an oblong adobe building," Spring later recalled, "[and] delivered to me a number of school books with the injunction to . . . supply them free of cost to children of indigent parents."[51] For the time being, the Board members worked out an agreement for the Sisters of St. Joseph to teach the girls.

On June 27, 1872, Larcena and Fisher watched their bright, pretty eleven-year-old, Mary Ann Page, receive scholarship awards at the close of St. Joseph's Academy's second term. Mary was not "crowned for good conduct," as Will Oury's daughter Louise was, but she won the first prize in her class for arithmetic and for reading. She also played a role in a skit, "The Queen of Flowers."[52] Beaming proudly at the enchanting young creature onstage, Fisher and Larcena could not know that in a few short years Mary would become the central figure in a real-life drama that would bring them all heartache and astound the whole town.

TWELVE: MARY PAGE

In September, 1876, Mary Ann Page turned fifteen. She was pretty enough to turn heads as she walked to the Congress Street School, her textbooks under her arm. Her white shirtwaist and ankle-length skirt fit gracefully over maturing curves. Larcena's daughter was becoming a young woman.

Mary's teacher, Mary Bernard Aguirre, could not have foreseen the far-reaching consequences when she chose fair-haired Mary to represent "Morning" in one of the "tableaux vivantes" that her class would perform for the townspeople as part of that year's Christmas celebration. "There was a romance begun the night of the tableaux," Mrs. Aguirre later wrote in her memoirs, "which ripened into a marriage and ended in murder for one, and a slow, awful death for the other."[1]

The tableau portraying "Night and Morning," illuminated by colored limelights imported from San Francisco, was on the stage at one end of the long, darkened room when Dr. John C. Handy, Tucson's most prominent physician, entered at the other end. The passion with which he reacted was characteristic of the big, handsome, thirty-two-year-old bachelor.[2] He was instantly "spellbound," he later told Mrs. Aguirre. She described the picture he saw:

"Night," a lovely dark-haired girl, was leaving the stage, looking back towards "Morning" as she came in; in filmy white, the morning star on her forehead and treading upon pink clouds, her arms were outstretched towards "Night," and she, a lovely pink and white of a girl, full of life and youth. . . . Though he had known the girl who represented "Morning" almost all of her life, he never had realized her beauty until then. He fell violently in love with her then and there and in a year they were married.[3]

"Violent" was a word aptly applied to the doctor although many of his admiring patients considered him saintly. The marriage of their daughter to this respected man eventually brought great sorrow to Larcena and Fisher, who at first probably considered it an excellent prospect for the girl. There were dangerous and implacable elements in Handy's personality when he was crossed or provoked.[4] Years later, Judge Richard E. Sloan commented, "I have never known a man who would go farther to avenge a fancied or real slight or injury than Dr. Handy."[5]

Handy had opened his office in Tucson in August, 1871, a year after Larcena and Fisher married.[6] The doctor was an intelligent and talented professional. Born in New Jersey and transplanted to California, he was only nineteen when he graduated from Medical College of the Pacific in San Francisco, the state's first medical school. In Arizona, he had served as a contract surgeon since 1866.[7] He was that rare white man, like Tom Jeffords, who had gained the Apaches' confidence. He had learned their language and acted as a military interpreter. Two Apaches guided him through hostile territory on his first visit to Tucson in 1870. The *Weekly Arizonan* reported at that time: "The Apaches regard the Doctor with a species of reverence because of his success in treating their diseases. He . . . is entrusted with full particulars regarding their laws, customs and traditions."[8]

From 1871 to 1892 Tucson considered John C. Handy its "foremost physician and surgeon." According to Dr. William V. Whitmore, who knew him well, "never have the poor of Pima County had more attentive and skillful service than during those

John Charles Handy, M.D., prominent Tucson physician (Marjorie Handy Hart Collection, Arizona Historical Society).

years. . . . Dr. Handy proved to be a distinctly high-class man, both as a physician and surgeon. He at once won the high respect and utmost confidence of the people."[9]

Mary was not yet seventeen when she married John Handy on July 17, 1878. For two weeks before the wedding, Tucson women talked of little else. Larcena and Fisher Scott decorated their garden lavishly with lamps and candles, hired musicians, and greeted a "gay and large assemblage," laden with gifts, on the appointed night. John E. Anderson, a young Presbyterian missionary who had just commenced building Tucson's first Protestant church, performed the ceremony. "The bridesmaids and groomsmen 'stood up' like soldiers," the *Arizona Weekly Star* declared, and the newlyweds and their guests danced away the balmy summer night.[10]

"The friends of the happy pair will join us in wishing Mr. and Mrs. Handy an unobstructed pathway of prosperity and happiness through life," the *Star* chirped blithely.[11] But none of the admiring girls who envied the bride on that gala evening would have wanted to be in her place at the end.

Things seemed to start out well enough. Mary gave birth to a baby in each of the next four years. The day after John Charles Handy, Jr., the fourth child, was born, on July 27, 1882, his proud father bought $10 worth of cigars.[12] Larcena became a busy grandmother as the young wife found herself inundated by motherhood. The two women now had six young children between them. Childcare left them little spare time, even though they had Mexican-born nursemaids to help tend the youngsters.

In spite of their domestic duties, it is likely that Larcena and Mary had been among the fascinated spectators who watched the first railroad train to Tucson chug in on March 20, 1880, bearing high officials of Southern Pacific. The whole town turned out for that glorious occasion. Dr. Handy and other important citizens had formed committees and prepared lavish celebration ceremonies. There were greetings and speeches to the crowds, a banquet at Levin's Park, and a grand ball.[13]

One of the speakers was William Sanders Oury, Tucson's

Sixteen-year-old Mary Ann Page dressed for her wedding, 1878 (Marshall L. Pennington).

earliest Anglo-American settler—the man who had buried John Page in Cañada del Oro. Oury reminded his large audience, "The pioneers of Arizona have spent the best years of their life in preparing the way for that progress which we now see consummated." He seemed to foresee that the agonies and exploits of frontiersmen like himself would be overlooked or degraded by swarms of ambitious newcomers, for he added, "Our last request is that you kindly avoid trampling in the dust the few remaining monuments of the first American settlements in Arizona."[14]

Frontier days had ended even before the coming of the railroad. Most of the hostile Indians had gone to reservations in 1874, a development that, according to historian Patrick Hamilton, began "one of the brightest periods in Arizona's history."[15] Security of life and property outside town limits had improved tremendously since then, although Geronimo had yet to be dealt with and highway holdups were still a problem.

The railroad hastened the modernization of Tucson. By 1884, Larcena could telephone Mary's residence or run water from a tap at her kitchen sink.[16] From her windows, she and Mary and their children could gaze down on the majestic brick Southern Pacific depot on the flat below. They could watch powerful steam locomotives hissing into the station and see rail cars disgorging their freight and passengers. The toot of train whistles soon replaced the clatter of the mule-drawn freight wagons that had once churned up dust in front of the Scott house.

Fisher's and Larcena's son, Will, was a schoolboy of thirteen in 1884, and their daughter, Georgie Hazel, was twelve.[17] The four Handy youngsters ranged in age from five to two at that time. We can imagine little Jack Handy clinging to his grandmother's hand as she and Mary took the children to play at Carrillo's Gardens, just one block south of the Scott home. The park was the pride and joy of Tucson. Leopoldo Carrillo had patterned it after elaborate parks in San Francisco, with beds of roses and a shady pavilion and rowboats gliding between miniature islands set in a sparkling lake.[18]

Further evidence of the passing of the frontier was the sight of Protestant churches in Tucson, a town once inhabited by roughnecks so unholy that J. Ross Browne had described it as a veritable "paradise of devils."[19] John Anderson, the Presbyterian missionary who performed the Handys' wedding ceremony, had erected a handsome adobe structure with Gothic arches and a sharply peaked roof that distinguished it from Tucson's earlier box-like, flat-topped buildings. When Congregationalists acquired the historic Anderson church, Larcena joined them and remained a faithful member for the rest of her life.[20]

These signs of civilization were somewhat misleading, however. Tucsonans clung to old habits until well after the turn of the century. Gambling halls stayed open and saloons flourished as before, despite earnest efforts by reform-minded women and a man or two. The "soiled doves" of Gay Alley still stood in their doorways just two or three blocks from Larcena's home. Businessmen, including Dr. Handy, still carried pistols and knives in their pockets as they went to work.

Larcena's husband, now called "Judge" Scott, shared the responsibility for keeping such things from getting out of hand. He had won election as a justice of the peace in 1883. He and Jimmie Lee had sold the Eagle Flour Mill ten years earlier, and Fisher was a mounted inspector with the U. S. Customs Service from then until 1881. He cut timber for awhile after that, and he and Lee continued to work the Naguila Mine as partners.[21]

Jimmie Lee died in 1884. Time had already set about rounding up the region's pioneers. Mercedes Shibell, Larcena's fellow captive in 1860, had died before her twenty-sixth birthday. Alcoholic Jack Swilling, who once prospected and tramped across New Mexico and Arizona with Fisher, had passed away in disrepute in 1878.[22]

Fearing that few such old-timers would be left to tell their stories in another decade or two, Charles D. Poston issued a Territory-wide call to his fellow survivors: "All those in favor of forming a Pioneer Association of historical and humanitarian purposes are requested to meet at the Palace Hotel, Tucson, on Thursday, the last day of January, 1884, at 8 o'clock, p.m."[23]

As a result of that meeting, Dr. John Handy and Judge William Fisher Scott were among fifty-nine men who became charter members of the Society of Arizona Pioneers (now the Arizona Historical Society). They chose William S. Oury as the first president.[24] John Handy later held that office.[25] Custom being what it was then, the "Pioneers" did not include women, although Larcena Pennington Scott, María Ramírez Lee, and other females outdid many of the members in frontier experience and years of residence in Arizona.

Dr. Handy's reputation acquired additional luster when the University of Arizona Board of Regents elected him chancellor in 1886. As such, he became ex-officio president of the Board. There was no university as yet, only a plot of ground, a legislative appropriation of $25,000, and a citizenry disappointed because territorial planners had not allocated a juicier plum to Tucson. The doctor took great interest in the plans for the university's first building but soon disagreed with other Board members as to its design. For the next six months he avoided their meetings. After he ignored a warning, the Board removed him from office.[26]

By this time, Larcena and Fisher were aware that the Handys' marriage was in a deplorable condition. Mary must often have been the subject of her mother's prayers because of it. Even had Mary tried to hide her troubles from Larcena and Fisher Scott, town gossip must have reached their ears. One cannot imagine them sitting idly by when they realized that their daughter's situation was intolerable. They had learned, however, that their influential son-in-law was strong-willed and could be highly irascible. He would not welcome interference in his personal affairs.

Pima County Treasurer Ben Heney, whose home was across the street from the Handy's, recalled later that Mary sometimes confided to his wife how Dr. Handy—"a big, powerful man"—abused her.[27] It seems to be characteristic of mistreated wives to blame themselves and postpone leaving their husbands, but the time finally came for young Mrs. Handy. Pregnant for the fifth time, she filed for divorce in December, 1888. The law firm of Jeffords & Franklin represented her. A rumor soon spread that

Dr. Handy had gone to the judge and lawyers and threatened to kill them if the case came to trial.[28] Mary dropped her suit a month after she filed it, and the couple continued to live unhappily together.[29]

The next four years brought Larcena as much despair as anything she had previously endured. Her heart ached at the pain, misery, and illness etching lines on her daughter's lovely face. She often found Mary, formerly so alert and intelligent, in a state of drug-induced confusion. Mary had started taking morphine to relieve her suffering. Whether John Handy himself or another doctor first treated her with the drug is uncertain. She could have simply bought it at a drugstore. Doctors were enthusiastic about the benefits of morphine and opium in the 1880s; both were readily available without prescription.[30]

By July, 1889, according to her own statement, Mary was a morphine addict and a prisoner, locked by her husband in a room of their home, shortly after the birth of her fifth child, Spencer.[31] Subsequent treatment to cure her addiction had left her "weak in body and mind." She was in a state of "delirium or . . . stupor," she later claimed, the day that John Handy unlocked the door and entered with a deed that would convey her interest in their house and lot to his mother, Roseanna Handy, as trustee for their children.[32]

Handy had already sent the four older children to his mother and sister in Oakland, California. Now he told Mary that the day before he had also sent the baby. He threatened to keep his wife locked up and separated from her infant forever unless she signed the deed. Fearful, dazed, scarcely comprehending what she was doing, Larcena's daughter wrote her signature.[33] John Handy filed that deed away. Two years later, he used it.

Little Spencer actually remained in Tucson for another year. That time went by without improvement in the Handys' relationship, and little if any in Mary's health. In July of 1890, John Handy himself filed for divorce and, six months later, a court order allowed him to place the baby in hospital custody, where Spencer may have remained until the lengthy lawsuit was concluded.[34]

People gossiped that Dr. Handy wanted a divorce so that he could marry another woman whom he had been seeing for some time. Some of his neighbors said that he maintained another household and that "his favorite diversion was getting the other woman and her child in his buggy and driving past his own house."[35] Persons claiming to be acquainted with the circumstances stated to the Tombstone *Prospector* that Handy was infatuated with one Pansy Smith, who had divorced her husband on account of the doctor. The *Prospector* criticized Handy for associating with another female when he already had a wife who was "a good, true woman and mother." He had abused his wife shamefully, the newspaper added.[36] There may have been more than rumor to the story: Dr. Handy's descendants speak of his illegitimate son who rose to prominence in Tucson, never knowing who his real father was.[37]

Mary had a hard time finding an attorney to represent her in the divorce suit brought by her husband. Fisher Scott, having learned some law while he was justice of the peace, did what he could to help her. It is likely that his ailing stepdaughter often leaned on his arm as she made her rounds of attorney's offices. C. W. Wright first took on Mary's defense and asked another lawyer, Ben Heney's brother Francis, to act as associate attorney.

Francis J. Heney was destined for national fame, and fifteen years later, he would be a public figure personally known and praised by President Theodore Roosevelt. Now, he reluctantly agreed to assist Wright. Then Wright withdrew from Mary's defense, and Heney refused to continue on his own. Mary next employed William Barnes, but he, too, soon dropped out, intimidated by Handy. It appeared that no lawyer dared incur the respected doctor's wrath.[38] Again and again Mary went back to Frank Heney; perhaps she sensed his sympathy. He finally told her he would think about representing her.

A month after filing for divorce, Dr. Handy went to his home on Stone Avenue and made an attempt to take one of his children, probably little Spencer, away with him. Mary resisted him with all the strength at her command. He filed a complaint in justice court, stating that she had threatened him with physical violence before and that on this occasion she assaulted him, grabbed him with her hands, and bit him on the arm. He wanted her restrained, claiming he was within his rights to take the child.[39] This episode must have angered Larcena and Fisher even as it saddened them.

Mary Handy, probably with Fisher's help, filed an answer in justice court the next day. She asserted that her husband had moved out after filing for divorce, but that he returned every hour of the day and every day to quarrel with her; that he would go through all the rooms and had assaulted, beaten and bruised her and threatened to continue to do so. She cited Judge Richard Sloan's order that the children should not be removed permanently from the home pending the outcome of the divorce and custody suit. She, in turn, asked to have John Handy restrained, fearing that he would do her great bodily harm.[40]

Dr. Handy happened to be the much-loved family physician of Brewster Cameron, clerk of the district court. Cameron was also a friend of Frank Heney. He was shocked and alarmed when Handy invited him into the back room of his medical office on various occasions and insisted that he deliver a message to Heney. The message was always the same: Frank Heney was not to take Mrs. Handy's case. Handy told Cameron, "If Frank Heney takes that case I will kill him!"[41] When the startled court clerk inquired why Mrs. Handy should not have a lawyer to represent her, the doctor retorted angrily, "She is a morphine fiend and a common slut. She does not deserve any."[42]

Each time Handy sent his ominous message, Cameron pleaded with Heney to stay out of the suit. Heney heard of Handy's threats from other sources, too, and he began to experience disagreeable encounters with the vindictive doctor as the case progressed. He told Cameron that Handy had tried several times to run him down with his buggy in the street, had publicly called him a coward and a son-of-a-bitch, and had tried to provoke a fight. Heney had little doubt that Handy meant to kill him. He began taking meals at Cameron's house and walking to the court-house in Cameron's company. Frightened by Handy's aggressive behavior, Cameron remonstrated with the doctor, "Your wife accuses you of cruelty. If you [try to] override the law it is bound to have an effect on the court and community."[43]

Dr. Handy's repeated attempts to cow Heney finally had the opposite effect. The lawyer agreed to help Larcena's desperate daughter. He explained to Cameron that "it was a duty he owed to himself, his profession, and the community."[44]

Francis J. Heney would not have impressed the casual observer as a man of courage. He was thirty-one years old at the time. He had a rather slight physique, a pleasant, bespectacled face, center-parted hair slicked back from his forehead, and he wore a high starched white collar under his chin. But he had a stiffer backbone than this mild appearance suggested. As a boy in a rough-and-tumble neighborhood in San Francisco, Heney had survived by becoming pugnacious. He earned his own education in spite of his father's opposition and refusal of support. He went to night school and gained acceptance to the University of California. There he earned a reputation for drinking and gambling and was expelled in his freshman year for fighting. He then studied law and was admitted to the California bar. He had moved to Arizona's dry climate for health reasons and was a relative newcomer among Tucson lawyers.[45]

During eight months of bitterly contested proceedings, various witnesses testified on Mary's behalf, including Fisher Scott, Mrs. Ben Heney, and Dr. Hiram Fenner. In the end, however, Handy obtained his divorce and custody of the five children. The judge ordered him to pay Mary $30 a month in alimony, decreed that she could retain the Handy home, and denied Frank Heney's prompt motion for a new trial.[46] Dr. Handy sent the baby, Spencer, to join the other children in Oakland.

Not content with partial victory, John Handy next tried to evict Mary from her house. He sued his ex-wife in justice court in July, 1891, for unlawful detainer of the dwelling, signing the complaint as agent for Roseanna Handy, his mother, guardian of the children. Fisher Scott, afraid that a fair hearing could not be held before the presiding justice, helped Mary obtain a change of

Dr. John Handy in the doorway of his Tucson office. The buggy in front may
be the one Handy used to intimidate Francis Heney (Arizona Historical Society). Below, Tucson's Congress Street School (built in 1875), where Handy
fell violently in love with student Mary Page Scott. The photo dates to about
1885 (Arizona Historical Society).

venue. The second justice dismissed the suit, but John Handy persisted. He appealed to superior court and presented the deed of relinquishment that he had forced his sick wife to sign two years earlier.[47]

Again Francis J. Heney represented Mary, and again Dr. Handy threatened to kill him. Heney started carrying a gun at his brother Ben's advice. According to Ben Heney, Handy sent word that he would "take Frank's gun away and kill him with it."[48] Six months after the divorce case ended, the eviction suit was still going on. Apprehension gnawed constantly at Frank Heney as Handy continued to display his animosity.

At noon on September 24, 1891, Frank Heney left his office to go to lunch. His secretary, Lautaro Roca, was to catch up and join him after finishing two or three more minutes of work. Heney later testified that as he walked along Court Street toward Pennington Street near the courthouse, he saw John Handy, still some distance away, walking toward him. The lawyer paused and spoke to a workman, hoping that Handy would ignore the two of them and that Roca would come along.[49]

John Handy walked on by, but suddenly whirled with a shout, grasped Heney by the neck, pushed him against a wall and struck at his face. Heney broke away, pulling his pistol from his pocket. Handy leaped on him again and grappled for the gun.[50] A few people just coming out of the courthouse heard a shot and, looking in its direction, noticed the desperate struggle. They saw big John Handy lift his smaller opponent from his feet, then fall backward to the ground with the lawyer on top of him.

A *Citizen* reporter who was one of the observers described the scene. Voices in the gathering crowd called out, "Don't shoot! Don't shoot!" Heney cried out several times, "If he will let go I won't shoot." But his enemy hung on grimly until a deputy sheriff and other onlookers took the gun and pried the two men apart. Heney's secretary, who had arrived by that time, removed a gun from Dr. Handy's pocket and handed it to the deputy.[51]

John Handy had been shot. The bullet had entered his abdomen, and, as it turned out, had pierced the intestines in more

Persons coming out of the Pima County Courthouse, corner of Pennington and Court Streets, saw Francis J. Heney and John C. Handy struggling nearby for the possession of a pistol. Photo taken about 1891 (A. S. Reynolds Collection, Arizona Historical Society).

than a dozen places and lodged near the base of his spine. Nevertheless the doctor walked with support to his office, a block away, where he inspected his own wound.[52] Other local doctors gathered around, but Handy insisted that Dr. George E. Goodfellow of Tombstone, a wizard with gunshot wounds, perform the necessary surgery. While waiting for the surgeon Handy dictated his will, acknowledged it before witnesses, and feebly marked an "x" as his signature.[53] He also told his version of the shooting to three persons standing over him. One of them wrote it down.

> About noon today, I was going to visit a very sick patient, and as I passed Frank Heney's office he came out . . . and when he saw me he drew a revolver and rushed up to me with it presented towards me and I commenced grabbing at it to keep him from shooting me, but he got the muzzle of it against my belley [sic] and fired . . . I did not strike him. . . . I did not do anything to him but to struggle with him to keep him from shooting me.[54]

Goodfellow made a legendary race against time from Tombstone to Tucson on a special Southern Pacific engine, but shortly after midnight, just as the surgeon completed the operation, John Handy died.[55] Notified by telegraph, Handy's sister, Cornelia Holbrook, arrived on the train from Oakland in time for his funeral four days later. A huge crowd of rich and poor attended the impressive Masonic services. For the sum of $27, which included his sister's berth and meals en route, Southern Pacific transported Handy's body to Oakland for burial.[56]

John C. Handy left all his property to be divided equally among his five children, naming Cornelia Holbrook as executrix of his will. Mary filed unsuccessful objections. The court accepted the will and made Mrs. Holbrook guardian of the five Handy children.[57]

A hearing determined that Francis J. Heney had committed justifiable homicide in self defense. After reading a transcript of witnesses' testimony in the *Arizona Daily Star,* even John Handy's friends, who included the *Star's* editor, agreed with the court's decision.[58]

Roseanna Handy, the doctor's mother, dropped the suit to evict Mary shortly after his death, but she still held the deed in which the young wife disclaimed her property rights. Mary sued to have it declared fraudulent and invalid. A year later, on December 15, 1892, Judge Richard Sloan approved her petition.[59] It was a small victory compared to the loss of her children. And by this time Mary was too near death to care.

Three months after he labored in vain to save John Handy's life, Dr. George Goodfellow had performed a vaginal hysterectomy—his first such operation—on Mary. The illness that had so weakened her proved to be cervical cancer. She recovered from the operation, somewhat to Goodfellow's surprise, but the malignancy recurred about four months later.[60] Longing to see her children once more, Mary wrote Cornelia Holbrook and Roseanna Handy, asking that they send the youngsters back to Tucson. They refused.[61]

Teacher Mary Aguirre, ending her tale of the ill-fated romance that began at her class Christmas program, wrote, "He was, after some years, murdered in cold blood, and she, a year after, died a lingering death."[62] There was little Larcena could do now for Mary except give whatever loving attention might comfort the thin, feeble invalid, the beloved child born to her at Mowry Mine in those fearful early days of the Civil War. At the age of thirty-one, on January 28, 1893, Mary Page Handy died.[63] Her funeral service was simple, her mourners few. The *Arizona Weekly Citizen* commented that throughout all her many sorrows she had the sympathy of the community and the admiration of close friends "for her sterling qualities of mind, and heart, and her great fortitude in tribulation."[64]

As that shocking chain of events drew to its sorrowful close, Larcena faced the unhappy prospect that she would never again see her five Handy grandchildren. But one of them—the little boy

Grandmother Roseanna Handy at her home in Oakland, California, with the five small children of Mary Page and John Handy, as well as two Holbrook cousins. John C. Handy, Jr., poses at the front right center. In the background, Roseanna holds Spencer (Marjorie Handy Hart Collection, Arizona Historical Society).

who bore his father's name—would return, hating the lawyer who had shot his father.

In the year that Mary Handy died, Frank Heney was appointed attorney general of Arizona Territory. Soon afterward, he resigned, returned to San Francisco, and built up a law practice there. From 1903 to 1905 he was the remarkably successful prosecutor for the United States Department of Justice in public land fraud cases in California and Oregon.[65] In the process, Heney and his associate, detective William J. Burns, earned the admiration and personal friendship of President Theodore Roosevelt.[66]

A crusading newspaper publisher, Fremont Older of the San Francisco *Bulletin,* and a wealthy San Francisco businessman, Rudolf Spreckels, decided in 1905 to get Heney and Burns to clean up corruption in their city's politics. Older and Spreckels consulted Roosevelt, who agreed that Heney and Burns were the best men in America for the job, and they convinced the district attorney, an honest official, to appoint Heney as a special prosecutor in his office.[67] Spreckels contributed a fund of $100,000 for expenses of the San Francisco Graft Prosecutions. Francis Heney agreed to do the job without pay, as his own civic contribution. He drew on the fund only for expenses.[68] During the next six years, as Heney and Burns exposed a sordid system of political bosses and bribery in the city, their names were constantly in the newspapers.

Larcena's five Handy grandchildren were growing up not far from Francis Heney while he was earning fame. For awhile they lived with their stern and uncompromising paternal grandmother, Roseanna Handy, at Fourteenth and Chestnut streets in Oakland. John Charles Handy, Jr., who was seven when he left Tucson for Oakland, rebelled against her strict, albeit well-meaning, domination. At the age of nine, according to family tradition, Jack, as he was called, crawled out his bedroom window in his underwear and hid in order to escape accompanying Roseanna to church.[69]

Grandmother Handy spoke of the children's mother disparagingly, if at all. She told them a twisted version of their father's death in which Francis J. Heney was a villainous murderer. She

Trix and Jack Handy in 1902 when they married (Marjorie Handy Hart Collection, Arizona Historical Society).

Francis J. Heney, the lawyer who d fended Mary in 1891 and was speci prosecutor in the San Francisco gra trials. From a group photo taken San Francisco about 1906 (Arizor Historical Society).

may have believed it. With no one to contradict that story, young Jack Handy believed it, too, and resolved that someday he would square accounts with Heney.

After a few years, Jack's aunt Cornelia Holbrook Crosby took the Handy children into her home in San Francisco.[70] Jack was even less happy with Cornelia than with Roseanna. At fourteen, he ran away and went to sea on a whaling ship. Back in San Francisco on April 13, 1902, three months before he was twenty, he married his nineteen-year-old grammar-school sweetheart, Beatrix Walter, nicknamed "Trixie" — a petite blue-eyed blonde with a nineteen-inch waist. She encouraged him to go back to Tucson.

When Larcena opened her door to her grandson's knock, he looked into the calm blue eyes of a tall, erect woman of sixty-five. Soft white hair framed her serene, almost unlined face. Jack introduced himself and his bride. Larcena hardly recognized the brown-haired, brown-eyed youth, now a sturdy six-feet-two — he had been so little when his father sent him away to Oakland. But one could see his resemblance to Dr. Handy.

Larcena's and Fisher's children, Will and Georgie, were grown and living in homes of their own by then, so there was room at the Scotts' for Jack and Trixie. The company of this lively, loving young couple brought a great deal of pleasure to Larcena. They stayed with the Scotts for the next two years, and there Jack found the warmth that he had lacked in Roseanna Handy's home.

Both Jack and wide-eyed Trixie felt intimidated by Tucson at first. They were astonished when Indians came to the house. Sometimes these rather forbidding swarthy visitors would sit and converse; at other times they just sat. The young couple grew to love Tucson, however, as the months went by. Trixie and Larcena developed a strong bond of affection. Jack got a job in Tucson as a fireman on the Southern Pacific Railroad. He had had little formal schooling, which ruled out some other employment opportunities, but he was bright and inquisitive. He read voraciously and taught himself so well that later in his life others considered him highly intellectual.

He fit comfortably into the Scott family circle. Larcena's son

Will—Jack's uncle—was now thirty, with a wife and children of his own. He and Jack became good friends. Will was a miner, as his father had been. Jack liked to go with him out to the Naguila Mine, in which Fisher still owned a half-interest.[71] The mine had never fully justified the once glorious expectations of the town's businessmen, and Fisher was again a justice of the peace. The position supported himself and Larcena, but the prosperity they had enjoyed thirty years earlier had gradually diminished.

Early in 1904, Jack and Trixie were expecting their first child. They yielded to the urgings of Trixie's father to return to San Francisco for the baby's birth. Their daughter Florence—Larcena's first great-grandchild—was born there in April, and a second baby girl, Marjorie, arrived fourteen months later. As far as is known, Larcena never saw Jack and his family after they left Tucson, but they kept in touch with her, their "Gramsy Scott." As Larcena may have suspected from their letters, her grandson and Trixie lived close to poverty for some time in San Francisco. For about eight years, until he got a good, steady position with Standard Oil Company, Jack worked as a chauffeur or took odd jobs. Sometimes he was unemployed, too proud to perform menial tasks.[72]

Francis J. Heney, the lawyer Jack had learned to hate, was front-page news in San Francisco in 1906. Jack must have seen the stories. Sentiment in San Francisco was divided: some of the newspapers praised Frank Heney and the reform effort; others reviled him. The *Examiner* ridiculed him as "Beany" in malicious cartoons.

One of Frank Heney's chief targets was Abraham Ruef, a brilliant young college graduate who had sacrificed scruples for money and power.[73] Heney publicly accused him of wrongdoing. Abe Ruef, looking for something that would damage the prosecutor's character and credibility, learned that Heney had shot Dr. Handy in Arizona fifteen years earlier. Ruef sent men to Tucson to dig up all the dirt they could. Then, in the *Chronicle,* he directed a sarcastic retort to Heney's published charges: "You lied . . . you showed the same courage which put a bullet into the body of Dr.

J. C. Handy of Tucson, Arizona, in 1891, for whose killing you . . . were acquitted because you were the only witness to the deed."[74]

It may have been Ruef who sent reporters from the San Francisco *Daily News* to Oakland to interview Roseanna Handy. She asserted, contrary to testimony in Heney's Tucson trial, that it was Heney who had often threatened to kill Handy and that her son had given his word not to molest the lawyer. There was pathos in her description of the respected doctor kissing his children goodbye as he left his house on the morning of the shooting, but actually they may have been with her in Oakland at the time. Roseanna claimed that on the fatal day, Heney stepped out of his office holding a gun as the doctor passed by, and, ignoring her son's pleas and raised arms, cold-bloodedly shot Handy again and again. He then, she added, contrived to escape punishment for this murder.[75]

Ruef's gang apparently plotted even more sinister tactics to silence Heney: rumors spread through the city that an attempt would be made to assassinate the special prosecutor. The *Examiner* scoffed at the idea that Heney would be killed. It printed a caricature of "Beany" with an "X" on his neck where the fatal bullet would strike. The cartoon proved prophetic.[76]

Ruef's gang next located John Handy, Jr., and proposed that he go to Tucson and swear out a warrant for Heney's arrest on the charge of murdering Dr. Handy. Instead, Jack went to Heney's office. His opportunity to square accounts was finally at hand. No details of their meeting exist in print, but imagination suggests that a secretary showed Jack in, announcing the name that after all these years still shivered down Frank Heney's spine.[77] The prosecutor, older and a bit heavier than in his Tucson days, rose to his feet behind his desk, staring through his glasses at his enemy's son, remembering how the raging doctor's hand and his own had gripped that pistol, feeling again the pressure of their locked bodies falling to the street in mortal struggle, the deadly shot echoing in his ears.

Before Jack at last was the man who had killed his father. He stood still, recalling how he had always felt about Francis Heney. During the time Jack had been with Larcena in Tucson, however, he had learned the full circumstances of that affair. He took two quick strides forward and seized the hand that the prosecutor held out to him. He thanked Heney for helping his mother at a terrible time in her life. Then he quickly explained the Ruef gang's evil intentions. The emotional meeting was the beginning of a deep, lifelong friendship between John Handy, Jr., and Francis J. Heney.[78]

Abe Ruef's trial began in 1908. On November 13, during a five-minute recess, Frank Heney remained seated at a table in the courtroom. His bodyguard stood near him. More than two hundred people milled around the room, waiting for the proceedings to resume. Heney's associates always believed that what happened next had been pre-arranged by the Ruef gang, though they were never able to prove the connection. In the confusion, no one paid attention to an ordinary-looking man who walked up to Heney's table, thrust a gun close to the prosecutor's head, and fired. Heney's bodyguard seized the assassin immediately, but Heney lay on the floor, apparently dead, blood gushing from his cheek.[79]

Miraculously, Heney lived, scarred, and permanently deafened in his left ear. His assailant killed himself, or was killed, in his jail cell. The jury found Abe Ruef guilty of graft and the judge sentenced him to fourteen years in San Quentin. Weakened by his injuries, Frank Heney continued the graft prosecutions, but he and his associates were unable to convict the wealthy, influential men whose bribes had corrupted Ruef and minor city officials.[80]

Encouraged by admirers, Heney ran for district attorney in 1909. He lost. He had made powerful political enemies in San Francisco during the graft prosecution. He ran an unsuccessful campaign for the Senate in 1914 and was defeated in a bid for the governorship of California in 1918. His first wife died. His law practice dwindled. During all these disheartening years his relationship with Jack Handy was like that of father and son.[81]

Heney eventually moved his practice to Los Angeles where he became a superior court judge. There, in 1937, he lay on his deathbed. Beside him sat Larcena's grandson Jack, now a balding "San Francisco oil company executive" of fifty-five, murmuring "tender words of encouragement to the man who was once his mortal enemy."[82] So stated the Los Angeles *Evening Herald Express*. Jack refused comment to reporters, but they found other informants, and when Judge Heney died, the newspaper, under the headline, "HENEY PALLBEARER TO BE SON OF MAN HE SHOT," related the "strange and dramatic saga of a man who forgave his father's killer."[83]

THIRTEEN: "TOWARD THE WESTERN SHORE"

By the year 1902, when John Handy, Jr. came to Tucson to visit Larcena and Fisher, there were not enough of the earliest pioneers remaining in Arizona to crowd a small room. And for those old-timers, life, like the setting sun, was "fast dipping toward the western shore," as the *Tucson Post* phrased it.[1] Larcena and Fisher were still clear-eyed and vigorous, but they were feeling the approach of their final years. They were aware that they were survivors. So few of their friends and neighbors remembered the perilous times before and during the Civil War. So few could even begin to understand what clinging to existence in that new and dangerous territory had meant. Only those who had lived through it could know. The newcomers — even their own descendants — never would.

Here and there an individual appeared who was eager to try. One was Larcena's new son-in-law, Professor Robert H. Forbes of the developing University of Arizona. Wisconsin-born and Harvard-educated, Forbes had come to the University to teach agriculture. A small dynamo of a man, he attacked his new career with the ferocity of a young lion, and after he met Larcena's good-looking daughter, Georgie Scott, he became fascinated by the history of the Penningtons.[2]

Georgie had grown up tall like her parents. She was a slender girl with "striking grey eyes," light brown hair, and regal dignity. She became a schoolteacher after training at a teacher's college in

Colorado. On January 15, 1902, she married Robert H. Forbes. According to Tucson folklore, Georgie accepted his proposal on the condition that he climb high, sheer Baboquivari Peak southwest of town. Five times between 1896 and 1898 he tried to reach the summit. He lighted a bonfire on the mountain the night of July 12, 1898, to signal success at last.[3] With similar tenacity, he forged a distinguished record of achievement in Arizona, Africa, and Jamaica and lived to be a hundred.

In his scientific, scholarly fashion, Robert Forbes began taking notes on his conversations with Larcena and Fisher Scott. As Larcena retold the story of her capture by Apaches, Georgie recorded it in her neat schoolteacher's handwriting for her husband. He corresponded with those Arizona old-timers he could track down and interviewed them — one-armed Silas St. John, who survived the ax murders at Dragoon Springs, Daniel E. Conner, who came with the Walker Party to the Hassayampa and laughed at the Indian arrow dangling from Jack Pennington's pants leg, Sabino Otero, who was Jim Pennington's friend, and Charles Genung, who pursued a killer to Tubac and found Larcena and her sisters there. Forbes photographed the Pennington's old stone house at the border, their homesites in Tubac and Sópori, and their former haunts in the Sonoita Valley. His diligence eventually resulted in a small booklet about the Penningtons in Arizona, published six years after Larcena's death.[4]

Forbes was keenly aware of his mother-in-law's eminence as a pioneer. It would have been hard to find another woman more qualified than Larcena to head a list of Arizona's early Anglo-American settlers. She had lived in the Territory longer than any others and had remained through all its worst times, when most fled to safer regions. She had experienced its horrors and survived them; she had known the splendors of its untrammeled wilderness. She had watched Tucson grow from a village of barely four hundred Spanish-speaking residents to a modern melting pot of over 5600.

Where wooden ox-carts from Mexico once creaked slowly past her door, a mule-drawn trolley now ran on steel rails all the way out to a modern university.[5] Automobiles sped down Main

Georgie Hazel Scott, later Mrs. Robert H. Forbes (Arizona Historical Society). Below, a triumphant Robert H. Forbes at the top of Baboquivari (Arizona Historical Society).

Street at the legal limit of seven miles an hour, or even faster. Highways were now free of hostile Apaches and Mexican bandits, although American train robbers occasionally tested law enforcement officers. Most Arizona towns and cities had arisen in Larcena's time. Phoenix, non-existent when her father was killed, was now the territorial capital, with a population almost as large as Tucson's.[6] Her life in Arizona had encompassed all these changes.

Her right to be considered a foremost pioneer was confirmed in December, 1902, when the newly formed Ladies' Auxiliary of the Society of Arizona Pioneers elected Larcena Pennington Scott its first president. Fisher and John Handy had become charter members of the Society in 1884. Since the beginning, members' wives had provided food and entertainment and attended the group's social functions, but women were never invited to membership. The male members, approving the formation of the Auxiliary, congratulated the ladies with a supper of tamales and enchiladas (furnished by the honorees), followed by dancing.[7]

Arizonans who had known Larcena and her father's family in the early days were scarce now. Newcomers sometimes asked for whom Josephine Canyon and Josephine Peak in the Santa Rita Mountains were named, and it was seldom that anyone could answer: "Why, that was for Elias Pennington's youngest girl. He brought twelve children to Arizona when it was just a wilderness—one of the first families to settle here."

That magnificent but merciless frontier had destroyed Elias and four of those children. All the surviving Penningtons except Larcena had escaped to Texas, but death finds everyone eventually. In Jack Pennington's case, in 1904, it was he who sought death.

John Parker Pennington, to whom his despairing sisters had turned in their bleakest hour, had spent the last ten years blind with cataracts. Larcena had tried to help him:

"My Dear Brother John," she wrote to him in 1901, "I saw an advertisement in a magazine that Dr. Oren O'Neal could cure cataracts by a mild medicine." She obtained a blank consultation form from O'Neal and enclosed it in her letter to Jack, asking him to have his daughters fill it out and return the form to her. "I will get Georgie to copy it," Larcena told her brother, "and I will send it to [O'Neal], that is if you wish me to."[8] Jack may not have returned the completed form, but he underwent an eye operation in Austin. It proved unsuccessful.[9]

Jack appeared to reconcile himself to his condition. He taught himself to move independently around his Georgetown farm, feeling along fence lines and familiar structures, even wandering over to the neighbors, who thought him jolly and congenial as always. But on the night of November 30, 1904, after spending a pleasant day with his family, he took his bed sheet and quietly groped his way to the corncrib in the barn. He climbed onto the thick rim of a wooden trough, knotted one end of the sheet around a rafter and the other around his neck. Then he jumped. His wife found him hanging there in the morning.[10]

So the early pioneers continued to diminish in number. Some of the old-timers who had known the Scotts and Jack and the other Penningtons in frontier days gathered at the Scott home on a late July evening in 1907 to help celebrate Larcena and Fisher's thirty-seventh wedding anniversary. The *Tucson Post* reported the occasion, describing Judge Scott as "over six feet tall . . . still a man of strength and vigor." Mrs. Scott, it said, was "a tall, white-haired, dignified lady" who had lived over fifty years in the Territory and saw her dear ones "go down before the relentless Apache." Her sufferings were "four-fold worse than the pangs of death."[11] With poetic truth the writer pointed out:

> Whatever Arizona had to show of frontier life they have seen. They paid to see the show with their own blood, and with the blood of kindred and friends that reddened the deserts and hills of Arizona.[12]

Larcena's husband somehow broke a hip about two years later. One wonders if he took a careless step on the rocks at the Naguila Mine. Fisher was never again able to get about. He spent

John Parker "Jack" Pennington with his wife Isabelle and children at Georgetown, Texas, in 1901, three years before his suicide (Marshall L. Pennington).

his days in a chair in their house, crippled in body but alert in mind.[13] Larcena spent hers caring for him and keeping him company, walking to the corner store to buy their simple necessities, and attending church on Sundays. Their children, Will Scott and Georgie Forbes, undoubtedly looked in on them often.

The dwindling group of pioneer survivors like Larcena and Fisher were special in the sense that only they could testify from personal experience to the old times. In September, 1910, when Larcena was seventy-three, the government called her as a witness in an Indian Depredations suit whereby another pioneer, lumberman Alphonse Lazard, sought reparations from the United States government for losses he had sustained long ago at the hands of Apaches. Most questions put to her were about her capture fifty years earlier.[14]

"Do you know the name of the chief that was with the Indians?" Harry Peyton, Lazard's attorney, asked her.

"That big chief was Skinimzin [sic], but I wont [sic] be sure," the court reporter wrote down her answer, spelling the difficult name as well as he could make it out.

John Stansbury, the government's lawyer, asked, "You of your own knowledge, personal knowledge, do not know who was the chief?"

"No, not of my own personal knowledge," she responded, "but Mr. Scott could tell you, he remembers all about it better than I do, he was out going all over the territory and he knew them and I did not, but his name was old Skiniminez [sic], I think." Eskiminzin had been a chief of the Pinals. Captain Richard S. Ewell of the First Dragoons at Fort Buchanan was satisfied beyond a doubt that Tonto Apaches, rather than Pinals, abducted Larcena and Mercedes, but the settlers were never convinced of that.

"When they could not carry me any further," she answered another question, "rather than leave me they tried to kill me, stripped me of my waist and beat me and took off [my] shoes and left me for dead, and I suppose I lay there for several days and when I came to I crawled along the best I could until I made it to camp, and it was a long time before I recovered." She did not mention her two weeks of thirst and hunger, her wounds and thorn-pierced feet, her terror. Just ". . . I crawled along the best I could," a matter-of-fact statement of what she had done to stay alive.

"Are you the woman they threw over that cliff?"

"Yes, sir."

"Was snow on the ground?"

"Yes . . . under the shade trees you would find snow."

"What direction were they going when they left you?"

"Going right north they took the little girl along; she was small and they could take her; her people had sent her to me; she was a Mexican girl; they carried her and could not carry me so left me for dead."

"Was the little girl recaptured?"

"Yes, Capt. Yewell [sic] recaptured her."

"Were any of the members of your family killed by the Indians at any time?"

"Yes, 4 of them, two brothers, my father and first husband were all killed by the Indians." Those days were so long in the past, time and change had finally erased the pain she had felt then.

The year 1912 brought another change, a great one for Arizona: on February 14 it was admitted as the 48th state of the Union. Exuberant crowds filled the streets of Tucson. Flags flew and bands marched in long parades and well-dressed men and women at banquet tables raised their glasses to a shining new era. Whistles tooted periodically, reminiscent of the thrilling blasts from Lee and Scott's new Eagle Flour Mill, once the pride of every Tucsonan. Many were the stories told of settlers' struggles and trials in frontier times. Fisher and Larcena probably celebrated quietly at home with a visit from Will and Georgie and old friends. But few of those were still alive. Some, like Tommy Farrell, lingered on in the Arizona Pioneer's Home in Prescott. Bill Kirkland, Will Oury, Charles Poston, and many others had already reached "the western shore."

Capitalizing on widespread current interest in Arizona's state-

"He finally threw her over the cliff": an illustration from "The Ordeal of Mrs. Page," a highly erroneous account by John A. Spring that ran in the February, 1912, issue of *Wide World Magazine* (Margo Hart Anderson Collection, Piedmont, California).

hood and history, *Wide World Magazine,* published in London and New York, printed in its February, 1912, issue a sensationalized and error-filled illustrated account of Larcena's capture by Apaches. It was written by pioneer John A. Spring, who might have consulted the subject herself if he had cared to prepare a more accurate story. Descendants of Larcena's grandson, John Handy, Jr., still treasure an original copy of that issue, which Jack must have read and saved.[15]

Larcena's final days now drifted uneventfully away, as withered leaves fallen into a slowly flowing stream disappear around a bend. On March 31, 1913, at the age of seventy-six, she died of unrecorded causes at home. She was laid to rest in Tucson's Evergreen Cemetery. A long obituary in the *Arizona Daily Star* praised her cheerful, naturally religious disposition, her admirable character, her courage.[16]

The Ladies' Auxiliary of the Society of Arizona Pioneers, which had made her honorary lifetime president, paid its respects at the Pioneers' next meeting. "If ever a person came up through great tribulation it was Mrs. Larcena A. Scott," said the speaker, giving the attentive members a brief recital of Larcena's experiences, a reminder of the dreadful price exacted from the early settlers.[17]

The *Star's* obituary summed up Larcena Pennington Page Scott well: "She combined the best qualities of the pioneer women who in the early days shared without flinching the difficulties and dangers endured by the men."[18] Her life demonstrates what pale demographics and statistics fail to make clear, what later generations can otherwise hardly comprehend: the stubborn courage, faith, and endurance that enabled Americans to leave comfort and safety behind, push westward into strange, unsettled lands, survive with few resources, refuse to surrender, and finally triumph over the obstacles that beset them.

William Fisher Scott lived not quite two years after Larcena's death. He passed away on December 31, 1914, at the age of eighty-three, and was buried beside her.[19] Scott Avenue, which crosses Pennington Street in downtown Tucson, bears his name.

First and honorary lifetime president of the Society of Arizona Pioneers Ladies Auxiliary: Larcena Pennington Page Scott, about 1902 (Arizona Historical Society).

Throngs of people come and go at that intersection, unaware of the significance of those street names honoring some of the earliest settlers of one of the last, the harshest, and the bloodiest American frontiers.

EPILOGUE

The old cemetery where Mary Ann Page Handy's body lay was abandoned by the time Fisher Scott died in 1915. It was about to be excavated in preparation for new business buildings on the site. Mary Ann's grave marker had disappeared, but a former caretaker located her remains for her half-sister, Georgie Forbes. Georgie and her husband had a small box containing them interred between Fisher's and Larcena's headstones in Evergreen Cemetery.[1]

The Forbeses' interest in completing a historical sketch of the Pennington family increased with Larcena's and Fisher's deaths. Five of those pioneer Penningtons were still alive, and Forbes was determined to find out what they could tell him about their early struggles. Amanda Jane Pennington Crumpton, who had been old enough when the family first came to Arizona to remember what it was like, was his best bet. He journeyed to Santa Cruz, California, in May, 1916, to interview her.

A now unknown accident had caused Amanda Jane to lose one foot sometime after she left Arizona. She got around on crutches. She and Billy Crumpton married in 1874.[2] They moved in 1882 to California, near Quincy, where Crumpton and their sons mined for gold.[3] After her husband's death in 1898, Amanda Jane and her five children moved to Santa Cruz. Robert Forbes got her story none too soon. She died of malaria in 1919,[4] the same year that the Arizona Archaeological and Historical Society published Forbes' little book, *The Penningtons, Pioneers of Early Arizona.*

Georgie's part in the research was to go to Georgetown, Texas, and talk to her Pennington relatives there. She stayed with Jack Pennington's married younger daughter, Flora Belle Rader, whose family was then living at his farm. The little Rader children giggled at Georgie's dignified manners and the way she pronounced their name "Rahder."[5] She may have spoken with Mary Frances and Josephine Pennington, also, although both had married and moved away from Jack's farm long before.

Georgie could not interview Caroline Pennington Nichols, although she was still alive. "Cas" never recovered her sanity after the birth of her twins. The diagnosis was "acute mania due to childbirth."[6] Her husband and children left Texas. Jack committed her to Austin State Hospital in January, 1877, two months before his first marriage. She was still there.[7] About 1932, Jack's grandchildren remember hearing that an aunt had recently died in a state institution. It was undoubtedly Caroline.[8]

There was no way to talk to Will Pennington, either—the only one of Larcena's brothers still alive. All Georgie could learn was that he had argued bitterly with Jack in 1877, after ten years of freighting and farming by his side. No one now can say just what it was all about, but Will is reported to have shouted angrily that he owed his sisters nothing, and the next morning he had vanished. So had the best wagon, mule teams, and tools. Will never returned to the farm. Jack never found a trace of his whereabouts, and for the next fifty years none of the Penningtons knew where Will was.[9]

On a winter day in the late 1920s the long-lost Will unexpectedly surfaced. He sought out his widowed younger sister, Mary Frances Pennington Randolph, in Martin County, Texas, where she lived with her oldest son, Thomas Henry Randolph. Both Will and Mary Frances were now in their seventies. She had never forgiven the manner of his departure from Jack's farm in 1877 and now greeted him with a noticeable lack of warmth. She let him stay the night, but, say descendants, refused to let him use one of her blankets on his bed.[10]

Rebuffed, but not completely discouraged, in 1928 Will sought out Sarah Josephine Elizabeth, his youngest sister, with better luck, or a better approach. Josie was living with her husband, Charles A. (Van) Gordon, on their farm at Brownwood, Texas.[11] By then, Will was a lonely old bachelor in failing health. He owned forty-eight acres of farmland at Tolar in Hood County, Texas, where he had spent the last fifty-five years; he had not been very far away while Jack searched vainly for him. Will now deeded his farmland to Josie and Van Gordon for $400 and the further consideration that they would care for and support him for the rest of his life, which they did. He lived only nine more months.[12] Six years later, in October, 1935, Josie herself passed away at the age of eighty-one.[13]

Mary Frances, the last survivor among the eight daughters and four sons Elias Pennington had brought to Arizona in 1857, died two months after Josie, in December, 1935.[14] Georgie and Robert Forbes, moved by the passing of these last of the pioneer Penningtons, had four handsome granite boulders engraved and taken to the old barbed-wire-fenced Sópori graveyard, near the crumbling ruin of the house where Elias and his family had once lived, and where the remains of Ann and James Pennington lay.

The infrequent visitor to this small isolated plot, on a flat, brushy hilltop beside the Arivaca Road, has a splendid panoramic view of the Santa Rita Mountains where Apaches captured Larcena and Mercedes in 1860.[15] Wild grasses grow among the twenty or more rock-covered mounds in the little cemetery. Most of them are unmarked, but a few that are identified have Spanish surnames from territorial and pre-territorial times. Larcena's daughter Georgie and her husband laid down one of their four memorial stones for Ann Pennington, one for James, and a third for Elias, Green, and Ellen.[16] Letters are chiseled into these stones deeply enough to last for centuries. The fourth chunk of granite, lying squarely in the graveyard gateway, admonishes all who enter:

> TREAD SOFTLY HERE
> THESE STONY MOUNDS
> SHELTER THE BONES OF
> ARIZONA'S OLDEST PIONEERS

NOTES

Abbreviations
AHF: Arizona Historical Foundation, Hayden Library, Arizona State University, Tempe
AHSL: Arizona Historical Society Library, Tucson
ASLA: Arizona State Library & Archives, Phoenix
MLP: Marshall Lee Pennington, Lubbock, Texas
VCR: Virginia Culin Roberts

1: Captured

1. Except as otherwise noted, the events and details related in this chapter are taken from the three most authoritative sources: (1) [Georgie Scott Forbes], "Mamma's Capture by Indians in the Spring of 1860," handwritten MS [ca. 1900], Forbes Collection, Box 3, AHSL; (2) "Mrs. Page's Personal Narrative, Tubac [Arizona], April 9, 1860," St. Louis *Missouri Republican,* May 8, 1860, as quoted in Constance Wynn Altshuler, *Latest from Arizona! The Hesperian Letters, 1859–1861* (Tucson: Arizona Pioneers' Historical Society, 1969), pp. 64–67; (3) Robert H. Forbes, *The Penningtons, Pioneers of Early Arizona* ([Tucson]: Arizona Archaeological and Historical Society, 1919), pp. 12–21.

2. *Tucson Weekly Arizonian,* 3 November 1859.

3. William Hudson Kirkland, "An account of the captives [sic] by Apache Indians of Mrs. John Page, nee Larcena Pennington, daughter of Mr. and Mrs. E. G. Pennington, and incidents connected therewith," MS, 3 September 1909, Ben and Fern Allen Collection, AHSL; *New York Times,* 12 April 1860, 5:2.

4. *Ibid.*

5. *Ibid.;* Forbes, *The Penningtons,* p. 12.

6. *Ibid.* The stagecoach driver mistakenly delivered the child to Mrs. Eliza

Heath, supervisor of the Canoa way station. The "station lady" assumed it was her personal obligation to take charge of the little girl and staunchly refused to turn her over to Larcena. Hard feelings arose between the two women, Kirkland said, until he arrived a few days later and settled the issue.

7. [Georgie Scott Forbes], "Mamma's Capture"; "Mrs. Page's Personal Narrative," Altshuler, *Latest from Arizona!,* p. 65.

8. *Daily Alta Californian,* 6 April 1860.

9. Kirkland, "An Account of the captives," MS 3 September 1909. Randall—"one of our best men," according to Phocion Way—worked at the Salero Mine in the summer of 1858, but left on 12 August to harvest crops at a ranch in which he was a partner with Kirkland. William A. Duffen, ed., "Overland Via 'Jackass Mail' in 1858, The Diary of Phocion R. Way " (Part IV), *Arizona and the West,* 2 (Winter 1960): 361. Larcena Page, interviewed by Thompson Turner in April 1860, is quoted as saying that William Randall was engaged in the lumber business with her husband: "Mrs. Page's Personal Narrative," Altshuler, *Latest from Arizona!,* p. 64.

10. For an authoritative description of Tonto Apaches in this time period, see E. R. Hagemann, ed., "Surgeon Smart and the Indians: An 1866 Apache Word List," *Journal of Arizona History,* 11 (Summer 1970): 135–36.

11. Kirkland MS, 3 September 1909.

12. *Ibid; New York Times,* 12 April 1860, 5:2.

13. "Mrs. Page's Personal Narrative," Altshuler, *Latest From Arizona!,* pp. 64–67. Obviously the party climbed high enough to find snow, but Larcena later said that the Indians kept mainly to the foothills.

14. [Georgie Scott Forbes], "Mama's Capture."

15. *Alphonse Lazard vs United States and the Apache Indians: Indian Depredations Claim No. 8773,* Testimony of Larcena A. Scott, taken at Tucson, Arizona, 20 September 1910, typescript of testimony in Forbes Collection, Box 3, AHSL.

16. [Georgie Scott Forbes], "Mama's Capture."

17. *Ibid.*

2: The Penningtons

1. Marriages and births recorded in the John Parker Pennington, II, Family Bible (original in Marshall L. Pennington Collection, Lubbock, Texas), as quoted by Marshall L. Pennington to VCR, Lubbock, Texas, 28 February 1981; *Census of the United States, 1860, Arizona Territory, New Mexico,* p. 35, photocopy of original returns, AHSL.

2. Elias G. Pennington was born in South Carolina 16 April 1809; Julia Ann Hood, his wife, was born in North Carolina 12 February 1815. John Parker Pennington, II, Family Bible.

3. *U.S. Census 1850, Fannin County, Texas,* Washington: U.S. National Archives, (microfilm 910, no. 5809 pt. 3), p. 167; John Parker Pennington, II, Family Bible.

4. Amanda Jane [Pennington] Crumpton to Robert H. Forbes, Santa Cruz, California, 18 May 1916, Interview notes in Forbes Collection, Box 3, Folder 3, AHSL.

5. Letter from J. Ross Browne, Tubac [Arizona], 5 February 1864, *San Francisco Bulletin,* 15 March 1864.

6. Forbes, Amanda Jane Crumpton Interview.

7. Browne, 5 February 1864.

8. H[enry] F[rank] Pennington to Mrs. Florence E. Drachman, Chicago, 22 June 1939, Forbes Collection, Box 3, AHSL. This interesting legend emanates from the Henry Frank Pennington branch of the Penningtons, which claims that their ancestor John was Elias Green Pennington's brother. Family genealogists from Elias' branch have so far been unable to produce other evidence that this is so, but the relationship is given some credence by Elias having named a son "John," and by the 1860 census showing that a John B. Pennington (possibly of the Henry Frank branch) was then living with Larcena and John Page in Arizona.

9. Forbes, Amanda J. Crumpton Interview.

10. Red River County Board of Land Commissioners, Clarksville, 8 January 1840, Certificate No. 698 to Elias Pennington (Red River County Clerk, Clarksville); Republic of Texas, Anson Jones, President, Land Patent No. 388 to Elias Pennington, 3 December 1845 (State of Texas, General Land Office, Austin).

11. Republic of Texas, County of Fannin, Surveys 1 May 1841 and 10 October 1842 by Samuel Erwin, D. S., for Elias G. Pennington (Red River County Clerk, Clarksville, Texas).

12. Rex W. Strickland, "History of Fannin County, Texas, 1836–1843," *Southwest Historical Quarterly, 33* (April 1930): 262–298, and 34 (July, 1930): 36–38.

13. John Parker Pennington, II, Family Bible.

14. Strickland, "History of Fannin County," pp. 36–38.

15. J. S. Newman, "A History of the Primitive Baptists of Texas, Oklahoma and Indian Territories" [Tioga, Texas], *Baptist Trumpet,* 1 (1906): 210–11.

16. Honey Grove Church, Jesse Buttler [sic], Moderator, and Walter Yeary, C.C., 12 May 1849, Certificate to E. G. Pennington, original in Marshall L. Pennington Collection, Lubbock, Texas.

17. Forbes, *The Penningtons, Pioneers of Early Arizona: A Historical Sketch* ([Tucson]: Archaeological and Historical Society, 1919), p. 1.

18. John Parker Pennington, II, Family Bible; *1850 Census Fannin County,* p. 167; *1860 Census Arizona Territory, New Mexico,* p. 35.

19. Marshall L. Pennington to VCR, 29 November 1979, author's files; Marshall L. Pennington to Eunice B. Rader, Lubbock, 16 February 1981, photocopy in author's files.

20. *History of Primitive Baptists,* p. 211; School attendance is indicated in the *1850 Census Fannin County,* p. 167.

21. State of Texas General Land Office, Austin, File 165 (Elias Pennington), Survey Plat. The Texas Pacific Company financed the Sonora Exploring and

Mining Company which came to Arizona in 1856 under Charles D. Poston and Samuel P. Heintzelman. A. W. Gressinger, *Charles D. Poston, Sunland Seer* (Globe, Arizona: Dale Stuart King, 1961), pp. 21–22.

22. Fannin County Clerk, Bonham, "Deeds," vol. C, pp. 5, 406, 408, vol. H, p. 549, vol. I, p. 34; Forbes, *The Penningtons,* p. 2.

23. John Parker Pennington, II, Family Bible; Forbes, *The Penningtons,* p. 2.

24. Forbes, *The Penningtons,* p. 3.

25. *Ibid.,* p. 2.

26. There was also a settlement named Keechi laid out in Leon County a year later (1857).

27. Forbes, *The Penningtons,* p. 2; The wagonmaster may have been Jesse Sutton, a farmer and stationkeeper at the "Desert Station" near Gila Bend on the Overland Mail Route. Sutton later employed Jack Pennington there. *1860 Census Arizona Territory, New Mexico,* p. 61; Virginia Culin Roberts, "Jack Pennington in Early Arizona," *Arizona and the West* 23 (Winter 1981): 320.

28. Forbes, Amanda Jane Crumpton Interview.

29. Benjamin Butler Harris, *The Gila Trail: The Texas Argonauts and the California Gold Rush,* Richard H. Dillon, ed. and anno. (Norman: University of Oklahoma Press, 1960), pp. 31–45; Maybelle Edwards Martin, ed., "From Texas to California in 1849: Diary of C. C. Cox," *Southwestern Historical Quarterly,* 29 (July, 1925): 27–28, 46.

30. Forbes, *The Penningtons,* p. 3.

31. *Ibid.*

32. The Penningtons more or less followed a trail blazed by Colonel Jack Hays in 1849, but little used until 1856 when James Birch laid out the San Antonio-San Diego Mail Stage Line along this route. Ralph Moody, *The Old Trails West* (New York: Thomas Y. Crowell Co., 1963), pp. 90–94; Forbes, *The Penningtons,* p. 3.

33. *Memorial and Petition to Congress from Citizens of Arizona Territory, Tubac, 27 February 1858* (Photostat from National Archives Record Group No. 46, Benjamin Sacks Collection, AHF).

34. Lee Myers, "Mangas Colorado's Favorite Ambush Site," *Old West* (Winter, 1968): 24–26, 73–76.

35. Roberts, "Jack Pennington in Early Arizona.," pp. 327–29.

36. Daniel Ellis Conner, *Joseph Reddeford Walker and the Arizona Adventure,* edited by Donald J. Berthrong and Odessa Davenport (Norman: University of Oklahoma Press, 1956), p. 61, fn 10; See also Byrd H. Granger, *Will C. Barnes' Arizona Place Names* (Tucson: University of Arizona Press, 1960), p. 36.

37. Ray Brandes, *Frontier Military Posts of Arizona* (Globe, Arizona: Dale Stuart King, 1960), p. 22.

38. Forbes, *The Penningtons,* p. 7.

39. Conner, *Joseph Reddeford Walker,* pp. 238–41.

40. A number of people died of "mountain fever" in Arizona towns in the 1880s and 1890s. Frances Quebbeman, *Medicine in Territorial Arizona* (Phoenix: Arizona Historical Foundation, 1966), p. 172; Brigham Young and other Mor-

mons are said to have had this disease in 1847, with "burning fever and delerium [sic]." Frank Waters, *The Earp Brothers of Tombstone: The Story of Mrs. Virgil Earp* (New York: Bramhall House, 1960), p. 16.

41. Dr. Lewis Kennon was with this garrison from approximately June 1856 until December 1857, when Lieut. Bernard J. D. Irwin relieved him. Quebbeman, *Medicine in Territorial Arizona,* p. 33.

42. James S. Hutchins, "Bald Head Ewell, Frontier Dragoon," *Arizoniana,* 3 (Spring 1962): 21.

43. Forbes, *The Penningtons,* p. 7.

44. Asst. Surgeon Bernard J. D. Irwin, "Sanitary Report, Fort Buchanan, Arizona," February 1859, *Senate Executive Documents,* 52: 207–20, Records of the Surgeon General's Office, United States 36th Congress, 1st Session, 6 August 1860, Serial No. 1035.

45. Forbes, *The Penningtons,* p. 10.

46. *1860 Census, Arizona Territory, New Mexico,* p. 69; Solomon Warner, Reminiscences, Ledger Book, p. 29, Warner Collection, Box 6, Folder 59, AHSL; Samuel Hughes, Account of trip from Tucson to Calabasas, Fort Buchanan, and intermediate points, 20, 21 September 1859, copy in R. H. Forbes Notebook, Forbes Collection, Box 3, AHSL.

47. H. B. Wharfield, *Fort Yuma on the Colorado River* (El Cajon, California: privately published, 1968), p. 87; Arthur Woodward, *The Great Western, Amazon of the Army* (San Francisco: Yerba Buena Chapter of E Clampus Vitus, 1961) [n.p.], p. 48.

48. O'Neil, *They Die But Once,* p. 40.

49. Irwin, "Sanitary Report, Fort Buchanan, Arizona," February 1859.

50. Bernard L. Fontana and J. Cameron Greenleaf, "Johnny Ward's Ranch: A Study in Historic Archaeology," *The Kiva, Journal of the [Arizona] Archaeological & Historical Society,* 28 (October-December 1962): 16.

51. Forbes, *The Penningtons,* p. 10.

3: Woman of Courage

1. R. S. Ewell, Captain First Dragoons, Commanding, to Lieutenant John D. Wilkins, Acting Assistant Adjutant General, Department of New Mexico, 10 April 1860, "Report in relation to two females captured by Tonto Apaches" (photocopy in Sacks Collection, AHF).

2. Constance Wynn Altshuler, *Chains of Command: Arizona and the Army, 1856-1875* (Tucson: Arizona Historical Society, 1981), pp. 4–11.

3. Ewell to Wilkins, 10 April 1860.

4. Ewell indicated in his 10 April report that he had first reported the capture on 17 March. *Ibid.* There was regular, monthly military mail service to and from department headquarters at Fort Thorn. Altshuler, *Chains of Command,* p. 6.

5. James S. Hutchins, "Bald Head Ewell, Frontier Dragoon," *Arizoniana,* 3 (Spring 1962): 20–21.

6. Ewell later determined "beyond a doubt" that the abductors were Tonto Apaches, rather than Pinals. Ewell to Wilkins, 10 April 1860.

7. "Highly Important from Arizona, Tubac, March 18, 1860," St. Louis *Missouri Republican*, 3 April 1860, as quoted in Constance Wynn Altshuler, *Latest From Arizona! The Hesperian Letters 1859-1861* (Tucson, Arizona: Arizona Pioneers' Historical Society, 1969), pp. 47–48.

8. Fifty-six settlers had lambasted the military system in New Mexico, of which Fort Buchanan was a part, in an 1858 petition which set forth grievances and requested a volunteer militia to replace the ineffective troops. *Memorial and Petition to Congress from Citizens of Arizona Territory, Tubac, 27 February 1858*, National Archives Record Group 46, photostat in Sacks Collection, AHF. (From 1856 to 1862, "Arizona Territory" designated the Gadsden Purchase region of Arizona, then still part of New Mexico Territory.)

9. Edward H. Spicer, *Cycles of Conquest* (Tucson: University of Arizona Press, 1962), pp. 243–44.

10. Ewell to Wilkins, 10 April 1860; Altshuler, *Latest From Arizona!*, pp. 36–41.

11. Altshuler, *Latest From Arizona!*, pp. 48, 250; Hutchins, *Bald Head Ewell*, p. 22.

12. William Hudson Kirkland, "An account of the captives [sic] by Apache Indians of Mrs. John Page, nee Larcena Pennington, daughter of Mr. and Mrs. E. G. Pennington, and incidents connected therewith," MS, 3 September 1909 (Ben and Fern Allen Collection, AHSL).

13. Edward F. Radeleff [Radcliff], "Heroic Mrs. Page," *Weekly Phoenix Herald*, 2 July 1891. "Radeleff" is shown as "Radcliff" in the *Census of the United States, 1860, Arizona Territory, New Mexico*, p. 41, and in the Tubac *Weekly Arizonian*, 19 May 1859.

14. Altshuler, *Latest from Arizona!*, p. 52.

15. *Ibid.*, pp. 47–48. Turner at first indicated the express arrived at Tubac on 18 March, but his later reports show that it was the 17th.

16. Edward F. Radeleff [Radcliff], "Heroic Mrs. Page."

17. Altshuler, *Latest from Arizona!*, pp. 47–48.

18. *Ibid.*, pp. 49-50; *New York Times*, 12 April 1860, 5:2, correspondence from Thompson Turner ("Hesperian"), Tubac, Friday, March 23, 1860.

19. *Ibid.*

20. *Ibid.*, p. 51.

21. *Ibid.*; Radcliff said twenty-five Papagos accompanied the group: Radeleff [Radcliff], "Heroic Mrs. Page."

22. Altshuler, *Latest from Arizona!*, pp. 51–52.

23. *Ibid.*

24. Radeleff [Radcliff], "Heroic Mrs. Page"; James H. Tevis, *Arizona in the '50's* (Albuquerque: University of New Mexico Press, 1954), pp. 70–71.

25. [Georgie Scott Forbes], "Mamma's Capture by Indians in the Spring of 1860," [n.d., ca. 1900], MS, Forbes Collection, Box 3, AHSL.

26. *Ibid.*

27. Ewell to Wilkins, 10 April 1860; Altshuler, *Latest from Arizona!*, p. 70.
28. St. Louis *Missouri Republican,* 8 May 1860; see also Altshuler, *Latest from Arizona!,* p. 66.
29. Ewell to Wilkins, 10 April 1860; Tevis, *Arizona in the '50's,* pp. 72–73.
30. San Francisco *Daily Alta California,* 6 April 1860.
31. [Georgie Scott Forbes], "Mamma's Capture."
32. *Ibid.*
33. *Ibid.*
34. *Missouri Republican,* 8 May 1860; see also Altshuler, *Latest from Arizona!,* p. 66.
35. Kirkland, MS, 3 September 1909; Jeff Ake said the man who carried Larcena was George Fulton: James Bradas O'Neil, *They Die But Once* (New York: Knight Publications, 1935), p. 35.
36. [Georgie Scott Forbes], "Mamma's Capture." Hampton Brown, a mulatto, and "Virgin Mary" (later Mrs. Cornelius Ramos) moved on to Prescott, Arizona, where she ran the first boarding house for miners and left her name on Virgin Mary Hill. Thomas Edwin Farish, *History of Arizona,* 8 vols. (San Francisco: Filmer Bros., 1914–1918), vol. 3, p. 212; "Virgin Mary" file, Sharlot Hall Museum, Prescott.
37. Kirkland MS 3 September 1909.
38. Radeleff [Radcliff], "Heroic Mrs. Page."
39. *New York Times,* 21 April 1860, 3:3.
40. B. Sachs, M. D., *Be It Enacted: The Creation of the Territory of Arizona* (Phoenix: Arizona Historical Foundation, 1964), p. 133.
41. *Ibid.*; Altshuler, *Latest from Arizona!,* p. 47, 55.
42. Tevis, *Arizona in the '50's,* p. 71.
43. Kirkland MS 3 September 1909.
44. *Ibid.*
45. *Missouri Republican,* 8 May 1860.
46. *Ibid.*; Altshuler, *Latest from Arizona!,* p. 69–70; Sachs, *Be It Enacted,* pp. 137–39, 149. Both the name "Ewell County" and the provisional government itself were short-lived.
47. Percy Gatling Hamlin, ed., *The Making of a Soldier: Letters of General. R. S. Ewell, 1817–1872* (Richmond, Virginia: Whittet & Shepperson, 1935), p. 95.
48. Radeleff [Radcliff], "Heroic Mrs. Page."
49. *Census of the United States, 1860, Arizona Territory, New Mexico* (photocopy of original returns, AHSL), p. 35.

4: Rough Times on the Border

1. *Thomas J. Cassner, Administrator, v. The United States et al., Indian Depredations No. 3112,* p. 180, Testimony of Annie M. [Ake] Davis, 3 December 1913.
2. *Census of the United States, 1860, Arizona Territory, New Mexico,* p. 30 (Sonorita [sic] Creek Settlement); "F. Biertu Journal, 1860–1861," MS HM4367, Huntington Library, San Marino, California, Sketch Map, p. 119

(reproduced in Virginia Culin Roberts, "Heroines on the Arizona Frontier," *Journal of Arizona History,* 23 [Spring 1982]: 18); James Bradas O'Neil, *They Die But Once* (New York: Knight Publications, 1935), p. 5.

3. *Census of the United States, 1860, Arizona Territory, New Mexico* (photocopy of original, AHSL), p. 35; *Thomas J. Cassner, Administrator, v. the United States, et al., Indian Depredations, No. 3112,* U.S. Court of Claims (Washington: Government Printing Office [24761–14], 1914), pp. 61–62, Testimony of Esther [Wadsworth] Martin, 25 August 1913; pp. 76–78, Esther Martin, 26 November 1913; pp. 158–59, 165–66, Charles H. [Jeff] Ake, 22 November 1913; pp. 169–73, Annie M. [Ake] Davis, 3 December 1913; p. 155, S. P. Campbell, 13 December 1913; see also Constance Wynn Altshuler, *Chains of Command: Arizona and the Army, 1856–1875* (Tucson: Arizona Historical Society, 1975), pp. 3, 4.

4. *Indian Depredations Claim No. 3112,* pp. 62, 66, Esther [Wadsworth] Martin, 26 August 1913. At age ninety-three, Charles H. [Jeff] Ake stated that his father arrived at Calabasas from California with government contracts already in hand (see O'Neil, *They Die But Once,* pp. 21–22). However, that contradicts his sworn testimony at age sixty-five in 1913 in *Indian Depredations Claim No. 3112,* p. 165.

5. *1860 Census, Arizona Territory, New Mexico,* pp. 9 (Tucson) and 35 (Middle Santa Cruz Settlement); O'Neil, *They Die But Once,* pp. 28–29.

6. *1860 Census, Arizona Territory, New Mexico,* p. 35.

7. *Census of the United States, 1850, San Diego County, California* (microfilm 002492, LDS Genealogical Society, Salt Lake City), p. 272. Although there are several John Pages listed in the 1850 California census, the author has so far been unable to identify John Hempstead Page among them.

8. O'Neil, *They Die But Once,* p. 31.

9. *Ibid.,* p. 20.

10. O'Neil, *They Die But Once,* pp. 28–29; Robert H. Forbes, *Crabb's Filibustering Expedition into Sonora, 1857* ([Tucson]: Arizona Silhouettes, 1952), Introduction [n. p.]; J. Y. Ainsa, *History of the Crabb Expedition into Northern Sonora* (Phoenix: self-published, 1951), pp. 5, 15. Ainsa reported that Crabb planned to locate 600 Caucasian American families in Sonora.

11. Forbes, *Crabb's Filibustering Expedition,* pp. 7–16; Ainsa, *History of the Crabb Expedition,* p. 4–10.

12. Ainsa, *History of the Crabb Expedition,* pp. 9–10; Forbes, *Crabb's Filibustering Expedition,* p. 39; O'Neil, *They Die But Once,* pp. 28–29.

13. Forbes, *Crabb's Filibustering Expedition,* pp. 13–15; Ainsa, *History of the Crabb Expedition,* pp. 13–18.

14. Forbes, *Crabb's Filibustering Expedition,* Introduction [n.p.], pp. 22–24, fn 31; Ainsa, *History of the Crabb Expedition,* p. 10, 13–18.

15. Forbes, *Crabb's Filibustering Expedition,* "Introduction" [n.p.], pp. 39–40; Ainsa, *History of the Crabb Expedition,* "Introduction."

16. Forbes, *Crabb's Filibustering Expedition,* pp. 2–6; June Caldwell, "Filibustering in Sonora 1841-1857," MS (C147j), [n.d.], AHSL.

17. O'Neil, *They Die But Once,* pp. 28–29.
18. Edward S. Wallace, "The Gray-eyed Man of Destiny," *American Heritage,* 9 (December 1957): 28.
19. O'Neil, *They Die But Once,* p. 28.
20. Diane M. T. North, *Samuel Peter Heintzelman and the Sonora Exploring & Mining Company* (Tucson: University of Arizona Press, 1980), p. 64; *1860 Census Arizona Territory, New Mexico,* Tucson, p. 5.
21. O'Neil, *They Die But Once,* p. 29.
22. Charles D. Poston to Sylvester Mowry, 5 August [1857], quoted in Sylvester Mowry, *Memoir of the Proposed Territory of Arizona* (Washington: Henry Polkinhorn, Printer, 1857), pp. 22–23. The letter's date of 1850, as printed in the *Memoir,* is an obvious typographical error.
23. Padrés' name has been misspelled Padraes, Padreos and Pedros in various sources. He delivered commodities to the Cerro Colorado Mine in the summer of 1858. (See North, *Samuel Peter Heintzelman,* p. 129.) An Arizona resident after 1860, Padrés engaged in freighting and mining.
24. Charles D. Poston to Sylvester Mowry, 15 August 1857, in Mowry, *Memoir* (1857), p. 20; "Our Arizona Correspondence," San Francisco *Daily Alta California,* 25 December 1857, identifies the five filibusters as "Curley, Davis, Ward, Casey and Burke." Solomon Warner, quoted in Cornelius C. Smith, Sr., "A History of the Oury Family" (unpublished MS, AHSL), pp. 77, 85–86, named J. G. (Billiard) Ward and one Redding as two of them. Jeff Ake stated that "a feller named Davis" and "a feller named Ward" came to Sonoita Valley with John Page, Bill Ake, and the other filibusters. He named Redding as one who left Sonoita Valley with the Akes in 1861. O'Neil, *They Die But Once,* pp. 28–30, 40.
25. *Daily Alta California,* 25 December 1857; Smith, "A History of the Oury Family," pp. 85–86; Poston to Mowry, 15 August 1857, in Mowry, *Memoir* (1857), pp. 20–21.
26. Poston to Mowry, 15 August 1857, in Mowry, *Memoir* (1857), pp. 20–21.
27. Robert H. Forbes, *The Penningtons: Pioneers of Early Arizona* ([Tucson]: Arizona Archaeological and Historical Society, 1919), pp. 7, 10; *Memorial and Petition to Congress from Citizens of Arizona Territory, Tubac, 27 February 1858* [n. p.], National Archives, Record Group No. 46 (photostat in Sacks Collection, AHF).
28. G[ranville] H. Oury to Sylvester Mowry, 17 October 1857, in Mowry, *Memoir* (1857), p. 21; *Memorial and Petition, Tubac, 27 February 1858*; Forbes, *The Penningtons,* p. 7.
29. Ray Brandes, *Frontier Military Posts of Arizona* (Globe, Arizona: Dale Stuart King, 1960), p. 22.
30. *Memorial and Petition, Tubac, 27 February 1858.*
31. *Ibid.*
32. Charles R. Ames, "Along the Mexican Border—Then and Now," *Journal of Arizona History,* 18 (Winter 1977): 432.

33. Charles D. Poston, "The Pennington Family," *Tucson Citizen,* 17 January 1896.

34. Robert H. Forbes, photograph of Pennington houses on the Santa Cruz, 1913, see Pictures-Places-Pennington Homes, photo files, AHSL; Robert H. Forbes, *The Penningtons, Pioneers of Early Arizona* ([Tucson]: Arizona Archaeological and Historical Society, 1919), illustration opposite p. 10. This site was later known as the "Stone House Ranch"; it became the property of Patrick J. Hand who deeded it in 1877 to Albert C. Benedict. Copy of deed in George McIntosh file, folder 34, MS 68, AHSL. The "stone house" appears on *Topographical Map, Nogales Quadrangle, Santa Cruz County, Arizona, USGS edition 1905,* reprinted 1916 (AHSL map files).

35. A. M. Gustafson, *John Spring's Arizona* (Tucson: University of Arizona Press, 1966), p. 130.

36. Topographical Map, Nogales Quadrangle, USGS 1905.

37. *Memorial and Petition to Congress, Tubac, 27 February 1858.*

38. *Ibid.*

39. *Ibid.* For more about the Army contract system and its problems see Darlis A. Miller, "Civilians and Military Supply in the Southwest," *Journal of Arizona History,* 23 (Summer 1982): 115–138.

40. Altshuler, *Chains of Command,* pp. 6–7.

41. *Ibid.,* pp. 6–7, 251.

42. *Memorial and Petition to Congress, Tubac, 27 February 1858.* On 25 February 1859, a year after this petition was signed, the House Committee on Territories discharged it and referred it to the Committee on Military Affairs and the Militia.

43. Altshuler, *Chains of Command,* p. 7; Constance Wynn Altshuler, *Starting With Defiance: Nineteenth Century Arizona Military Posts* (Tucson: Arizona Historical Society, 1983), p. 19.

44. Forbes, *The Penningtons,* p. 8.

45. A note to this effect was added after Elias Pennington's name by the census enumerator in *1860 Census, Arizona Territory, New Mexico* (photocopy of original returns, AHSL), p. 34.

46. Robert H. Forbes, *The Penningtons,* pp. 26; Washington, D.C., United States Court of Claims, *Indian Depredations No. 7363, William F. Scott, Administrator, vs. U.S. and Apache Indians,* filed 5 April 1893, testimony of Edward N. Fish, pp. 26–27, copy of proceedings in Robert H. Forbes files, Box 3, AHSL.

47. Bert M. Fireman, *Arizona Historic Land* (New York: Alfred A. Knopf, 1982), p. 150; Charles H. Dunning with Edward H. Peplow, Jr., *Rock to Riches* (Phoenix: Southwest Publishing Co., 1959), p. 60.

48. W. Hubert Curry, *Sun Rising on the West, the Saga of Henry Clay and Elizabeth Smith* (Crosbyton, Texas: Crosby County Pioneer Memorial, 1979), pp. 9–22.

49. Amanda Jane [Pennington] Crumpton to Robert H. Forbes, Santa Cruz,

California, 18 May 1916, Interview Notes in Forbes Collection, Box 3, Folder 3, AHSL; Forbes, *The Penningtons,* p. 12.

50. Amanda Jane [Pennington] Crumpton Interview.

51. *Ibid.*; Handwriting practice paper, Forbes Collection, Box 3, Folder 3, AHSL.

52. Amanda Jane [Pennington] Crumpton Interview.

53. William A. Duffen, ed., "Overland Via 'Jackass Mail': The Diary of Phocion R. Way," *Arizona and the West,* 2 (Winter 1960): 355.

54. *Ibid.*

55. Gressinger, *Charles D. Poston, Sunland Seer,* pp. 30–34.

56. Duffen, "Diary of Phocion R. Way," *Arizona and the West,* 2 (Autumn 1960): 280.

57. *Ibid.*

58. Duffen, "Diary of Phocion R. Way," *Arizona and the West,* 2 (Winter, 1960): 354.

5: Murders and Marriages

1. "Pennington Chronology," Robert H. Forbes notes, Box 3, Folder 3, AHSL. The exact date of the move is unknown.

2. Elias G. Pennington, Homestead Notice filed 30 December 1865, Pima County, Arizona Territory, *Land Claims Book 1,* p. 59.

3. Bernard L. Fontana, "Calabasas of the Rio Rico," *The Smoke Signal* (Tucson: Tucson Corral of the Westerners), 24 (Fall 1971): 1–86. The Gándara Hacienda now belongs to the Arizona Historical Society.

4. Amanda Jane [Pennington] Crumpton to Robert H. Forbes, Santa Cruz, California, 18 May 1916, Interview Notes in Forbes Collection, Box 3, Folder 3, AHSL; Robert H. Forbes photograph of Gándara Hacienda, Pictures-Places-Pennington Homes, photo files, AHSL.

5. Curry, *Sun Rising on the West, The Saga of Henry Clay and Elizabeth Smith* (Crosbyton, Texas: Crosby County Pioneer Memorial, 1979), p. 24; see also Hattie M. Anderson, ed., "Mining and Indian Fighting in Arizona and New Mexico, 1858–1861: — Memoirs of Hank Smith," *Panhandle Plains Historical Review,* 1 (1928): 75–77.

6. Curry, *Sun Rising on the West,* p. 25; see also Anderson, "Mining and Indian Fighting," pp. 77–78.

7. C. D. Poston, 5 August 1857, in Sylvester Mowry, *Memoir of the Proposed Territory of Arizona* (Washington, D.C.: Henry Polkinghorn, Printer, 1857), p. 22; C. D. Poston, 15 August 1857, Ibid., p. 21. For more about the oppressive tax on Mexican imports see "Our Arizona Correspondence," *Daily Alta Californian,* 15 December 1857.

8. James Bradas O'Neil, *They Die But Once* (New York: Knight Publications, 1935), p. 28.

9. Diane M. T. North, *Samuel Peter Heintzelman and the Sonora Exploring &*

Mining Company (Tucson: University of Arizona Press, 1980), pp. 127, 129, 134, 135.

10. I. V. D. Reeve, Brevet Lieutenant Colonel, U.S. A., to Lieutenant J. D. Wilkins, Acting Assistant Adjutant General, 20 May 1859, Washington, D.C., National Archives, Records Group 98, Records of the War Department, U.S. Army Commands, Letters Received Department of New Mexico, Box 12, R 22-1859 (photocopy of original in Sacks Collection, Folder Fort Buchanan 1859, AHF).

11. O'Neil, *They Die But Once,* p. 35; Randall is named as a partner in Constance Wynn Altshuler, *Latest from Arizona! The Hesperian Letters, 1859–1861* (Tucson: The Arizona Pioneers' Historical Society, 1969), p. 64.

12. Tubac *Weekly Arizonian,* 3 March 1859.

13. Charles D. Poston, "Early Matrimony in Southern Arizona," *Prescott Morning Courier,* 28 May 1891.

14. *Weekly Arizonian,* Tubac, 14 April 1859.

15. O'Neil, *They Die But Once,* p. 5.

16. James W. Byrkit, "The Word on the Frontier: Anglo Protestant Churches in Arizona, 1859-1899," *Journal of Arizona History,* 21 (Spring 1980): 64.

17. *Weekly Arizonian,* 3 March 1859.

18. Altshuler, *Latest From Arizona!,* p. 247–48.

19. *Weekly Arizonian,* 12 May and 19 May 1859.

20. Tubac *Weekly Arizonian,* 12 May 1859 and 19 May 1859; *Sacramento Union,* 25 May 1859. Greenbury Byrd was no angel; pioneer Solomon Warner criticized his actions after the shooting of Edward Miles. See Cornelius C. Smith, Jr., *William Sanders Oury, History-Maker of the Southwest* (Tucson: University of Arizona Press, 1967), pp. 98–99.

21. Roscoe P. Conkling and Margaret B. Conkling, *The Butterfield Overland Mail 1857–1869,* 3 vols. (Glendale, California: Arthur H. Clark Company, 1947), vol. 2, pp. 141–46.

22. *Ibid.*

23. Reeve to Wilkins, 20 May 1859.

24. *Weekly Arizonian,* 19 May 1859.

25. *Ibid.*; San Francisco *Weekly Alta Californian,* 28 May 1859.

26. *Sacramento Union,* 25 May 1859.

27. *Weekly Arizonian,* 19 May 1859.

28. *Weekly Arizonian,* 12 May 1859; F. Biertu Journal, 1860–61 (Huntington Library, San Marino, California, MS HM4367), sketch map p. 119, reproduced in Virginia Culin Roberts, "Heroines on the Arizona Frontier," *Journal of Arizona History,* 23 (Spring 1982): 18.

29. Ashworth is shown as "Ash" on the Biertu map (see note 28); O'Neil, *They Die But Once,* p. 35.

30. *Weekly Arizonian,* 12 May 1859.

31. *Weekly Arizonian,* 19 May 1859; Solomon Warner, Handwritten Rem-

iniscences in Ledger Book, p. 85 (Warner Collection, Box 6, Folder 59, AHSL). The Carea mentioned in the article may have been a misspelling of "Carillo."

32. *Weekly Arizonian,* 19 May 1859.
33. Reeve to Wilkins, 20 May 1859.
34. *Ibid.*
35. *Ibid.*
36. *Weekly Arizonian,* 19 May 1859.
37. *Ibid.*
38. *Ibid.*
39. *Ibid.*
40. New York *Daily Tribune,* 9 June 1859 (typescript, Hayden Collection, Greenbury Byrd File, AHSL).
41. *Weekly Arizonian,* 19 May 1859.
42. Reeve to Wilkins, 20 May 1859.
43. Marriage record, John Parker Pennington, II, Family Bible, Marshall L. Pennington Collection, Lubbock, Texas.
44. *Census of the United States, 1860, Arizona Territory, New Mexico* (photocopy of original, AHSL), p. 34. In 1857 at Tubac Charles Burr signed the so-called "Kippen Memorial," a petition to Congress. See B. Sachs, M.D., *Be It Enacted: The Creation of the Territory of Arizona* (Phoenix: Arizona Historical Foundation, 1964), Appendix A, p. 121.
45. O'Neil, *They Die But Once,* p. 34; Jerry Thompson, "The Vulture over the Carrion: Captain James 'Paddy' Graydon and the Civil War in the Territory of New Mexico," *Journal of Arizona History,* 23 (Winter 1983): 385.
46. *Weekly Arizonian,* 21 April 1859.
47. *Weekly Arizonian,* 19 May 1859.
48. *Ibid.*
49. *Ibid.*
50. *Ibid.*
51. *Ibid.,* 26 May 1859.
52. *Ibid.,* 2 June 1859.
53. *Ibid.,* 19 May 1859.
54. *Ibid.,* 2 June 1859.
55. *Ibid.,* 9 June 1859.
56. *Ibid.,* 23 June 1859.
57. *Ibid.,* 9 June 1859.
58. Tucson *Weekly Arizonian,* 29 September 1859, "A Letter from the Obiquitous [sic]." (The *Weekly Arizonian* was moved from Tubac to Tucson about 1 August 1859.)
59. Samuel W. Cozzens wrote several books including *The Marvelous Country, or, Three Years in Arizona and New Mexico* (Boston: Lee & Shepard, 1876 [first edition 1873]), a partially fictionized and occasionally erroneous account which was also published in London.
60. The trial record for the "Sonoita Murders" case is in *Mining Claims Book*

2, p. 7, Recorder's Office, Dona Ana County, Las Cruces, New Mexico. (The office has two different record books with that title.)

61. Altshuler, *Latest From Arizona!,* pp. 247–48; Elizabeth R. Brownell, *They Lived in Tubac* (Tucson: Westernlore Press, 1986), pp. 16–18.

62. Anderson, ed., "Mining and Indian Fighting," pp. 80–87.

63. Robert H. Forbes Notebook, Forbes Collection, Box 3, AHSL, entry for 13 June 1915.

64. Tucson *Weekly Arizonian,* 4 August 1859.

65. Tubac *Weekly Arizonian,* 30 June 1859.

66. Tucson *Weekly Arizonian,* 15 September 1859; Frances Quebbeman, *Medicine in Territorial Arizona* (Phoenix: Arizona Historical Foundation, 1966), pp.37–38.

67. Tucson *Weekly Arizonian,* 4 August 1859 and 18 August 1859. A man named Page (no first name given) appears in several of Phocion Way's diary entries in the summer and fall of 1858. See William A. Duffen, ed., "Overland Via Jackass Mail: The Diary of Phocion R. Way," *Arizona and the West,* 2 (Winter 1960): 353–70, passim. It has been assumed (erroneously, in the author's opinion) that this man was John Hempstead Page: see *Ibid.,* p. 356, fn. 6. The *Arizonian* of 4 August refers specifically to Edward G. Page of the Salero (Santa Rita) Mine.

68. Tucson *Weekly Arizonian,* 20 October 1859.

69. Anderson, ed., "Mining and Indian Fighting," p. 79.

70. *Ibid.,* pp. 79–80.

71. Tucson *Weekly Arizonian,* 20 October 1859.

72. Anderson, ed., "Mining and Indian Fighting," p. 79.

73. Tucson *Weekly Arizonian,* 20 October 1859.

74. *Ibid.,* 8 December 1859.

75. When James Pennington later recorded his claim he stated, ". . . I have lived upon the same at all times only such as I was compelled to leave on account of Indians and the unsettled condition of the country." Pima County, Arizona, *Land Claims Number 1,* p. 51.

76. John Parker Pennington, II, Family Bible, Marshall L. Pennington collection, Houston, Texas.

6: Lonely Graves

1. Minutes, Society of Arizona Pioneers (Arizona Historical Society), as quoted in C. L. Sonnichsen, *Pioneer Heritage: The First Century of the Arizona Historical Society* (Tucson: The Arizona Historical Society, 1984), p. 19.

2. *Ibid,* p. 4.

3. St. Louis *Missouri Republican,* 14 April 1860, as quoted in Constance Wynn Altshuler, *Latest from Arizona! The Hesperian Letters, 1859–1861* (Tucson: Arizona Pioneers' Historical Society, 1969), p. 60.

4. *Missouri Republican,* 25 May 1860, 17 June 1860, 27 June 1860, and 9 July 1860, all as quoted in Altshuler, *Latest from Arizona!,* pp. 81, 90, 96, 100.

5. *Missouri Republican,* 8 May 1860, 3 June 1860, 5 June 1860, 27 June 1860, all as quoted in Altshuler, *Latest from Arizona!,* pp. 68–69, 84, 87–88, 95.

6. References to these pioneer memoirs, including those of James Tevis, Charles Genung, Edward Radcliff, and William H. Kirkland, will be found in the chapter notes and bibliography.

7. Ben and Fern Allen Collection, William Hudson Kirkland files, AHSL.

8. *United States Census 1860, Arizona Territory, New Mexico,* photocopy of original returns, AHSL; *Missouri Republican,* 3 June 1860, as quoted in Altshuler, *Latest from Arizona!,* p. 85.

9. Tucson *Weekly Arizonian,* 9 February 1861, advertisement.

10. *Missouri Republican,* 12 May 1860, 5 June 1860, and 17 June 1860, all as quoted in Altshuler, *Latest from Arizona!,* pp. 72, 88, 90, 92.

11. *Missouri Republican,* 16 May 1860 and 3 June 1860, as quoted in Altshuler, *Latest from Arizona!,* pp. 77, 86; James Bradas O'Neil, *They Die But Once* (New York: Knight Publications, 1935), p. 28; *1860 Census, Arizona Territory, New Mexico,* San Pedro Settlement, p. 25.

12. *Missouri Republican,* 27 June 1860, 9 July 1860, 6 August 1860, 4 September 1860, 12 September 1860, all as quoted in Altshuler, *Latest from Arizona!,* pp. 96, 100, 106, 114, 116.

13. *Missouri Republican,* 17 June 1860, 20 June 1860, both as quoted in Altshuler, *Latest from Arizona!,* pp. 91, 93.

14. W. Hubert Curry, *Sun Rising on the West, the Saga of Henry Clay and Elizabeth Smith* (Crosbyton, Texas: Crosby County Pioneer Memorial, 1979), pp. 34–35; Hattie M. Anderson, ed., "Mining and Indian Fighting in Arizona and New Mexico, 1858–1861: — Memoirs of Hank Smith," *Panhandle Plains Historical Review,* 1 (1928): 75–77; Virginia Culin Roberts, "Jack Pennington in Early Arizona," *Arizona and the West,* 23 (Winter 1981): 324.

15. *Missouri Republican,* 20 June 1860, as quoted in Altshuler, *Latest from Arizona!,* p. 93.

16. The name was Pino Alto at that time.

17. *Missouri Republican,* 27 June 1860, as quoted in Altshuler, *Latest from Arizona!,* p. 96.

18. *United States Census 1860, New Mexico* (Salt Lake City: Church of Latter Day Saints Genealogical Library Microfilm 653, Roll 712), Doña Ana County, p. 147, (Overland Mail Line), line 19; *1860 Census Arizona Territory, New Mexico,* p. 34.

19. *Missouri Republican,* 16 August 1860, as quoted in Altshuler, *Latest from Arizona!,* p. 107–08.

20. Percy Gatling Hamlin, comp., ed., *The Making of a Soldier: Letters of General R. S. Ewell, 1817–1872* (Richmond, Virginia: Whittet & Shepperson, 1935), letter of 26 October 1859.

21. The census taker on September 1 listed Page, Dennison and Pennington as farmers, Hutton as a bricklayer (*1860 Census Arizona Territory, New Mexico,* p. 35). Dennison and Pennington were about Larcena's age. Both had been born in Virginia where, according to legend, Elias Pennington had relatives. Elias had given the middle name Dennison to his daughter Margaret. It was a pioneer tendency for family members to migrate together, and Dennison is said to have come to Arizona in 1857, the year that Larcena came.

22. The Prescott *Arizona Miner,* October 8, 1870, obituary of William E. Dennison.

23. "Letter from Arizona," San Francisco *Evening Bulletin,* 26 September 1860 (Microfilm Roll 3490, Reel 11, AHSL).

24. *Missouri Republican,* 4 October 1860, as quoted in Altshuler, *Latest from Arizona!,* p. 121–22.

25. Constance Wynn Altshuler, *Starting With Defiance: Nineteenth Century Arizona Military Posts* (Tucson: Arizona Historical Society, 1983), p. 18; *Missouri Republican,* 17 October 1860 and 27 November 1860, as quoted in Altshuler, *Latest from Arizona!,* pp. 130, 141.

26. *Missouri Republican,* 15 October 1860, as quoted in Altshuler, *Latest from Arizona!,* p. 128.

27. Hamlin, *The Making of a Soldier,* letter of 10 June 1857.

28. San Francisco *Evening Bulletin,* 4 December 1860, as quoted in Altshuler, *Latest from Arizona!,* p. 152.

29. *Ibid.*; *Missouri Republican,* 27 August 1860, 4 December 1860, and 23 January 1861, as quoted in Altshuler, *Latest from Arizona!,* pp. 111, 152, 156.

30. Mesilla *Times,* 24 January 1861, as reported in San Francisco *Herald,* 6 February 1861.

31. *Missouri Republican,* 11 February 1861 and San Francisco *Evening Bulletin,* 18 March 1861, as quoted in Altshuler, *Latest from Arizona!,* pp. 166, 181.

32. Hamlin, *The Making of a Soldier,* letter of 22 January 1861.

33. *Ibid.,* p. 99.

34. *Missouri Republican,* 5 February 1861, as quoted in Altshuler, *Latest from Arizona!,* p. 163.

35. *Ibid.*; *Evening Bulletin,* 16 January 1861, as quoted in Altshuler, *Latest from Arizona!,* p. 159; *Missouri Republican,* 25 January 1861, as quoted in Altshuler, *Latest from Arizona!,* p. 165.

36. *Missouri Republican,* 28 February 1861, as quoted in Altshuler, *Latest from Arizona!,* p. 170.

37. The captured boy is thought to have grown up among the Indians, being later known as Mickey Free, an Apache scout.

38. *Missouri Republican,* 11 February 1861 and 28 February 1861, as quoted in Altshuler, *Latest from Arizona!,* pp. 165, 169–73; *Evening Bulletin,* 2 March 1861 and 6 March 1861, as quoted in Altshuler, *Latest from Arizona!,* pp. 174–78; Altshuler, *Latest from Arizona!,* pp. 220–27.

39. Sacramento *Union,* 7 March 1861.

40. *Ibid.*

41. *Missouri Republican,* 28 February 1861, as quoted in Altshuler, *Latest from Arizona!,* p. 173; *Evening Bulletin,* 2 March 1861 and 6 March 1861, as quoted in Altshuler, *Latest from Arizona!,* pp. 174–78.

42. *Union,* 7 March 1861, as quoted in Altshuler, *Latest from Arizona!,* p. 237.

43. "Samaniego's Ranch," in Section 13, T 10 S, R 14 E., Gila & Salt River Meridian (now in Pinal County), and early roads are marked on a map signed by Surveyor General Royal A. Johnson, Tucson, 19 July 1884.

44. William S. Oury, "The Sequel of the Cochise Outbreak of 1861," Tucson *Arizona Weekly Star,* 27 July 1877 and 2 August 1877.

45. *Ibid.*

46. *Union,* 7 March 1861 and 14 March 1861, as quoted by Altshuler, *Latest from Arizona!,* pp. 237–39.

47. Oury, "Sequel of the Cochise Outbreak"; *Union,* 7 March 1861 and 14 March 1861, as quoted by Altshuler, *Latest from Arizona!,* pp. 237–39.

48. *Ibid.,* p. 236.

49. Oury, "Sequel of the Cochise Outbreak."

50. For more about Oury, see Cornelius C. Smith, Jr., *William Sanders Oury: History-Maker of the Southwest* (Tucson: University of Arizona Press, 1967).

51. Oury, "Sequel of the Cochise Outbreak."

52. *Ibid.*

53. *Ibid.*

54. *Union,* 14 March 1861, as quoted in Altshuler, *Latest from Arizona!,* p. 239.

55. Oury, "Sequel of the Cochise Outbreak." An unsigned note added to a typed biographical sheet in the John Hempstead Page file (Hayden Collection, AHSL) reads: "Buried where he fell near Samaniego's ranch."

56. Robert H. Forbes Notebook, Notes on conversation with Mrs. Scott [Larcena Pennington Page Scott] January 19, 1913, in Forbes Collection, Box 3, Folder 3, AHSL.

7: The Great Exodus

1. Robert H. Forbes, handwritten draft for "The Penningtons," Forbes Collection, Box 3, Folder 3, AHSL.

2. San Francisco *Evening Bulletin,* 15 April 1861, as quoted in Constance Wynn Altshuler, *Latest from Arizona! The Hesperian Letters, 1859–1861* (Tucson: Arizona Pioneers' Historical Society, 1969), p. 192.

3. *Ibid.,* p. 193; *Evening Bulletin,* 3 April 1861, as quoted in Altshuler, *Latest from Arizona!,* p. 184; St. Louis *Missouri Republican,* 25 April 1861, as quoted in Altshuler, *Latest from Arizona!,* p. 189. For more about stage and mail service to Arizona during this period, see Altshuler, *Latest from Arizona!,* pp. 211–13.

4. *Missouri Republican,* 25 April 1861, as quoted in Altshuler, *Latest from Arizona!,* p. 190.

5. A. W. Evans, First Lieutenant 7th Infantry, to Lieutenant G. Chapin, Adjt 7th Infantry, Fort Buchanan, 20 Mar 1861, National Archives Record Group 98, Records of the War Department, U.S. Army Commands, Letters Received

Department of New Mexico, 1 E 1861 (handwritten copy in Sacks Collection, Folder 5066, AHF).

6. Samuel Robinson, "Arizona in 1861: A Contemporary Account," intro. and anno. by Constance Wynn Altshuler, *Journal of Arizona History*, 25 (Spring 1984): 21–30. This comprises a letter and diary written by Robinson.

7. *Ibid.*, pp. 29–30.

8. *Ibid.*, pp. 32–36; Altshuler, *Latest From Arizona!*, pp. 198–99.

9. Robinson, "Arizona in 1861," pp. 37 (4 May), 41 (21 May), 45–48 (9–15 June), 51–52 (25, 28 June). Roods has also been spelled Rhodes. *Ibid.*, p. 72, fn. 34.

10. *Census of the United States, 1860, Arizona Territory, New Mexico* (photocopy of original returns, AHSL), p. 9. The first daughter of Missouri Ann Bacon Kirkland was also called Lizzie, which suggests a relationship to Lizzie Bacon Ake.

11. Robinson, "Arizona in 1861," pp. 49 (19, 20 June), 51 (25 June).

12. *Ibid.*, pp. 50–52 (21–30 June).

13. Jeff Ake stated that he heard that Lizzie's brother later waylaid and killed Bill Ake and was sentenced to hang. James Bradas O'Neil, *They Die But Once* (New York: Knight Publications, 1935) p. 30; Rafael Pumpelly, *My Reminiscences* (New York: Henry Holt and Company, 1918), vol. 1, pp. 236–37.

14. Robinson, "Arizona in 1861," p. 54 (4 July).

15. *Missouri Republican*, 25 April 1861, as quoted in Altshuler, *Latest from Arizona!*, p. 190.

16. Robinson, "Arizona in 1861," p. 42 (27 May).

17. Tucson *Arizonian*, 10 August 1861.

18. Robinson, "Arizona in 1861," pp. 51–52 (25, 28, 29 June), 54–57 (15, 17 July).

19. *Ibid.*, p. 67 (14 August).

20. *Weekly Arizonian*, 9 February 1861 (photostat, AHSL), advertisement; Gilbert J. Pedersen, "A Yankee in Arizona: The Misfortunes of William S. Grant, 1860–61," *Journal of Arizona History*, 16 (Summer 1975): 132–33, 137.

21. Robinson, "Arizona in 1861," pp. 54–57 (15, 17 July).

22. *Ibid.*, p. 58 (20, 21 July).

23. *Ibid.*, p. 57–58 (18, 19 July). Jeff Ake reported that officers told the settlers to take all the surplus they wanted, but his veracity is suspect. O'Neil, *They Die But Once*, p. 40.

24. Robinson, "Arizona in 1861," p. 60 (24 July); Constance Wynn Altshuler, *Starting With Defiance: Nineteenth Century Arizona Military Posts* (Tucson: Arizona Historical Society, 1983), p. 21.

25. Jerry Thompson, "The Vulture over the Carrion: Captain James 'Paddy' Graydon and the Civil War in the Territory of New Mexico," *Journal of Arizona History*, 24 (Winter 1983): 387–404. Thompson errs in saying that Graydon was in charge of the cattle herds with the Ake-Wadsworth wagon train; there is no evidence that Graydon even traveled with the Ake-Wadsworth party.

26. Robinson, "Arizona in 1861," p. 60 (24 July).

27. *Ibid.*, pp. 60 (24, 25 July).

28. Amanda Jane [Pennington] Crumpton to Robert H. Forbes, Santa Cruz, California, 18 May 1916, Interview Notes in Forbes Collection, Box 3, Folder 3, AHSL.

29. Poston made his way through northern Sonora and on to Fort Yuma, the California coast, his home state of Kentucky, and New York, returning later to Arizona. A. W. Gressinger, *Charles D. Poston, Sunland Seer* (Globe, Arizona: Dale Stuart King, 1961), pp. 67–78.

30. Robinson, "Arizona in 1861," pp. 61 (25 July), 62 (27 July).

31. *Ibid.*, p. 62–63 (5 August).

32. *Arizonian,* 10 August 1861, "Troubles at Tubac."

33. Robinson, "Arizona in 1861," p. 63 (6 August). Granville H. Oury led the Americans who came from Tucson to help defend Tubac, according to the *Arizonian,* 10 August 1861.

34. Robinson, "Arizona in 1861," p. 61 (25 July), pp. 62–64 (5, 6 August).

35. *Ibid.*, p. 64 (7 August).

36. *Ibid.*, (8 August).

37. Altshuler, *Latest from Arizona!,* pp. 10–11.

38. *Arizonian,* 10 August 1861.

39. Robinson, "Arizona in 1861," p. 67 (14–17 August).

40. F. Biertu Journal, 1860–61, MS HM4367, Huntington Library, San Marino, California, Sketch Map, p. 119 (reproduced in Virginia Culin Roberts, "Heroines on the Arizona Frontier," *Journal of Arizona History,* 23 [Spring 1982]: 18).

41. *Census of the United States, 1860, Arizona Territory, New Mexico* (photocopy of original, AHSL), p. 35; *Thomas J. Cassner, Administrator, v. The United States et al., Indian Depredations, No. 3112,* U.S. Court of Claims (Washington: Government Printing Office [24761–14], 1914), pp. 61–62, Testimony of Esther [Wadsworth] Martin, 25 August 1913; pp. 76–78, Esther Martin, 26 November 1913; pp. 158–59, 165–66, Charles H. [Jeff] Ake, 22 November 1913; pp. 169–73, Annie M. [Ake] Davis, 3 December 1913; p. 155 S. P. Campbell, 13 December 1893.

42. *Indian Depredations Claim No. 3112,* p. 173, Annie M. Davis, 3 December 1913.

43. William Wadsworth became the first county clerk when Orange County was created from Jefferson County, Texas, in 1852. Molly Theriot, Orange County Clerk, to VCR, Orange, Texas, 19 November 1981; District Court, Orange County, Texas, Fall 1856, *No. 60, Divorce, Altha C. Wadsworth vs William W. Wadsworth;* District Court, Orange County, Texas, 24 September 1855, *No. 49, Divorce, Charles H. Saxon vs Ester [sic] Saxon;* Indian Depredations Claim No. 3112, p. 77, Esther [Wadsworth] Martin, 26 November 1913.

44. *1860 Census, Arizona Territory, New Mexico,* p. 35.

45. J. Ross Browne, *A Tour Through Arizona, 1864* (New York: Harper & Brothers, 1869), p. 154.

46. *Thomas J. Cassner, Administrator, v. The United States et al., Indian Depredations, No. 3112,* U.S. Court of Claims (Washington: Government Printing Office, [24761–14] 1914), p. 8, Affidavit of Mary B. Ake. The Akes had a vested interest in these large numbers. William F. Scott, an objective observer, testified that he had seen five to six hundred cattle in the Ake-Wadsworth herd, about a dozen sheep, and no goats. *Ibid.*, pp. 116–20.

47. *Ibid.*, p. 8, Mary B. Ake, and p. 46, Deposition of Thomas Farrell.

48. The actual number of men in the party is not known. Jeff Ake and Thomas Farrell were both over eighty, many years later, when Ake stated forty-seven and Farrell estimated nineteen plus the two Ake boys. *Ibid.*, p. 47, Deposition of Thomas Farrell; O'Neil, *They Die But Once,* p. 40.

49. Daniel Ellis Conner, *Joseph Reddeford Walker and the Arizona Adventure* (Norman: University of Oklahoma Press, 1956), pp. 36–37.

50. Dan Thrapp, *Victorio and the Mimbres Apaches* (Norman: University of Oklahoma Press, 1974), pp. 73–77; W. Hubert Curry, *Sun Rising on the West, the Saga of Henry Clay and Elizabeth Smith* (Crosbyton, Texas: Crosby County Pioneer Memorial, 1979), pp. 43–44, quoting Paul I. Wellman.

51. Curry, *Sun Rising on the West,* p. 65; Hattie M. Anderson, "With the Confederates in New Mexico during the Civil War: — Memoirs of Hank Smith," *Panhandle-Plains Historical Review,* 2 (1929): 65.

52. William F. Scott, Paper read before Society of Arizona Pioneers, 6 July 1894, typescript in William F. Scott file, AHSL.

53. New Orleans *Daily Delta,* 2 April 1861, quoting the *Mesilla Times,* 9 March 1861.

54. Scott, Paper, 6 July 1894.

55. U.S. War Department, *War of the Rebellion,* Series I, Vol. IX (Washington: Government Printing Office, 1883), p. 677, Colonel J. M. Chivington to Brigadier General E. R. S. Canby, U.S. A., Fort Craig, New Mexico, 11 June 1862.

56. *Mesilla Times,* 17 August 1861; U.S. National Archives M-318, microfilm 1694, "Compiled Service Records of Confederate Soldiers Who Served in Organizations from Territory of Arizona."

57. *Indian Depredations No. 3112,* p. 47, Deposition of Thomas Farrell.

58. Scott, Paper, 6 July 1894.

59. O'Neil, *They Die But Once,* p. 41; *Indian Depredations No. 3112,* p. 47, Deposition of Thomas Farrell; Scott, Paper, 6 July 1894.

60. *Mesilla Times,* 27 July 1861; Los Angeles *Semi-Weekly Southern News,* 6 September 1861; New Orleans *Sunday Delta,* 25 August 1861, an account based on the *Mesilla Times,* 4 August 1861.

8: Fisher Scott

1. The eyewitness accounts of Scott and Smith, both written years later, differ in many respects. Smith's sequence of events is demonstrably faulty. The author has reconstructed the actions of the Arizona Guards by comparing these accounts and considering testimony in the Ake depredation claim. William Fisher Scott, Paper read before Society of Arizona Pioneers, 6 July 1894, typescript in William F. Scott file, AHSL; *Thomas J. Cassner, Administrator, v. The United States et al., Indian Depredations, No. 3112,* U.S. Court of Claims (Washington: Government Printing Office [24761–14], 1914), p. 116, Deposition of William F. Scott; Hattie M. Anderson, "Mining and Indian Fighting in Arizona and New Mexico, 1858–1861: — Memoirs of Hank Smith," *Panhandle-Plains Historical Review,* 1 (1928): 101–02; W. Hubert Curry, *Sun Rising on the West, the Saga of Henry Clay and Elizabeth Smith* (Crosbyton, Texas: Crosby County Pioneer Memorial, 1979), p. 54; Microfilm, U.S. National Archives M–318, Film 1694, "Compiled service records of Confederate soldiers who served in organizations from the Territory of Arizona." Although Pennington is not named in the incomplete muster rolls, Smith's memoirs indicate that Jack also joined.

2. William F. Scott Portrait File, AHSL; William F. Scott Biographical File, Hayden Collection, AHSL.

3. Scott, Paper, 6 July 1894; *Mesilla Times,* 1 November 1860; Anderson, "Mining and Indian Fighting," pp. 106–07; Curry, *Sun Rising on the West,* pp. 60–61. Hank Smith has the exploration venture out of sequence in his memoirs. George Frazer had previously explored the Black River and San Francisco River area as early as 1852.

4. *Indian Depredations No. 3112,* pp. 47–48, Deposition of Thomas Farrell, p. 176, Deposition of Annie M. [Ake] Davis, pp. 61–80, Deposition of Esther [Wadsworth] Martin, pp. 39–45, Deposition of Charles [Jeff] Ake.

5. *Ibid.,* pp. 47–48, Deposition of Thomas Farrell.

6. *Ibid.,* pp. 17, 21, Deposition of Mariano Madrid.

7. James Bradas O'Neil, *They Die But Once* (New York: Knight Publications, 1935), p. 42.

8. *Indian Depredations No. 3112,* pp. 69–80, Deposition of Esther [Wadsworth] Martin.

9. *Ibid.,* p. 39, Deposition of Charles H. [Jeff] Ake; O'Neil, *They Die But Once,* p. 42.

10. *Ibid.*

11. John P. Pennington, II, to Barry Pennington, Georgetown, Texas, 14 March 1954, copy in author's files. Jack Pennington's grandsons still treasure the rifle believed to be the one he used at Cooke's Canyon. MLP to Clark Pennington, Lubbock, Texas, 14 Dec 1979, copy in author's files.

12. O'Neil, *They Die But Once,* pp. 42–44. Cherokee [Chickasaw] Brown may have been the "Sonoita Murderer" who shot up the mescal distillery in 1859 and escaped arrest.

13. *Indian Depredations Claim No. 3112,* p. 48, Deposition of Thomas Farrell.

14. *Ibid.*

15. *Ibid.,* p. 64, Deposition of Esther [Wadsworth] Martin; O'Neil, *They Die But Once,* p. 44.

16. *Ibid.,* p. 15, Deposition of Mariano Madrid.

17. *Ibid.*, p. 48, Deposition of Thomas Farrell.

18. *Ibid.*, p. 49.

19. *Ibid.*, p. 162, Deposition of Charles H. [Jeff] Ake, p. 116, Deposition of William F. Scott.

20. August 27 is shown as the enlistment date in Mastin's company for Zimmer, Sharp, and others who were undoubtedly in the Ake-Wadsworth party. Microfilm, U.S. National Archives M-318, Film 1694, "Compiled service records of Confederate soldiers who served in organizations from the Territory of Arizona."

21. *Indian Depredations No. 3112,* p. 117, Deposition of William F. Scott.

22. *Ibid.*; Scott, Paper, 6 July 1894; Anderson, "Mining and Indian Fighting," pp. 101–04; Curry, *Sun Rising on the West,* p. 55.

23. *Indian Depredations No. 3112,* pp. 116–17, Deposition of William F. Scott. Despite testimony to the contrary, Jeff Ake testified that no cattle were recovered, but his family stood to gain financially by so stating.

24. *Ibid.*, p. 48, Deposition of Thomas Farrell.

25. *Mesilla Times,* 3 September 1861, as quoted in the New Orleans *Daily Picayune,* 1 November 1861.

26. Scott, Paper, 6 July 1894; *Indian Depredations No. 3112,* p. 49, Deposition of Thomas Farrell.

27. *Indian Depredations No. 3112,* pp. 67–68, Deposition of Esther [Wadsworth] Martin.

28. *Ibid.*, p. 64. About four years after the ambush, Esther Wadsworth married a discharged Union soldier, John [Jack] Martin, and with him operated a small cattle ranch, dairy, stage station, inn, government forage agency, and post office at Aleman, on the Jornada del Muerto north of Las Cruces. See Joan Jensen and Darlis A. Miller, eds., *New Mexico Women: Intercultural Perspectives* (Albuquerque: University of New Mexico Press, 1986), pp. 145–46.

29. Scott, Paper, 6 July 1894.

30. New Orleans *Daily Picayune,* 1 November 1861, from the *Mesilla Times,* 3 October 1861.

31. *Ibid.*; Scott, Paper, 6 July 1894; Anderson, "Mining and Indian Fighting," p. 100; Curry, *Sun Rising on the West,* pp. 52–53.

32. Houston *Tri-Weekly Telegraph,* 1 November 1861; "Obituary," *Mesilla Times,* p. 2, undated fragment, Special Collections, New Mexico State University Library, Las Cruces.

33. Colonel John R. Baylor to Headquarters, San Antonio, Doña Ana, Arizona, 12 October 1861, Microfilm, U.S. National Archives M-318, Film 1694, "Compiled service records of Confederate soldiers who served in organizations from the Territory of Arizona."

34. New Orleans *Daily Delta,* 31 October 1861.

35. Microfilm, U.S. National Archives M-318, Film 1694, "Compiled service records of Confederate soldiers who served in Arizona."

36. *Indian Depredations No. 3112,* p. 71, Deposition of Esther [Wadsworth]

Martin. Military records, admittedly incomplete, do not show John Parker Pennington serving with Confederate or Federal troops.

37. *Mesilla Times,* 15 January 1862.

38. *Indian Depredations No. 3112,* pp. 117–18, Deposition of William F. Scott, pp. 157–65, Deposition of Charles H. [Jeff] Ake; O'Neil, *They Die But Once,* p. 46.

39. *Mesilla Times,* 12 December 1861.

40. Arthur A. Wright, *The Civil War in the Southwest* (Denver: Big Mountain Press, 1964), p. 53.

9: Nomads of War

1. Bernard Fontana, "The Mowry Mine, 1858–1958," *The Kiva,* 23 (February 1958): 14–15.

2. *Ibid.*

3. B. Sacks, "Sylvester Mowry, Libertine, Artilleryman, Entrepreneur," *American West,* 1 (Summer 1964): 14–24.

4. Sydney W. Mowry to E. J. Bricknall, Fort Yuma, 8 April 1856, typescript in Sylvester Mowry Biographical File, AHSL.

5. J. Ross Browne, *A Tour through Arizona—1864* (New York: Harper & Brothers, 1869), p. 203.

6. [Robert H. Forbes], Note for epitaph of Mary Ann Page, Forbes Collection, AHSL. "Patagonia" in 1861 referred to the Mowry Mine. The Arizona town of the same name did not exist until forty years later.

7. Robert H. Forbes, *The Penningtons, Pioneers of Early Arizona* ([Tucson]: Arizona Archaeological and Historical Society, 1919), p. 22.

8. S. Hunter, Captain Company A, to Col. John R. Baylor, 5 April 1862, U.S. War Department, *The War of the Rebellion: A Compilation of the Official Records of the Union and Confederate Armies,* Ser. I, Vol. IX (Washington: Government Printing Office, 1883), pp. 707–08.

9. C. L. Sonnichsen, *Tucson* (Norman: University of Oklahoma Press, 1982), pp. 61–64; Boyd Finch, "Sherod Hunter and the Confederates in Arizona," *Journal of Arizona History,* 10 (Autumn 1969): 158–63.

10. Arthur A. Wright, *The Civil War in the Southwest* (Denver: Big Mountain Press, 1964), pp. 53–100; Jay J. Wagoner, *Arizona Territory 1863–1912: A Political History* (Tucson: University of Arizona Press, 1980), pp. 3–13.

11. Wagoner, *Arizona Territory 1863–1912,* pp. 14–16; Constance Wynn Altshuler, *Latest from Arizona!* (Tucson: Arizona Pioneers' Historical Society, 1969), p. 267; Frank C. Lockwood, "Palatine Robinson," Tucson *Arizona Daily Star,* 22 December 1940.

12. *San Francisco Bulletin,* 15 March 1864, Letter from J. Ross Browne, Tubac, 5 February 1864.

13. Microfilm, U.S. National Archives M–318, Film 1694, "Compiled service records of Confederate soldiers who served in organizations from the Territory of Arizona," (see W. F. Scott, J. W. Swilling, Henry C. Smith). Union

Colonel J. M. Chivington wrote to Brigadier General Edward R. S. Canby on 11 June 1862, "The Arizona Guards, who were raised for the protection of the settlements against the Indians, and who are more than half Northern and Union men, are pressed into the Confederate service." *War of the Rebellion*, Ser. I, Vol. IX, p. 677.

14. William F. Scott, Paper read before Society of Arizona Pioneers, 6 July 1894, typescript in William F. Scott File, AHSL.

15. "Compiled Service Records of Confederate Soldiers," microfilm.

16. W. Hubert Curry, *Sun Rising on the West, the Saga of Henry Clay and Elizabeth Smith* (Crosbyton, Texas: Crosby County Pioneer Memorial, 1979), p. 104–05.

17. Sidney DeLong, *History of Arizona* (San Francisco: The Whitaker & Ray Company, 1905), p. 168–69.

18. Daniel Ellis Conner, *Joseph Reddeford Walker and the Arizona Adventure*, edited by Donald J. Berthrong and Odessa Davenport (Norman: University of Oklahoma Press, 1956), p. 34.

19. *Ibid.* See also Bil Gilbert, *Westering Man: The Life of Joseph Walker, Master of the Frontier* (New York: Atheneum Press, 1983), pp. 264–66.

20. Conner, *Joseph Reddeford Walker,* pp. 98–105.

21. "Journal of the Pioneer and Walker Mining Districts, 1863–65," p. 249 (original, Office of the Yavapai County Recorder, Prescott, Arizona).

22. Jack may have been the John Pennington to whom Walker transferred claim number 14 on the Oolkilsipava on July 6th. *Ibid.*, p. 256; Virginia Culin Roberts, "Jack Pennington in Early Arizona", *Journal of Arizona History,* 23 (Spring 1982): 330.

23. Augustus Brichta, "Reminiscences of an old Pioneer," MS B849-2, AHSL.

24. Wagoner, *Arizona Territory 1863–1912,* pp. 28–38; Thomas Edwin Farish, *History of Arizona,* 8 vols. (San Francisco: Filmer Bros., 1914–1918), vol. 3, pp. 191–216.

25. William F. Scott File, Hayden Collection, AHSL; Major Theodore Coult to Captain J. F. Bennett, 14 October 1863, as quoted in Constance Wynn Altshuler, *Chains of Command: Arizona and the Army, 1856–1875* (Tucson: Arizona Historical Society, 1981), p. 32.

26. Robert H. Forbes, Notebook, Box 3, Folder 3, AHSL.

27. Arizona Territory, County of Pima, Probate Court: *Estate of E. G. Pennington, Deceased,* filed 4 April 1892, Deposition of William F. Scott, 16 January 1893, p. 1.

28. Forbes, Notebook.

29. Forbes, "Pennington Chronology," Forbes Collection, Box 3, Folder 3, AHSL; Altshuler, *Chains of Command,* pp. 27–87, passim.

30. J. Ross Browne, *A Tour Through Arizona—1864,* p. 134.

31. Forbes, *The Penningtons,* p. 9; Amanda Jane [Pennington] Crumpton to Robert H. Forbes, Santa Cruz, California, 18 May, 1916, Interview Notes in Forbes Collection, Box 3, folder 3, AHSL.

32. *San Francisco Bulletin,* March 15, 1864, Letter from J. Ross Browne, Tubac, 5 February 1864; Browne, *A Tour Through Arizona — 1864,* p. 155.

33. Lina Fergusson Browne, ed., *J. Ross Browne, His Letters, Journals & Writings* (Albuquerque: University of New Mexico Press, 1969), pp. 290–91.

34. Forbes, *The Penningtons,* pp. 25–29.

35. Forbes Notebook; William F. Scott File, Hayden Collection, AHSL; Charles Trumbull Hayden, Deed to James Lee and William F. Scott, 13 November 1866, *Pima County Book of Deeds No. 1* , pp. 78, 79, Pima County Recorder's Office, Tucson. Two brothers named Rowlett had built the Silver Lake mill six years earlier, damming the Santa Cruz River a mile and a half south of Tucson to create a lake which provided water power. They imported improved milling stones from San Francisco. All this was quite an industrial advance for the village where for almost a hundred years plodding burros had furnished the energy that ground flour. W. S. Grant, a government contractor from Maine, bought and expanded the Rowletts' mill and also built the Tucson Mill. But when Union soldiers evacuated Fort Breckenridge in 1861 they burned the mills and wrecked everything in Tucson that might possibly aid the Confederates. Grant left town, never to return. Soldiers of Carleton's California Column partially repaired one of the mills and operated it for a short time in 1862. Gilbert J. Pedersen, "A Yankee in Arizona: The Misfortunes of William S. Grant, 1860–1861," *Journal of Arizona History,* 16 (Summer 1975): 129–37; Bernice Cosulich, *Tucson* (Tucson: Arizona Silhouettes, 1953), pp. 271–74.

36. Farish, *History of Arizona,* vol. 3, p. 193. Farish gives the name of William F. Scol (an obvious misspelling) of Tucson as one of three appraisers.

37. Constance Wynn Altshuler, *Starting With Defiance: Nineteenth Century Arizona Military Posts* (Tucson: Arizona Historical Society, 1983), pp. 27, 58; Altshuler, *Chains of Command,* pp. 36, 37.

38. The record of Scott's purchase reads, in part, "Bought on April 27, 1864 from John gaber, place known as the labor del toreon . . . on east side of S Cr Riv about 2 mi above . . . Tubac" [sic], *Pima County Deeds 1855–1872,* p. 19, original, ASLA.

39. Forbes, *The Penningtons,* p. 34; Photograph by Robert H. Forbes, "Pictures — Places — Pennington Homes," AHSL. The restored Pennington house in Tubac is, as of this writing, the Cabot Art Gallery. See Elizabeth R. Brownell, *They Lived in Tubac* (Tucson: Westernlore Press, 1986), p. 42.

40. J. Ross Browne, *Adventures in Apache Country: A Tour of Arizona — 1864,* re-edition annotated by Donald M. Powell (Tucson: University of Arizona Press, 1974), p. 144.

41. *Ibid.,* p. 147.

42. Forbes, *The Penningtons,* p. 26.

43. C. B. Genung, "Early Days in Arizona," Prescott *Mining Review,* 20 May 1911, copy in Genung Notebook, Sharlot Hall Museum, Prescott.

44. Prescott *Arizona Miner,* April 6, 1864.

45. *Ibid.* The cavalry was camped at Reventon, near Tubac, in July, 1864, according to *Will C. Barnes' Arizona Place Names,* revised and enlarged by Byrd H. Granger (Tucson: University of Arizona Press, 1979), p. 323.

46. C. B. Genung to Robert H. Forbes, Mullen's Well, 25 June 1913, Interview Notes in Forbes Collection, Box 3, folder 3, AHSL. Although there was also a John F. Pennington mining near Prescott in 1864, Genung told Forbes that the "Jack" in this story was Mrs. Page's brother.

47. Genung, "Early Days in Arizona."

48. Genung to Forbes, Interview 25 June 1913.

49. *Ibid.*

50. D. E. Conner to R. H. Forbes, Elsinore, California, October 5, 1915, letter in Forbes Collection, Box 3, Folder 3, AHSL; Conner, *Joseph Reddeford Walker,* p. 153.

51. Genung, "Early Days in Arizona."

52. Genung to Forbes, Interview, 25 June 1913.

53. Genung, "Early Days in Arizona."

54. Shirley Brueggeman to VCR, Loma, Colorado, 21 Nov 1981, author's files. Mrs. Brueggeman is a granddaughter of Abner Nichols and a later wife.

55. *Ibid.*; *Special Arizona Census 1866,* Pima County, p. 50, persons no. 1532, 1533, 1534, photostat of original at AHSL; *Estate of E. G. Pennington, Deceased,* Deposition of William F. Scott, 16 January 1893, p. 11.

56. Wagoner, *Arizona Territory 1863–1912,* pp. 34–60.

57. Forbes, *The Penningtons,* p. 26.

10: A Shattered Family

1. Constance Wynn Altshuler, *Chains of Command: Arizona and the Army, 1856–1875* (Tucson: Arizona Historical Society, 1981), pp. 40–48, map p. 42. When Mason took command, Arizona Territory had Fort Whipple, Camp Tubac (Camp Cameron), Fort Goodwin, Fort Mohave, and Fort Bowie. He added Camp Lincoln (Camp Verde), Camp Date Creek, Camp Wallen, Fort Mason, and a detachment at La Paz.

2. *Ibid.,* pp. 40–48.

3. Thomas Edwin Farish, *History of Arizona,* 8 vols. (San Francisco: Filmer Bros., 1914–1918), vol. 4, p. 267; *William F. Scott, Administrator [Estate of E. G. Pennington, Deceased], Plaintiff, vs. U.S. and Apache Indians, Defendant, Indian Depredations No. 7363,* U.S. Court of Claims, Washington, D.C., filed 5 April 1893, typescript of proceedings, pp. 26–28, Deposition of Edward N. Fish, Forbes Collection, Box 3, Folder 6, AHSL.

4. *Special Arizona Census 1866,* Pima County, p. 57, photostat of original, AHSL; Amanda Jane [Pennington] Crumpton to Robert H. Forbes, Santa Cruz, California, 18 May 1916, Interview Notes in Forbes Collection, Box 3, Folder 3, AHSL; Deed from Christopher C. Dodson to William S. Oury, 27 January 1866, *Pima County, A.T.: Book of Deeds No. 1,* pp. 18–19, Pima County Recorder's Office, Tucson.

5. Forbes Notebook, Forbes Collection, Box 3, Folder 3, AHSL, entry of 27

July 1913; U.S. Department of Agriculture, Forest Service; Map, *Tumacacori Forest Reserve, Arizona,* 6 November 1906, see Twp 20S R12E, "Pennington."

6. J. Ross Browne, *A Tour Through Arizona—1864 (New York: Harper & Brothers, 1869), p. 260; Territory of New Mexico Deed Book 1851–1861,* copied 1882, pp. 20–24, ASLA; Tubac *Weekly Arizonian,* 9 June 1859.

7. Tubac *Weekly Arizonian,* 21 July 1859.

8. *T. J. Cassner, Administrator, vs The United States et al., Indian Depredations, No. 3112,* United States Court of Claims (Washington: Government Printing Office, 1915), p. 46, Deposition of Thomas Farrell.

9. Browne, *A Tour Through Arizona—1864,* pp. 260–61.

10. Sabino Otero to Robert H. Forbes, Tubac, 13 July 1913, Interview Notes in Forbes Notebook, Forbes Collection, Box 3, Folder 3, AHSL.

11. Robert H. Forbes, *The Penningtons, Pioneers of Early Arizona* ([Tucson], Arizona Archaeological and Historical Society, 1919), p. 31.

12. *Ibid.,* pp. 30–32; Field trip, May, 1979, by the author.

13. Ellen Pennington's family school is mentioned in Douglas D. Martin, *The Lamp in the Desert: the Story of the University of Arizona* (Tucson: University of Arizona Press, 1960), p. 17.

14. Amanda Jane [Pennington] Crumpton Interview, 18 May 1916.

15. *Special Arizona Census 1866,* Third Judicial District, Wickenburg [n.p.]. Number 168 (total of heads of families) is at the top of the page on which Jack Pennington is listed.

16. *Special Arizona Census 1866,* Pima County, Punta del Agua [n.p.], persons numbered 1853–1857.

17. *Scott vs U.S. and Apache Indians, Indian Depredations No. 7363,* typescript p. 8, Deposition of William F. Scott.

18. Altshuler, *Chains of Command,* p. 61; Altshuler, *Starting With Defiance: Nineteenth Century Arizona Military Posts* (Tucson: Arizona Historical Society, 1983), p. 42.

19. Forbes, *The Penningtons,* p. 33.

20. Samuel Robinson Diary, typescript, p. 19, AHSL; see also Samuel Robinson, "Arizona in 1861: A Contemporary Account," intro. and anno. by Constance Wynn Altshuler, *Journal of Arizona History,* 25 (Spring 1984): 54.

21. Amanda Jane [Pennington] Crumpton Interview, 18 May 1916.

22. Santa Cruz County Recorder, Santa Cruz, California, *SC 15–19 Deaths,* p. 379, Amandy [sic] Jane Crumpton, 10 Nov 1919.

23. *Special Arizona Census 1866,* Pima County, Sópori, [n.p.]. Person no. 1137, "W. A. Compton" is likely to have been W. A. Crumpton (one of that census-taker's many errors); *Census of Arizona Territory 1864,* Third Judicial District, photostat of original returns, AHSL, p. 15, person no. 426: Wm. A. Crumpton, blacksmith, age 29, born Alabama, resident of Arizona two years, value of personal property $42.

24. John Parker Pennington, II, Family Bible, Marshall L. Pennington to VCR, Lubbock, Texas, 28 February 1981.

25. *Census of Arizona Territory 1864,* Third Judicial District, p. 34, person no.

935: "Underwin Barrette [sic]," miner, age 31, born Arkansas, resident of Arizona three years, value of real estate $300., personal property $50.

26. Underwood C. Barnett Biographical File, Hayden Collection, AHSL; Daniel E. Conner, *Joseph Reddeford Walker and the Arizona Adventure,* ed. by Donald J. Berthrong and Odessa Davenport (Norman: University of Oklahoma Press, 1956), p. 333.

27. William A. Bell, *New Tracks in North America,* 2 vols. (London: Chapman & Hall, 1869), vol. 2, pp. 93–102.

28. *Ibid.,* pp. 100–02. Bell's version of Larcena's capture by Apaches is highly erroneous and unreliable.

29. *Ibid.*

30. John Parker Pennington, II, to Marshall Lee Pennington, 30 December 1959, copy in author's files.

31. John T. Smith as quoted in Elizabeth R. Brownell, *They Lived in Tubac* (Tucson: Westernlore Press, 1986), pp. 51, 53.

32. John Parker Pennington, II, to M. L. Pennington, 30 December 1859; Virginia Culin Roberts, "Jack Pennington in Early Arizona," *Arizona and the West,* 23 (Winter 1981): 330.

33. Washington, D.C., U.S. National Archives: Microfilm, *Ninth Decennial Census of the United States, 1870,* Bell County, Texas, p. 41; Nichols Family Records, Shirley Nichols Brueggeman to VCR, Loma, Colorado, 21 November 1981, letter in author's files.

34. Amanda Jane [Pennington] Crumpton Interview, 18 May 1916.

35. A. M. Gustafson, ed., *John Spring's Arizona* (Tucson: University of Arizona Press, 1966), pp. 164–65.

36. Brownell, *They Lived in Tubac* p. 52.

37. James A. Serven, "The Military Posts on Sonoita Creek," *Brand Book 2* (Tucson: The Tucson Corral of the Westerners, Inc., 1971), p. 41.

38. Amanda Jane [Pennington] Crumpton Interview, 18 May 1916; *Scott vs U.S. and Apache Indians, Indian Depredations No. 7363,* typescript pp. 3–4, Deposition of William F. Scott; Forbes, *The Penningtons,* p. 29.

39. *Scott vs U.S. and Apache Indians, Indian Depredations No. 7363,* typescript pp. 3–4, Deposition of William F. Scott.

40. Sabino Otero Interview, 13 July 1913.

41. "Genealogy," Mercedes Shibell Gould Boxed Material, AHSL; Charles A. Shibell Biographical File, AHSL.

42. Forbes, *The Penningtons,* p. 35.

43. *Scott vs U.S. and Apache Indians, Indian Depredations No. 7363,* typescript p. 32, Deposition of Thomas Hughes; Mary Gardner Kane to Robert H. Forbes, Interview, 8 December 1914, Forbes Collection, Box 3, Folder 3, AHSL.

44. Gustafson, *John Spring's Arizona,* p. 157.

45. *Scott vs U.S. and Apache Indians, Indian Depredations No. 7363,* typescript pp. 1–13, Deposition of William F. Scott.

46. Forbes, *The Penningtons,* p. 10.

47. Elias Pennington was cultivating the second farm below William Morgan's place on Sonoita Creek. Thomas Hughes stated that Elias leased these fields. *Scott vs U.S. and Apache Indians, Indian Depredations No. 7363,* Depositions of William Morgan, typescript p. 20, Thomas Hughes, p. 33. According to Jane Pennington, the site had belonged to "Uncle Billy" Finley in earlier days. Amanda Jane [Pennington] Crumpton Interview, 18 May 1916.

48. Mary Gardner Kane Interview, 8 December 1914.

49. *Scott vs U.S. and Apache Indians, Indian Depredations Claim No. 7363,* typescript p. 33, Deposition of Thomas Hughes; Serven, "Military Posts on Sonoita Creek," p. 42.

50. Charles A. Shibell to the Society of Arizona Pioneers, paper read 8 November 1887, Records of the Society of Arizona Pioneers, AHSL.

51. Underwood C. Barnett Biographical File, AHSL; Gustafson, *John Spring's Arizona,* p. 146.

52. *Scott vs U.S. and Apache Indians, Indian Depredations Claim No. 7363,* typescript pp. 29–34, Deposition of Thomas Hughes.

53. *Ibid.,* typescript pp. 14–18, Deposition of José L. Andrade.

54. Tucson *Weekly Arizonian,* 19 June 1869; Forbes, *The Penningtons,* p. 35.

55. *Scott vs U.S. and Apache Indians, Indian Depredations Claim No. 7363,* typescript pp. 14–18, Depositions of José L. Andrade, and pp. 19–22, William Morgan; Forbes, *The Penningtons,* p. 35; Tucson *Weekly Arizonian,* 19 June 1869, reported the number of Apache attackers as forty.

56. *Scott vs U.S. and Apache Indians, Indian Depredations Claim No. 7363,* typescript pp. 14–18, Depositions of José L. Andrade, and pp. 19–22, William Morgan; Forbes, *The Penningtons,* p. 35.

57. *Scott vs U.S. and Apache Indians, Indian Depredations Claim No. 7363,* typescript p. 6, Deposition of William F. Scott, p. 16, José L. Andrade, p. 21, William Morgan, and p. 31, Thomas Hughes.

58. Charles D. Poston, "The Pennington Family," *Tucson Citizen,* 17 January 1896.

59. Forbes, *The Penningtons,* p. 37.

60. *Federal Census 1870, Arizona Territory,* Pima County, Tucson, p. 45, photostat of original returns, AHSL. Margaret Pennington is listed as head of the household in this census.

61. L. E. Barnett to "Dear Sisters," Tubac, A. T., 1 October 1869, Forbes Collection, Box 3, Folder 3, AHSL.

62. *Ibid.*

63. Altshuler, *Chains of Command,* p. 49.

64. Underwood C. Barnett Biographical File, AHSL.

65. Forbes, *The Penningtons,* p. 37.

66. "Record Kept by William Whelan, Point of Mountain Station, 1869," 27 December 1869, original handwritten log, AHSL.

67. *Ibid.,* 28 December 1869.

68. Forbes, *The Penningtons,* p. 37.

69. Amanda Jane [Pennington] Crumpton Interview, 18 May 1916.

70. The *Weekly Arizonian,* 12 March 1870.

71. *Ibid.*

72. *Weekly Arizonian,* 26 March 1870.

73. *Federal Census 1870, Arizona Territory,* Pima County, Tucson, photostat of original returns, AHSL.

74. *Weekly Arizonan,* 6 August 1870.

75. William A. Crumpton and John Parker "Jack" Pennington jointly owned the Georgetown farm. Eunice B. Rader to Marshall L. Pennington, Georgetown, Texas, 3 December 1979, copy in author's files. Miss Rader is a granddaughter of John Parker Pennington.

76. Edward H. Hall's *Guide to the Great West* (New York: D. Appleton & Co., 1866), p. 87.

77. Forbes, *The Penningtons,* caption opposite p. 41.

11: New Love, New Life

1. *Weekly Arizonan,* Tucson, 6 August 1870.

2. *Ibid.*; The Penningtons were still in Tucson on June 13, 1870, when Assistant Marshal Charles A. Shibell made his 1870 Census enumeration. *Ninth Decennial Census of the United States, 1870, Arizona Territory,* Tucson, p. 45, photocopy of original returns, AHSL.

3. The Scott address was 300–302 South Main Street. The number was later changed to 256. *Arizona Daily Star,* 1 January 1915, Obituary of William Fisher Scott; G. W. Barter, comp. & pub., *Directory of the City of Tucson* (San Francisco: H. S. Crocker & Co., Printers, 1881), p. 106; Pima County Abstract Co., *City of Tucson General & Business Directory for 1897–1898* ([Tucson]: The Citizen Printing & Publishing Co. [1897]), p. 100.

4. *Weekly Arizonan,* 6 August 1870.

5. *Weekly Arizonan,* 29 October 1870.

6. Fisher Scott became a citizen in March 1867: William F. Scott File, Hayden Collection, AHSL; see also *1870 Census Arizona,* Tucson, photocopy of original, p. 68. James Lee became a citizen in April 1870: James Lee File, Hayden Collection, AHSL.

7. James Lee File, Hayden Collection, AHSL.

8. Bernice Cosulich, "Mrs. Moss Sees 50-year Change," typescript [n.d.], James Lee File, Hayden Collection, AHSL.

9. James E. Officer and Henry F. Dobyns, "Teodoro Ramírez: Early Citizen of Tucson," *Journal of Arizona History,* 25 (Autumn 1984): 221–44.

10. *1870 Census Arizona,* Tucson, photocopy of original, p. 67.

11. Cosulich, "Mrs. Moss Sees 50-Year Change."

12. *1870 Census Arizona,* Tucson, photocopy of original, pp. 67–68.

13. Cosulich, "Mrs. Moss Sees 50-Year Change."

14. *1870 Census Arizona,* Tucson, photocopy of original, p. 68.

15. *Arizona Weekly Star,* Tucson, 19 December 1878.

16. *Ninth Decennial Census of the United States, 1870, Arizona* (Washington: U.S. Government Printing Office, 1965), pp. 162–98, passim; Don Bufkin, "From Mud Village to Modern Metropolis: The Urbanization of Tucson," *Journal of Arizona History,* 22 (Spring 1981): 90.

17. C. C. Smith, anno., "Some Unpublished History of the Southwest" [Diary of Mrs. Granville Oury], *Arizona Historical Review,* 6 (January 1935): 61.

18. M. D. Pennington to "Brother and Sister," Georgetown, Texas, 21 February 1872, original letter in Forbes Collection, Box 3, AHSL.

19. Bernice Cosulich, *Tucson* (Tucson: Arizona Silhouettes, 1953), p. 96.

20. A. M. Gustafson, *John Spring's Arizona* (Tucson: University of Arizona Press, 1966), p. 189.

21. Josephine Clifford [McCrackin], *Overland Tales* (Philadelphia: J. Fagan & Son, Stereotypers, 1877), pp. 266–69.

22. *Ibid.*

23. John H. Marion, *Notes of travel through the Territory of Arizona, being an account of the trip made by General George Stoneman and others in Autumn of 1870* (Prescott: Office of the Arizona Miner, 1870), pp. 11–12.

24. C. L. Sonnichsen, *Tucson* (Norman: University of Oklahoma Press, 1982), pp. 50–51.

25. *Weekly Arizonan,* 7 February 1869, Advertisement.

26. Cosulich, *Tucson,* p. 228; see also Sonnichsen, *Tucson,* pp. 72–74.

27. *Arizona Citizen,* 24 December 1870.

28. *Memorial and Affidavits Showing Outrages Perpetrated by the Apache Indians in the Territory of Arizona During the Years 1869 and 1870* (San Francisco: Francis & Valentine, 1871), published by authority of the Legislature of the Territory of Arizona, p. 5, as quoted in Jay J. Wagoner, *Arizona Territory 1863–1912: A Political History* (Tucson: University of Arizona Press, 1980), pp. 103–04.

29. Obituary, *Weekly Arizona Miner,* 8 October 1870.

30. *Weekly Arizonian,* 11 March 1871.

31. Biographical sketch, William F. Scott File, Hayden Collection, AHSL.

32. *Memorial and Affidavits Showing Outrages,* p. 5, as quoted in Wagoner, *Arizona Territory 1863–1912,* pp. 102–105.

33. Camp Grant, near the site of old Fort Breckenridge, is not to be confused with the Fort Grant built later in a different location.

34. Constance Wynn Altshuler, *Chains of Command: Arizona and the Army, 1856–1875* (Tucson: The Arizona Historical Society, 1981), pp. 190–91.

35. C. C. Smith, *William Sanders Oury: History-Maker of the Southwest* (Tucson: University of Arizona Press, 1967), p. 189.

36. Altshuler, *Chains of Command,* p. 193.

37. Smith, *William Sanders Oury,* p. 189.

38. Altshuler, *Chains of Command,* p. 195.

39. James R. Hastings, "The Tragedy at Camp Grant in 1871," *Arizona and the West,* 1 (Summer 1959): 152.

40. *Ibid.*, pp. 146–60; Smith, *William Sanders Oury,* pp. 192–95; Altshuler, *Chains of Command,* pp. 194–95; *Arizona Citizen,* 7 September 1872.

41. *Arizona Citizen,* 28 October 1871.

42. Smith, *William Sanders Oury,* pp. 200–01.

43. Mrs. Samuel Hughes, "Reminiscences," *Arizona Historical Review,* 6 (April 1935): 71–73.

44. Gravestone of William Pennington Scott, Evergreen Cemetery, Tucson.

45. M. D. Pennington to "Brother and Sister" [Fisher and Larcena Scott], Georgetown, Texas, 21 February 1872, original in Forbes Collection, Box 3, Folder 3, AHSL.

46. *Ibid.*

47. Gravestone, Pennington Cemetery, Georgetown, Texas; Marshall L. Pennington, "Elias Green Pennington and Immediate Family," unpublished table of statistics, 28 February 1981, copy in author's files.

48. John G. Capron to S. R. De Long [San Diego, n.d.], John G. Capron File, Hayden Collection, AHSL.

49. *Arizona Citizen,* 2 March 1872.

50. Wagoner, *Arizona Territory 1863–1912,* p. 107.

51. Gustafson, *John Spring's Arizona,* pp. 238–39.

52. *Arizona Citizen,* 6 July 1872.

12: Mary Page

1. Mamie Bernard Aguirre, "Spanish Trader's Bride," *Westport Historical Quarterly,* 4 (December 1968): 5–23. Mary B. ("Mamie") Aguirre, daughter of Westport, Missouri, merchant, Joab Bernard, and widow of trader Epifanio Aguirre, began teaching in Tucson in April, 1876. In 1896 she became professor of Spanish at the University of Arizona. In the fall of 1986 she was selected for the Arizona Women's Hall of Fame. So closely do details of Mrs. Aguirre's story fit Mary Ann Page and Doctor John C. Handy that their identification with it is inescapable, even though the teacher did not name the persons involved.

2. John C. Handy was born in Newark, New Jersey, 20 October 1844. [W. V. Whitmore], "John Charles Handy, M. D. (Tucson, 1871–1891), typescript in Handy Collection, MS H236j, AHSL.

3. Aguirre, "Spanish Trader's Bride," pp. 22–23.

4. Dr. Handy once angrily attacked another Tucson physician, verbally and physically, for what Handy considered professional incompetence. J. C. Martin, "Turbulent as the Times," *Arizona Daily Star,* 12 November 1972. While Handy was contract surgeon at Camp Thomas, he shot the post trader, who had insulted him. When the man died, Handy turned himself in to authorities, who released him without charges. Tucson *Weekly Arizonan,* 26 November 1870, 3 December 1870.

5. Richard E. Sloan, *Memories of an Arizona Judge* (Stanford University: Stanford University Press, 1932), pp. 124–25.

6. Tucson *Arizona Citizen,* 12 August 1871.

7. Frances Quebbeman, *Medicine in Territorial Arizona* (Phoenix: Arizona Historical Foundation, 1966), p. 346.

8. *Weekly Arizonan,* Tucson, 3 December 1870.

9. [Whitmore], "John Charles Handy, M.D." For more about Dr. Handy's many achievements, see Quebbeman, *Medicine in Territorial Arizona,* passim; Virginia Culin Roberts, "Mary Page and the Lawyer Who Dared to Defend Her," *Journal of Arizona History,* 30 (Winter 1989): 365–90; Sister Alberta Cammack, "A Faithful Account of the Life and Death of Doctor John Charles Handy," *The Smoke Signal,* no. 52 (Tucson Corral of the Westerners, 1989), pp. 36–40; Sister Aloysia Ames, CSJ, *The St. Mary's I Knew* (Tucson: St. Mary's Hospital, 1970), p. 17; Betty Leavengood, "Dr. Handy and Mr. Hyde," *Old West* (Winter 1987).

10. Tucson *Arizona Weekly Star,* 25 July 1878.

11. *Ibid.*

12. Handy family records, including Dr. John C. Handy's account ledgers, are in the possession of descendants Marjorie Handy Hart and Margo Hart Anderson, Piedmont, California; Margo H. Anderson to VCR, Piedmont, 20 February 1988. The five children of John C. and Mary P. Handy were: Charles, born 1879, Mabel, 1880, William, 1881, John Charles, Jr., 1882, Spencer, 1889.

13. G. W. Barter, comp. and pub., *Directory of the City of Tucson, 1881* (San Francisco: H. S. Crocker & Co., Printers, 1881), p. 21; Sonnichsen, *Tucson,* pp. 102–05.

14. C. L. Sonnichsen, *Pioneer Heritage: The First Century of the Arizona Historical Society* (Tucson: Arizona Historical Society, 1984), p. 1, quoting Oury.

15. Patrick Hamilton, *The Resources of Arizona* (San Francisco: A. L. Bancroft & Company, Printers, 1884), p. 147.

16. Sonnichsen, *Tucson,* pp. 107–12. The Handy home was on Stone Avenue near McCormick Street. *Tucson and Tombstone City Directory, 1883–1884,* (Tucson: Cobler & Co., 1883), p. 56.

17. Georgie (Georgia) Hazel Scott was born 6 October 1872. The *Arizona Citizen,* 11 October 1873.

18. Leopoldo Carrillo Biographical File, AHSL; "Pictures, Places, Tucson: Carrillo's Gardens," AHSL photograph files.

19. J. Ross Browne, *A Tour Through Arizona — 1864* (New York: Harper & Brothers, 1869), p. 22.

20. *Tucson & Tombstone General & Business Directory for 1883, 1884,* p. 25; *Arizona Daily Star,* 1 April 1913, Obituary of Larcena Scott.

21. Scott and Lee sold the mill to Edward Nye Fish. Cosulich, *Tucson* (Tucson: Arizona Silhouettes, 1953), p. 276; William F. Scott Biographical File, Hayden Collection, AHSL; Pima County, Arizona, *Marriages,* Book 1, Office of the Clerk of Court, Tucson; Scott was Pima County Road Overseer in 1888: *Pima County, Arizona, Territorial Records,* vol. 37 (1864–1923), Bond of W. F. Scott, July 13, 1888 (University of Arizona Library, Special Collections).

22. James Lee File, Charles A. Shibell File, John W. Swilling File, all in Hayden Collection, AHSL.

23. Sonnichsen, *Pioneer Heritage,* p. 7, quoting Poston.

24. *Ibid.*, pp. 7–11; William F. Scott Biographical File.

25. John C. Handy Obituary, San Francisco *Chronicle,* 3 October, 1891.

26. Douglas D. Martin, *The Lamp in the Desert: The Story of the University of Arizona* (Tucson: University of Arizona Press, 1960), 32.

27. Cosulich, *Tucson,* p. 138.

28. *Ibid.*

29. *Civil Actions,* #1720, Docket Vol. 4, p. 226, Mary Handy, Plaintiff, vs J. C. Handy, Defendant, Divorce (Pima County Archives, Tucson, Arizona.) The Court granted Mary Handy permission to withdraw all files from the record on 27 May 1889.

30. Meg Cox, "The Drug Trade," *Wall Street Journal,* 3 December 1984.

31. Pima County, Arizona Territory, First Judicial District Court: *Civil Action #2040,* Mary Handy, Plaintiff, vs Rosa Anna Handy for herself and as Trustee, Defendant, Complaint filed 14 January 1892, microfilm, Office of the Pima County Clerk of Court.

32. *Ibid.*

33. *Ibid.*

34. Pima County, Arizona Territory, First Judicial District Court: *Civil Actions,* Docket vol. 4, p. 377, 427, #1867, J. C. Handy, Plaintiff, vs Mary Handy, Defendant, Pima County Archives, Tucson.

35. Eleanor Sloan, Secretary of the Arizona Pioneers' Historical Society, undated addendum to [Whitmore], "John Charles Handy, M. D.," p. 5.

36. Tombstone *Prospector,* 25 September 1891.

37. The illegitimate son left relatives in Tucson, and for that reason Handy descendants decline to name him. Margo Anderson (great-granddaughter of John C. and Mary Page Handy) to VCR, Piedmont, California, 7 May 1980 (letter in author's files).

38. *Arizona Daily Star,* 4 October 1891, testimony of Brewster Cameron, and 8 October 1891, testimony of Francis J. Heney. The Heney brothers were born in New York, brought up and educated in San Francisco, and came to Tucson some years before the shooting. Cosulich, *Tucson,* p. 138–39, quoting Ben Heney.

39. Peace Bond, John C. Handy, Plaintiff, 27 August 1890, Microfilm, Territorial Records, 1889, Criminal Cases No. 256 to A-446, Box C/3R, Office of the Clerk of Superior Court, Pima County, Tucson, Arizona.

40. *Ibid.*, Mary Handy, Cross-complaint, 28 August 1890.

41. *Arizona Daily Star,* 4 October 1891.

42. *Ibid.*

43. *Ibid.*

44. *Ibid.*

45. Walton Bean, *Boss Ruef's San Francisco: The Story of the Union Labor Party,*

Big Business, and the Graft Prosecution (Berkeley: The University of California, 1952), pp. 69–70.

46. Pima County, Arizona Territory: *Civil Actions,* #1867, Docket, vol. 4, p. 377; Receipt for one month's alimony, 3 June 1891, Handy Collection, File H2368-3, AHSL.

47. Pima County, Territory of Arizona, Justice's Court, Precinct No. 1: *#6993, Rosa Anna Handy, Plaintiff, v. Mary Handy, Defendant,* 1 July 1891, dismissed 6 July 1891, tried in First Judicial District Court as *Civil Actions #1980, Rosa Anna Handy, Plaintiff, vs Mary Handy, Defendant,* microfilm, Office of the Clerk of Superior Court of Pima County, Tucson, Arizona; *Civil Actions Docket,* vol. 5, p. 5, #1980, Rosa Anna Handy, Plaintiff, vs Mary Handy, Defendant, Pima County Archives, Tucson.

48. Cosulich, *Tucson,* pp. 138–39, quoting Ben Heney.

49. *Ibid.,* p. 140; *Arizona Daily Star,* 8 October 1981; *Arizona Weekly Citizen,* 3 October 1891.

50. *Arizona Daily Star,* 8 October 1891.

51. *Arizona Daily Citizen,* 24 September 1891.

52. *Ibid.*

53. *J. C. Handy, Deceased, No. 542,* "Will", filed 25 September 1891, Probate Court of Pima County, Territory of Arizona.

54. Unsigned statement attributed to Doctor John Charles Handy, 24 September 1891, handwritten, presumably by one of three witnesses named (Mrs. M. J. Smith, George Holbrook, H. W. Maxwell), on document photo negatives B92109, B92110, and B92111, Henry and Albert Buehman Memorial Collection, AHS.

55. [Whitmore], "John Charles Handy, M. D.," 3, 4; John W. Kennedy, "The First University Chancellor," *Arizona Medicine,* 23 (April 1966): 277; Cosulich, *Tucson,* p. 141.

56. Cosulich, *Tucson,* p. 142, quoting Harry A. Drachman; *J. C. Handy, Deceased, Probate No. 542,* Final Account of Cornelia H. Crosby, Executrix, filed 11 February 1901.

57. *J. C. Handy, Deceased.*

58. *Arizona Daily Star,* 4-8 October 1891; *Arizona Weekly Citizen,* 10 October 1891.

59. Pima County, Territory of Arizona, First Judicial District: *Civil Suit #2040,* Mary Handy, Plaintiff, vs Rosa Anna Handy, Defendant, microfilm, Office of the Clerk of Superior Court of Pima County, Tucson, Arizona.

60. W. V. Whitmore, M. D., "Early Medical Conditions in Arizona," *Southwestern Medicine,* 11 (April 1927): 160. Dr. Goodfellow had moved to Tucson to take Handy's position as Southern Pacific surgeon.

61. Margo H. Anderson to VCR, Interview 26 February 1989.

62. Aguirre, "Spanish Trader's Bride," pp. 22–23.

63. *Arizona Daily Citizen,* 28 January 1893.

64. *Arizona Weekly Citizen,* 4 February 1893.

65. Bean, *Boss Ruef's San Francisco,* p. 70.

66. *Ibid.*, p. 70–71; Franklin Hichborn, *"The System" as Uncovered by the San Francisco Graft Prosecution* (San Francisco: James H. Barry Company, 1915), passim; Lately Thomas, *A Debonair Scoundrel: An Episode in the Moral History of San Francisco* (New York: Holt, Rinehart and Winston, 1962), passim.

67. Bean, *Boss Ruef's San Francisco,* pp. 72–75.

68. *Ibid.*, p. 153.

69. Unless otherwise indicated, foregoing and following information about John C. Handy, Jr., and his wife comes from their surviving daughter, Marjorie Handy Hart and her daughter Margo Hart Anderson of Piedmont, California, in various interviews with and letters to the author. Interviews: Margo H. Anderson to VCR, Tucson, 22 February 1979 and 1 August 1988. Letters in author's files: Margo H. Anderson to VCR, Piedmont, 7 May 1980, 20 February 1988, 30 August 1988.

70. After Cornelia Handy Holbrook's first husband died she married a man named Crosby. Margo Anderson to VCR, Interview, 1 Aug 1988.

71. *Ibid.* After W. F. Scott's death, William P. Scott inherited the half-interest in the Naguila Mine. Superior Court, Pima County, Arizona, No. 3412, *Estate of William P. Scott, Deceased,* filed 16 March 1924.

72. None of John Handy, Jr.'s, brothers or his sister had offspring, nor did his older daughter, Florence. Therefore, as of this writing, the living descendants of Mary Ann Page and Dr. John Charles Handy consist of Marjorie Handy Hart, her two daughters, Margo Anderson and Marcia Pollack, and three girls and a boy in the next generation. Margo Anderson to VCR, 20 February 1988.

73. Hichborn, *"The System,"* passim; Thomas, *A Debonair Scoundrel,* passim.

74. Hichborn, *"The System,"* pp. 76, 263 (fn 282), and 20 (fn 13, quoting the San Francisco *Chronicle,* 7 November 1905); Bean, *Boss Ruef's San Francisco,* p. 68.

75. San Francisco *Daily News,* Fourth Year [1906], undated fragment, photocopy in Francis J. Heney File, AHSL.

76. Hichborn, *"The System,"* pp. 252, 263 (fn 282); See also Lincoln Steffens, *The Autobiography of Lincoln Steffens* (New York: Harcourt, Brace & World, 1931), pp. 567–70; Los Angeles Evening *Herald-Express,* 1 November 1937.

77. According to Handy family tradition, when John C. Handy, Jr., entered Francis Heney's San Francisco law office, Heney was clutching a pistol concealed in a half-opened desk drawer. Margo H. Anderson Interview, 26 February 1989.

78. Los Angeles Evening *Herald-Express,* 1 November 1937; Margo Anderson to VCR, Interviews, 22 February 1979 and 1 August 1988.

79. The Los Angeles Evening *Herald-Express,* 1 November 1937, stated that John Handy, Jr., was Heney's bodyguard, but Handy descendants cannot confirm that, nor do Heney's meticulous records of persons he employed during the prosecutions. See Hichborn, *"The System,"* Appendix.

80. Hichborn, *"The System,"* pp. 370–87; Thomas, *A Debonair Scoundrel,* pp. 399–401.

81. Bean, *Boss Ruef's San Francisco,* pp 305–06; Thomas, *A Debonair Scoundrel,* pp. 399–401. So close was the relationship between the Handys and Heneys that when Jack's older daughter, Florence, married in 1934, the second Mrs. Heney went with the newlyweds on their honeymoon in Carmel. Margo H. Anderson, Interview, 22 February 1979, and Letter, 7 May 1980.

82. Los Angeles Evening *Herald Express,* 1 November 1937.

83. *Ibid.* John C. Handy, Jr., died of a heart attack on 4 April 1959 in Empalme, Mexico. He was en route from Guadalajara to Nogales to join family members at the Circle Z Ranch in Sonoita Valley, Arizona. Margo H. Anderson Interview, 26 February 1989.

13: "Toward the Western Shore"

1. *Tucson Post,* 3 August 1907.

2. Charles C. Colley, *The Century of Robert H. Forbes* (Tucson: Arizona Historical Society, 1977), pp. 4–6.

3. *Ibid.*

4. Robert H. Forbes Collection, Box 3, AHSL; Robert H. Forbes, *The Penningtons, Pioneers of Early Arizona* ([Tucson]: Arizona Archaeological and Historical Society, 1919).

5. Don Bufkin, "From Mud Village to Modern Metropolis: The Urbanization of Tucson," *The Journal of Arizona History,* 22 (Spring 1981): 73, 91.

6. Bradford Luckingham, "Urban Development in Arizona: The Rise of Phoenix," *The Journal of Arizona History,* 22 (Summer 1981): 205.

7. C. L. Sonnichsen, *Pioneer Heritage* (Tucson: The Arizona Historical Society, 1984), p. 58. Teacher Mary Bernard Aguirre was elected vice-president of the Auxiliary.

8. L. A. Scott to Mr. John P. Pennington, Tucson, A. T., 27 March 1901, original letter in collection of Eunice B. Rader, Georgetown, Texas, copy in author's files.

9. Marshall L. Pennington to VCR, Lubbock, 28 November 1979, letter in author's files; Virginia Culin Roberts, "Jack Pennington in Early Arizona," *Arizona and the West,* 23 (Winter 1981): 333.

10. *Williamson Sun,* Georgetown, Texas, 1 December 1904; Virginia Culin Roberts, "Jack Pennington in Early Arizona," p. 333. Jack married Emily Jane McAllister in 1877. She died three years later, leaving an infant daughter, Mittie. He married Isabelle Purcell in 1882, and with her had a daughter, Flora Belle, and a son, John Parker Pennington, II. *Williamson County [Texas] Marriage Records, vols. 3–5 (1868–1885),* vol. 4, p. 245, #489 (Salt Lake City: LDS Genealogical Library, microfilm 1,007,900), John P. Pennington to Emily Jane McAllister, 6 March 1877; Marshall L. Pennington to VCR, 28 November 1979.

11. *Tucson Post,* 3 August 1907.

12. *Ibid.*

13. *Thomas J. Cassner, Administrator, vs The United States et al., Indian Dep-*

redations, No. 3112, U.S. Court of Claims, p. 120, Deposition of William F. Scott, October, 1913 (Washington: Government Printing Office, [24761-14] 1914).

14. The questions and answers that follow in the text are quoted from *Alphonse Lazard vs United States and Apache Indians, Indian Depredations Claim No. 8773,* Testimony of Larcena A. [sic] Scott, typescript in Forbes Collection, Box 3, AHSL.

15. John A. Spring, "The Ordeal of Mrs. Page," *Wide World Magazine* (February 1912): 362–67. Despite numerous errors of fact, Spring must have furnished the statement of total veracity required by the magazine editors.

16. *Arizona Daily Star,* 1 April 1913.

17. "Obituary of Mrs. Scott," read by Mrs. S. R. De Long at the Arizona Pioneer's Historical Society meeting 4 May 1913, Clipping [n.p., n.d.], Records of the Arizona Historical Society, AHSL.

18. *Arizona Daily Star,* 1 April 1913.

19. Obituaries, *Arizona Daily Star,* 1 January 1915 and *Tucson Citizen,* 1 January 1915.

Epilogue

1. O. C. Parker Undertaking Co. to R. H. Forbes, Receipt for Removing Remains, 27 May 1915, together with an unsigned account [attributed to Forbes] dated April 1955, about finding and moving Mary Ann's remains. Forbes Collection, Box 3, AHSL.

2. Amanda Jane Pennington married William Wallace Alexander Crumpton, 27 October 1874. *Williamson County Marriage Records, v. 3–5, (1868–1885),* Microfilm #1,007,900, LDS Genealogical Library, Salt Lake City, vol. 4, p. 117, #227; Amanda Jane [Pennington] Crumpton to Robert H. Forbes, Santa Cruz, California, 18 May 1916, Interview Notes in Forbes Collection, Box 3, Folder 3, AHSL.

3. Marvin Cook (Crumpton's grandson-in-law) to VCR, Eugene, Oregon, 10 July 1979, letter in author's files.

4. Plumas County, California, *Register of Deaths,* vol. 1, p. C-1, William A. Crumpton; Santa Cruz County, California, *Deaths, 1915–19,* p. 379, Amanda Jane Crumpton.

5. Eunice B. Rader to Marshall L. Pennington, Georgetown, 2 September 1979 (copy in author's files).

6. Abner Nichols took his three older children with him to Colorado about 1874, leaving his twins temporarily in Texas. When he returned to get them, one of the twins had died, and the family caring for the other had moved away. Shirley Nichols Brueggeman to VCR, Loma, Colorado, 21 November 1981.

7. Anita I. Sharp, Medical Records Librarian, Austin State Hospital, to Mrs. Ruth Rader Lesesne, 4 December 1979 (copy in author's files).

8. Marshall Lee Pennington to Mrs. J. R. Lesesne, Lubbock, Texas, 26 No-

vember 1979, copy of letter in author's files. The Austin State Hospital has withheld information about Caroline Nichols's death.

9. John Parker Pennington, II, to Marshall L. Pennington, Georgetown, Texas, Interview, 30 December 1959, photocopy of interview notes in author's files; also Eunice B. Rader to Marshall L. Pennington, Georgetown, Texas, 2 September 1979.

10. Mary Frances Pennington married William M. Randolph, 18 June 1877. *Williamson County Marriage Records,* vol. 4, p. 257, #513, Williamson County Courthouse, Georgetown, Texas; Nelle (Mrs. Robert) Drummond to VCR, Midland, Texas, 14 December 1979 (letter in author's files).

11. *Williamson County, Texas, Marriage Records, v. 3–5, (1868–1885),* Microfilm #1,007,900, LDS Genealogical Library, Salt Lake City, vol. 5, p. 111, #221.

12. Hood County Courthouse, Granbury, Texas, Recorder's Office, *Deed,* W. H. Pennington to C. A. Gordon, 31 October 1928; Obituary of William H. Pennington, *Brownwood* (Texas) *Bulletin,* 20 July 1929.

13. Obituary of Sarah Josephine E. Gordon, *Brownwood* (Texas) *Banner,* 31 October 1935.

14. Nelle Drummond to VCR, Midland, Texas, 14 December 1979.

15. Memorial stones, Sópori Ranch graveyard (also known as the "Pennington Cemetery").

16. Shortly after the completion of the Southern Pacific Railroad to Tucson in 1880, the government transferred human remains, most of them unidentified, from the abandoned Fort Crittenden Cemetery to the San Francisco National Cemetery at the Presidio. Forbes concluded that the bones of Elias and Green Pennington were among them. He was unable to locate Ellen Barnett's grave in Tucson. R. H. Forbes, "Note on the Penningtons (Following visit of R. H. Forbes to the National Cemetery at San Francisco August 28, 1933)," Forbes Collection, Box 3, AHSL; Jas. H. Laubach, Lt. Colonel, Q. M. Corps, to Dr. Robert H. Forbes, War Department, Washington, D.C., 17 October 1933, Forbes Collection, Box 3, AHSL.

BIBLIOGRAPHY

Interviews

Margo Hart Anderson. Interviews with author, Tucson, 22 February 1979, and Piedmont, California, 1 August 1988, and 26 February 1989.

Amanda Jane [Pennington] Crumpton. Interview with Robert H. Forbes, Santa Cruz, California, 18 May 1916. Forbes Collection, Box 3, Arizona Historical Society.

Charles B. Genung. Interview with Robert H. Forbes, Mullin's Well, Arizona, 25 June 1913. Forbes Collection, Box 3, Arizona Historical Society.

Mary Gardner Kane. Interview with Robert H. Forbes, [Sonoita Valley], 8 December 1914. Forbes Collection, Box 3, Arizona Historical Society.

Sabino Otero. Interview with Robert H. Forbes, Tubac, Arizona, 13 July 1913. Forbes Collection, Box 3, Arizona Historical Society.

John Parker Pennington, II. Interview with Marshall Lee Pennington, Georgetown, Texas, 30 December 1959. Photocopy of interview notes in author's files.

Marshall L. Pennington. Interviews with author, Tucson, 5, 6, 7, 8, and 11 February 1980.

Letters

Margo Hart Anderson to the author, Piedmont, California, 7 May 1980, 20 February 1988, and 30 August 1988.

L. E. Barnett to her sisters, Tubac, 1 October 1869. Forbes Collection, Box 3, Arizona Historical Society.

J. Ross Browne to San Francisco *Bulletin*, Tubac, 5 February 1864. San Francisco *Bulletin*, 15 March 1864.

Shirley Nichols Brueggeman to the author, Loma, Colorado, 21 November 1981.

John G. Capron to S. R. DeLong [San Diego, n.d.]. John G. Capron File, Hayden Collection, Arizona Historical Society.

D. E. Conner to R. H. Forbes, Elsinore, California, 5 October 1915. Forbes Collection, Box 3, Arizona Historical Society.

Marvin Cook to the author, Eugene, Oregon, 10 July 1979.

Nelle Drummond to the author, Midland, Texas, 14 December 1979.

Jas. H. Laubach, Lt. Colonel, Q. M. Corps, to Robert H. Forbes, War Department, Washington, D. C., 17 October 1933. Forbes Collection, Box 3, Arizona Historical Society.

Sydney W. [Sylvester] Mowry to E. J. Bricknall, Fort Yuma, California, 8 April 1856. Typescript in Sylvester Mowry Biographical File, Arizona Historical Society.

H[enry] F[rank] Pennington to Mrs. Florence E. Drachman, Chicago, 22 June 1939. Forbes Collection, Box 3, Arizona Historical Society.

John P. Pennington, II, to Barry Pennington, Georgetown, Texas, 14 March 1954. Photocopy in author's files.

Marshall L. Pennington to the author, Lubbock, Texas, 29 November 1979, and numerous other letters in author's files.

_____ to Mrs. J. R. Lesesne, Lubbock, Texas, 26 November 1979. Photocopy in author's files.

_____ to Clark Pennington, Lubbock, Texas, 14 December 1979. Photocopy in author's files.

_____ to Eunice B. Rader, Lubbock, 16 February 1981. Photocopy in author's files.

Margaret D. Pennington to "Brother and Sister" [W. F. and Larcena Scott], Georgetown, Texas, 21 February 1872. Forbes Collection, Box 3, Arizona Historical Society.

Eunice B. Rader to Marshall L. Pennington, Georgetown, Texas, 2 September 1979. Photocopy in author's files.

_____ to Marshall L. Pennington, Georgetown, Texas, 3 December 1979. Photocopy in author's files.

Samuel Robinson to John R. Robinson, Santa Rita, Arizona, 17 March 1861. Typescript, Arizona Historical Society.

Larcena A. Scott to Mr. John P. Pennington, Tucson, A.T., 27 March 1901. Photocopy in author's files.

Anita I. Sharp, Medical Records Librarian, Austin State Hospital, to Ruth Rader Lesesne, 4 December 1979. Photocopy in author's files.

Molly Theriot, Orange County Clerk, to the author, Orange, Texas, 19 November 1981.

Newspapers

Alta California (San Francisco).

Arizona Citizen (Tucson).

Arizona Daily Star (Tucson).

Arizona Miner (Prescott).

Brownwood [Texas] *Banner.*

Brownwood [Texas] *Bulletin.*

Civilian and Gazette (Galveston).

Daily Delta (New Orleans).

Daily Picayune (New Orleans).

Daily Tribune (New York).

Evening Herald Express (Los Angeles).

Mesilla [New Mexico] *Times.*

Missouri Republican (St. Louis).

New York Times.

Prospector (Tombstone).

Rocky Mountain News (Denver).

Sacramento Union.

San Francisco Chronicle.

San Francisco Evening Bulletin.

San Francisco Herald.

San Francisco Daily News (later *San Francisco News*).

Semi-Weekly Southern News (Los Angeles).

Tri-Weekly Telegraph (Houston).

Tucson Post.

Weekly Arizonian (Tubac).

Weekly Arizonian and *Weekly Arizonan* (Tucson).

Williamson County Sun (Georgetown, Texas).

Manuscripts, Journals, Notes, and Miscellaneous Items

Barnett, Underwood C. Hayden File. Arizona Historical Society.

Biertu, F. Journal, 1860–61. MS HM4367. Huntington Library, San Marino, California.

Brichta, Augustus. "Reminiscences of an old Pioneer." MS B849–2. Small Collection, Arizona Historical Society.

Caldwell, June. "Filibustering in Sonora 1841-1857." MS C147j. Arizona Historical Society.

Carrillo, Leopoldo. Biographical File. Arizona Historical Society.

Cosulich, Bernice. "Mrs. Moss Sees 50-year change." MS [n.d.]. Typescript in James Lee File, Hayden Collection, Arizona Historical Society.

Dennison, William E. Hayden File. Arizona Historical Society.

[Forbes, Georgie Scott]. "Mamma's Capture by Indians in the Spring of 1860," [c. 1900]. MS. Forbes Collection, Box 3, Arizona Historical Society.

Forbes, Robert H. Handwritten draft for "The Penningtons, Pioneers of Early Arizona." Forbes Collection, Box 3, Arizona Historical Society.

——————— . Miscellaneous Notes. Forbes Collection, Box 3, Arizona Historical Society.

——————— . *Pictures-Places-Pennington Homes*. Photo files. Arizona Historical Society.

"Genealogy." Mercedes Shibell Gould Boxed Material. Arizona Historical Society.

Handy, Dr. John Charles. Account Ledger, photographs, and other family records. Margo H. Anderson Collection, Piedmont, California.

——————— . Biographical File. Arizona Historical Society.

Hughes, Samuel. Account of trip from Tucson to Calabasas, Fort Buchanan, and intermediate points, 20, 21 September 1859. Biographical File. Arizona Historical Society.

Kirkland, William Hudson. "An account of the captives [sic] by Apache Indians of Mrs. John Page, nee Larcena Pennington, daughter of Mr. and Mrs. E. G. Pennington, and incidents connected therewith," 3 September 1909. MS. Ben and Fern Allen Collection, Arizona Historical Society.

Lee, James. Hayden File. Arizona Historical Society.

Pennington, Elias G. Hayden File. Arizona Historical Society.

Pennington Gravestones. Sópori Cemetery, Santa Cruz County, Arizona.

Pennington, Marshall L. "Elias Green Pennington and Immediate Family." Table of statistics, 28 February 1981. Copy in author's files.

"Pictures, Places, Tucson: Carrillo's Gardens." Photograph file. Arizona Historical Society.

Receipt. O. C. Parker Undertaking to Robert H. Forbes. Forbes Collection, Box 3, Arizona Historical Society.

Robinson, Samuel. Diary, 1861. Typescript, Arizona Historical Society.

Scott, William F. Paper read before Society of Arizona Pioneers, 6 July 1894. Typescript in William F. Scott Biographical File, Arizona Historical Society.

Shibell, Charles A. Biographical File. Arizona Historical Society.

_____ . Paper read before Society of Arizona Pioneers, 8 November 1887. Records of the Society of Arizona Pioneers, Arizona Historical Society.

Smith, Cornelius C., Sr. "A History of the Oury Family." MS. Arizona Historical Society.

Warner, Solomon. Reminiscences. Warner Collection, Box 6, Folder 59, Arizona Historical Society.

Whelan, William. "Record Kept by William Whelan, Point of Mountain Station, 1869." Handwritten log, Arizona Historical Society.

[Whitmore, Dr. William V.] "John Charles Handy, M. D." MS [n.d.]. Handy Collection, Arizona Historical Society.

Documents and Archival Materials

Arizona Territorial Government. *Special Census, 1866.* Photostat of original at Arizona Historical Society.

Barter, G. W., comp. & pub. *Directory of the City of Tucson.* San Francisco: H. S. Crocker & Co., Printers, 1881.

District Court, Orange County, Texas. *Charles H. Saxon vs Ester [sic] Saxon, No. 49.* Divorce, 24 September 1855. County Clerk's Office, Orange. Photocopies in author's files.

_____ . *Altha C. Wadsworth vs William W. Wadsworth, No. 60.* Divorce, Fall Term 1856. County Clerk's Office, Orange. Photocopies in author's files.

Dona Ana County, New Mexico. *Mining Claims, Book 2.* (One of two books with that title.) County Recorder's Office, Las Cruces.

Evans, A. W., First Lieutenant, 7th Infantry. Report to Lieutenant G. Chapin, Adjutant, 7th Infantry, Fort Buchanan, 20 Mar 1861. National Archives, Records Group 98, Records of the War Department, U. S. Army Commands, Letters Received Department of New Mexico, 1 E 1861. Handwritten copy in Sacks Collection, Folder 5066, Arizona Historical Foundation, Tempe.

Ewell, R. S., Captain First Dragoons, Commanding [Fort Buchanan, N. M.]. "Report in relation to two females captured by Tonto Apaches," 10 April

1860. Report to Lieutenant John D. Wilkins, Acting Assistant Adjutant General, Department of New Mexico. Photocopy in Sacks Collection, Arizona Historical Foundation, Tempe.

Family Bible, John Parker Pennington, II. Marshall L. Pennington Collection, Lubbock, Texas.

Fannin County, Texas. *Deeds,* vols. C, H, and I. County Clerk's Office, Bonham.

Forbes, Robert H. "Notes and papers re the Penningtons." Forbes Collection, Box 3, Arizona Historical Society.

Hand, Patrick J. to Albert C. Benedict, 5 December 1877. *Deed.* George McIntosh file (MS 68), Arizona Historical Society.

Hood County, Texas. *Deed.* W. H. Pennington to C. A. Gordon, 31 October 1928. County Recorder's Office, Granbury.

Honey Grove [Texas] Church, Jesse Buttler [sic], Moderator, and Walter Yeary, C.C. Membership certificate issued to E. G. Pennington, 12 May 1849. Marshall L. Pennington Collection, Lubbock, Texas. Copy in author's files.

Irwin, Bernard J. D., Assistant Surgeon. "Sanitary Report, Fort Buchanan, Arizona," February 1859. 36th Cong., 1st sess., 6 August 1860. Records of the Surgeon General's Office, Senate Executive Documents 52, Serial No. 1035.

Johnson, Royal A., Surveyor General. General Land Office Map, T 10 S, R 14 E, Gila and Salt River Meridian, Arizona, 19 July 1884. Federal Bureau of Land Management, Phoenix.

Journal of the Pioneer and Walker Mining Districts 1863-1865. Yavapai County Recorder's Office, Prescott, Arizona. (Transcription of the same, Phoenix: Works Progress Administration, Arizona Statewide Archival and Records Project, Historical Records Survey Projects, August 1941.)

Memorial and Petition to Congress from Citizens of Arizona Territory, Tubac, 27 February 1858. National Archives Records Group No. 46. Photostat of original in Benjamin Sacks Collection, Arizona Historical Foundation, Tempe.

Page, John Hempstead. Hayden File. Arizona Historical Society.

Pennington, Elias G. Hayden File. Arizona Historical Society.

Pennington, Elias. Survey Plat, filed 10 August 1841. File 165. State of Texas, General Land Office, Austin.

Pima County Abstract Co., comp. *City of Tucson General & Business Directory for 1897 and 1898.* Tucson: Citizen Printing & Publishing Co., ed. and printers.

Pima County, Arizona, Superior Court. *Estate of William P. Scott, Deceased, No. 3412.* Filed 16 March 1924. Microfilm, Pima County Clerk of Court.

Pima County, Arizona, Territorial Records. Special Collections, University of Arizona.

Pima County, Arizona Territory. *Deeds,* No. 1. County Recorder's Office, Tucson.

Pima County, Arizona Territory. Land Claims, No. 1. County Recorder's Office, Tucson.

Pima County, Arizona Territory. *Marriages,* Book 1. Pima County Clerk of Court, Tucson.

Pima County, Arizona Territory, First Judicial District Court. *Civil Actions Docket,* Vols. 4 and 5. Pima County Archives, Tucson.

——————— . *Civil Actions.* Cases No. 1720, 1867, 1980, and 2040. Microfilm. Pima County Clerk of Court, Tucson.

Pima County, Arizona Territory, Probate Court. *Estate of J. C. Handy, Deceased, No. 542.* Microfilm. Pima County Clerk of Court, Tucson.

——————— . *Estate of E. G. Pennington, Deceased,* filed 4 April 1892. Typescript. Elias G. Pennington Biographical File, Arizona Historical Society.

Pima County Deeds 1855–1872. Arizona State Library and Archives.

Plumas County, California. *Register of Deaths,* vol. 1. County Recorder, Quincy.

Records of the Arizona Historical Society, Tucson.

Red River County [Texas] Board of Land Commissioners. Certificate No. 698 to Elias Pennington, 8 January 1840. Red River County Clerk, Clarksville.

Reeve, I. V. D., Brevet Lieutenant Colonel, U. S. A. Letter to Lieutenant J. D. Wilkins, Acting Assistant Adjutant General, 20 May 1859. Washington, D. C., National Archives, Records Group 98, Records of the War Department, U. S. Army Commands, Letters Received Department of New Mexico, Box 12, R 22–1859. Photocopy of original in Sacks Collection, Folder Fort Buchanan 1859, Arizona Historical Foundation, Tempe.

Republic of Texas, Anson Jones, President. Land Patent No. 388 to Elias Pennington, 3 December 1845. State of Texas, General Land Office, Austin.

Republic of Texas, County of Fannin. Surveys by Samuel Erwin, D. S., for Elias G. Pennington, 1 May 1841 and 10 October 1842. Red River County Clerk, Clarksville.

Santa Cruz County, California. *Deaths, 1915–1919.* SC 15–19. County Recorder's Office, Santa Cruz.

Territory of New Mexico Deed Book 1851–1861. Copied 1882. Arizona State Library & Archives, Phoenix.

Tucson & Tombstone General & Business Directory for 1883 & 1884. Tucson: Cobler & Co., Daily Citizen Steam Printing, 1883.

United States Court of Claims. *Thomas J. Cassner, Administrator, v. The United States et al., Indian Depredations, No. 3112.* Washington: Government Printing Office, (No. 24761–14) 1914.

——————— . *Alphonse Lazard vs United States and the Apache Indians: Indian Depredations Claim No. 8773.* Larcena A. Scott's testimony, Tucson, 20 September 1910. Typescript. Forbes Collection, Box 3, Arizona Historical Society.

——————— . *William F. Scott, Administrator of the Estate of Elias G. Pennington, deceased, vs the United States and Apache Indians: Indian Depredations Claim No. 7363.* Record of proceedings, 16 and 17 January 1893. Typescript. Robert H. Forbes Collection, Box 3, Arizona Historical Society.

U. S. Department of Agriculture. *Tumacacori Forest Reserve, Arizona.* Forest Service Map, 6 November 1906. Arizona Historical Society.

U. S. Government. *Census of Arizona Territory 1864.* Photostat of original returns, Arizona Historical Society.

——————— . Federal Census, 1850, Fannin County, Texas. Microfilm 910, no. 5809 pt. 3, U. S. National Archives, Washington.

——————— . Federal Census, 1850, San Diego County, California. Microfilm 002492. LDS Genealogical Library, Salt Lake City.

——————— . Federal Census, 1860, Arizona Territory, New Mexico. Photocopy of original returns at Arizona Historical Society.

——————— . Federal Census, 1860, Dona Ana County, New Mexico. Microfilm 653, Roll 712. LDS Genealogical Library, Salt Lake City.

——————— . Federal Census, 1870, Bell County, Texas. Microfilm, U. S. National Archives.

——————— . Federal Census, 1870, Pima County, Arizona Territory. Photostat of original returns, Arizona Historical Society.

——————— . "Ninth Decennial Census of the United States, 1870, Arizona." Washington: U. S. Government Printing Office, 1965.

U. S. G. S. "Nogales Quadrangle, Santa Cruz County, Arizona." Topographical map, 1905 edition. Arizona Historical Society.

U. S. National Archives. "Compiled Service Records of Confederate Soldiers Who Served in Organizations from Territory of Arizona." Microfilm M–318, #1694.

U. S. War Department. *The War of the Rebellion: A Compilation of the Official Records of the Union and Confederate Armies,* series I, vol. IX. Washington: Government Printing Office, 1883.

"*Williamson County*" [Texas] "*Marriage Records, vols. 3-5 (1868-1885).*" Microfilm. Salt Lake City: LDS Genealogical Library.

"*Williamson County*" [Texas] "*Marriage Records,*" vol. 4. Williamson County Courthouse, Georgetown, Texas.

Books, Monographs, and Articles

Aguirre, Mamie Bernard. "Spanish Trader's Bride," *Westport Historical Quarterly,* vol. 4 (December 1968).

Ainsa, J. Y. *History of the Crabb Expedition into Northern Sonora.* Phoenix: self-published, 1951.

Altshuler, Constance Wynn. *Latest from Arizona! The Hesperian Letters, 1859-1861.* Tucson: Arizona Pioneers' Historical Society, 1969.

_____ . *Chains of Command: Arizona and the Army, 1856–1875.* Tucson: Arizona Historical Society, 1981.

_____ . *Starting with Defiance: Nineteenth Century Arizona Military Posts.* Tucson: Arizona Historical Society, 1983.

Ames, Charles R. "Along the Mexican Border—Then and Now," *The Journal of Arizona History,* vol. 18 (Winter 1977).

Ames, Sister Aloysia, CSJ. *The St. Mary's I Knew.* Tucson: St. Mary's Hospital of Tucson, Inc., 1970.

Anderson, Hattie M., ed. "Mining and Indian Fighting in Arizona and New Mexico, 1858-1861:—Memoirs of Hank Smith," *Panhandle-Plains Historical Review,* vol. 1 (1928).

_____ . "With the Confederates in New Mexico during the Civil War—Memoirs of Hank Smith," *Panhandle-Plains Historical Review,* vol. 2 (1929).

Bean, Walton. *Boss Ruef's San Francisco: The Story of the Union Labor Party, Big Business, and the Graft Prosecution.* Berkeley and Los Angeles: University of California Press, 1952.

Bell, William A. *New Tracks in North America,* vol. 2. London: Chapman & Hall, 1869.

Brandes, Ray. *Frontier Military Posts of Arizona.* Globe, Arizona: Dale Stuart King, 1960.

Browne, J. Ross. *A Tour through Arizona, 1864.* New York: Harper & Brothers, 1869. See also the edition, *Adventures in Apache Country: A Tour through Arizona—1864,* Donald M. Powell, ed. Tucson: University of Arizona Press, 1974.

Browne, Lina Fergusson, ed. *J. Ross Browne, His Letters, Journals & Writings.* Albuquerque: University of New Mexico Press, 1969.

Brownell, Elizabeth R. *They Lived in Tubac.* Tucson: Westernlore Press, 1986.

Bufkin, Don. "From Mud Village to Modern Metropolis: The Urbanization of Tucson," *Journal of Arizona History,* vol. 22 (Spring 1981).

Byrkit, James W. "The Word on the Frontier: Anglo Protestant Churches in Arizona, 1859–1899," *Journal of Arizona History*, vol. 21 (Spring 1980).

Cammack, Sister Alberta. "A Faithful Account of the Life and Death of Doctor John Charles Handy," *The Smoke Signal*, no. 52. Tucson: Tucson Corral of the Westerners, Inc., 1989.

Clifford [McCrackin], Josephine. *Overland Tales*. Philadelphia: J. Fagan & Son, Stereotypers, 1877.

Colley, Charles C. *The Century of Robert H. Forbes*. Tucson: Arizona Historical Society, 1977.

Conkling, Roscoe P. and Margaret B. Conkling. *The Butterfield Overland Mail 1857–1869*. 3 vols. Glendale, California: Arthur H. Clark Company, 1947.

Conner, Daniel Ellis. *Joseph Reddeford Walker and the Arizona Adventure*. Edited by Donald J. Berthrong and Odessa Davenport. Norman: University of Oklahoma Press, 1956.

Cosulich, Bernice. *Tucson*. Tucson: Arizona Silhouettes, 1953.

Cox, Meg. "The Drug Trade," *Wall Street Journal*, 3 December 1984.

Cozzens, Samuel W. *The Marvelous Country, or, Three Years in Arizona and New Mexico*. Boston: Lee & Shepard, 1876. (First edition 1873.)

Curry, W. Hubert. *Sun Rising on the West, the Saga of Henry Clay and Elizabeth Smith*. Crosbyton, Texas: Crosby County Pioneer Memorial, 1979.

DeLong, Sidney. *History of Arizona*. San Francisco: The Whitaker & Ray Company, 1905.

Duffen, William A., ed. "Overland Via 'Jackass Mail': The Diary of Phocion R. Way," *Arizona and the West*, vol. 2 (Winter 1960).

Dunning, Charles H. with Edward H. Peplow, Jr. *Rock to Riches*. Phoenix: Southwest Publishing Co., 1959.

E[hrenberg], Herman and Chas. D. P[oston], "Murders in Arizona," *The Arizonian* (Tucson), 10 August, 1861.

Farish, Thomas Edwin. *History of Arizona*. 8 vols. San Francisco: Filmer Bros, 1914–1918.

Finch, Boyd. "Sherod Hunter and the Confederates in Arizona," *Journal of Arizona History*, vol. 10 (Autumn 1969).

Fireman, Bert M. *Arizona Historic Land*. New York: Alfred A. Knopf, 1982.

Fontana, Bernard L. "Calabasas of the Rio Rico," *The Smoke Signal*, vol. 24 (Fall 1971). Tucson: Tucson Corral of the Westerners.

_____ and J. Cameron Greenleaf. "Johnny Ward's Ranch: A Study in Historic Archaeology," *The Kiva*, vol. 28 (October-December 1962).

_____ . "The Mowry Mine 1858-1958," *The Kiva,* vol. 23 (February 1958).

Forbes, Robert H. *The Penningtons, Pioneers of Early Arizona.* [Tucson]: Arizona Archaeological and Historical Society, 1919.

_____ . *Crabb's Filibustering Expedition into Sonora, 1857.* [Tucson]: Arizona Silhouettes, 1952.

Genung, C. B. "Early Days in Arizona," Prescott *Mining Review,* 20 May 1911. Copy in Genung Notebook, Sharlot Hall Museum, Prescott.

Gilbert, Bil. *Westering Man: The Life of Joseph Walker, Master of the Frontier.* New York: Atheneum Press, 1983.

Granger, Byrd H. *Will C. Barnes' Arizona Place Names.* Tucson: University of Arizona Press, 1960.

Gressinger, A. W. *Charles D. Poston, Sunland Seer.* Globe, Arizona: Dale Stuart King, 1961.

Gustafson, A. M., ed. *John Spring's Arizona.* Tucson: University of Arizona Press, 1966.

Hagemann, E. R., ed. "Surgeon Smart and the Indians: An 1866 Apache Word List," *Journal of Arizona History,* vol. 11 (Summer 1970).

Hall, Edward H. *Hall's Guide to the Great West.* New York: D. Appleton & Co., 1866.

Hamilton, Patrick. *The Resources of Arizona.* San Francisco: A. L. Bancroft & Company, Printers, Third Edition, 1884.

Hamlin, Percy Gatling, ed. *The Making of a Soldier: Letters of General R. S. Ewell, 1817–1872.* Richmond, Virginia: Whittet & Shepperson, 1935.

Harris, Benjamin Butler. *The Gila Trail: The Texas Argonauts and the California Gold Rush.* Edited and annotated by Richard H. Dillon. Norman: University of Oklahoma Press, 1960.

Hastings, James R. "The Tragedy at Camp Grant in 1871," *Arizona and the West,* vol. 1 (Summer 1959).

Hichborn, Franklin. *"The System" as Uncovered by the San Francisco Graft Prosecution.* San Francisco: James H. Barry Company, 1915.

Hughes, Mrs. Samuel. "Reminiscences," *Arizona Historical Review,* vol. 6 (April 1935).

Hutchins, James S. "Bald Head Ewell, Frontier Dragoon," *Arizoniana,* vol. 3 (Spring 1962).

Jensen, Joan and Darlis A. Miller, eds. *New Mexico Women: Intercultural Perspectives.* Albuquerque: University of New Mexico Press, 1986.

Kennedy, John W. "The First University Chancellor," *Arizona Medicine,* vol. 23 (April 1966).

Leavengood, Betty. "Dr. Handy and Mr. Hyde," *Old West,* Winter, 1987.

Lockwood, Frank C. "Palatine Robinson," *Arizona Daily Star* (Tucson), 22 December 1940.

Luckingham, Bradford. "Urban Development in Arizona: The Rise of Phoenix," *Journal of Arizona History,* vol. 22 (Summer 1981).

Marion, John H. "Notes of travel through the Territory of Arizona, being an account of the trip made by General George Stoneman and others in Autumn of 1870." Prescott: Office of the *Arizona Miner,* 1870.

Martin, Douglas D. *The Lamp in the Desert: the Story of the University of Arizona.* Tucson: University of Arizona Press, 1960.

Martin, J. C. "Turbulent as the Times," *Arizona Daily Star,* 12 November 1972.

Martin, Maybelle Edwards, ed. "From Texas to California in 1849: Diary of C. C. Cox," *Southwestern Historical Quarterly,* vol. 29 (July 1925).

Miller, Darlis A. "Civilians and Military Supply in the Southwest," *Journal of Arizona History,* vol. 23 (Summer 1982).

Moody, Ralph. *The Old Trails West.* New York: Thomas Y. Crowell Co., 1963.

Mowry, Sylvester. *Memoir of the Proposed Territory of Arizona.* Washington: Henry Polkinhorn, Printer, 1857.

Myers, Lee. "Mangas Colorado's Favorite Ambush Site," *Old West,* vol. 5 (Winter 1968).

Newman, J. S. "A History of the Primitive Baptists of Texas, Oklahoma and Indian Territories" [Tioga, Texas], *Baptist Trumpet,* vol. 1 (1906).

North, Diane M. T. *Samuel Peter Heintzelman and the Sonora Exploring & Mining Company.* Tucson: University of Arizona Press, 1980.

Officer, James E. and Henry F. Dobyns. "Teodoro Ramírez: Early Citizen of Tucson," *Journal of Arizona History,* vol. 25 (Autumn 1984).

O'Neil, James Bradas. *They Die But Once.* New York: Knight Publications, 1935.

Oury, William S. "The Sequel of the Cochise Outbreak of 1861," *Arizona Weekly Star* (Tucson), 27 July 1877 and 2 August 1877.

Peale, Norman Vincent. *Sin, Sex and Self-Control.* New York: Doubleday & Co., 1965.

Poston, Charles D. "Her First Wedding — Reception on a Wood Pile," *Morning Courier* (Prescott), 28 May 1891.

—————— . "The Pennington Family," *Arizona Citizen* (Tucson), 17 January 1896.

Pumpelly, Rafael. *Across America and Asia.* New York: Leypoldt & Holt, 1870, Third Edition, Revised.

―――――――――. *My Reminiscences,* vol. 1. New York: Henry Holt and Company, 1918.

Quebbeman, Frances. *Medicine in Territorial Arizona.* Phoenix: Arizona Historical Foundation, 1966.

Radeleff [Radcliff], Edward F. "Heroic Mrs. Page," *Weekly Phoenix Herald,* 2 July 1891.

Roberts, Virginia Culin. "Heroines of the Arizona Frontier," *Journal of Arizona History,* vol. 23 (Spring 1982).

―――――――――. "Jack Pennington in Early Arizona," *Arizona and the West,* vol. 23 (Winter 1981).

―――――――――. "Mary Page Handy and the Lawyer Who Dared to Defend Her," *The Journal of Arizona History,* vol. 30 (Winter 1989).

Robinson, Samuel. "Arizona in 1861, A Contemporary Account," *Journal of Arizona History,* vol. 25 (Spring 1984). Introduction and annotation by Constance Wynn Altshuler.

Sacks, B. *Be It Enacted: The Creation of the Territory of Arizona.* Phoenix: Arizona Historical Foundation, 1964.

―――――――――. "Sylvester Mowry: Libertine, Artilleryman, Entrepreneur," *American West,* vol. 1 (Summer 1964).

Sandwich, Brian. *The Great Western, Legendary Lady of the Southwest.* El Paso: Texas Western Press, 1991.

Sayner, Donald B. and Robert P. Hale, comps. *Arizona's First Newspaper "The Weekly Arizonian," Edward E. Cross, Editor, Tubac.* Tucson: University of Arizona Department of Biology and Arizona Historical Society, 1977.

Serven, James A. "The Military Posts on Sonoita Creek," *Brand Book 2.* Tucson: The Tucson Corral of the Westerners, Inc., 1971.

Sloan, Richard E. *Memories of an Arizona Judge.* Stanford University: Stanford University Press, 1932.

Smith, C. C., anno. "Some Unpublished History of the Southwest," *Arizona Historical Review,* vol. 6 (January 1935). (Diary of Malvina Oury, 1865.)

Smith, Cornelius C., Jr. *William Sanders Oury, History-Maker of the Southwest.* Tucson: University of Arizona Press, 1967.

Sonnichsen, C. L. *Pioneer Heritage: The First Century of the Arizona Historical Society.* Tucson: The Arizona Historical Society, 1984.

―――――――――. *Tucson: The Life and Times of an American City.* Norman: University of Oklahoma Press, 1982.

Spicer, Edward H. *Cycles of Conquest*. Tucson: University of Arizona Press, 1962.

Spring, John A. "The Ordeal of Mrs. Page," *Wide World Magazine,* February 1912.

Steffens, Lincoln. *The Autobiography of Lincoln Steffens*. New York: Harcourt, Brace & World, 1931.

Strickland, Rex W. "History of Fannin County, Texas, 1836–1843," *Southwest Historical Quarterly,* vols. 33 (April 1930) and 34 (July 1930).

Tevis, James H. *Arizona in the 50's*. Albuquerque: University of New Mexico Press, 1954.

Thomas, Lately. *A Debonair Scoundrel: An Episode in the Moral History of San Francisco*. New York: Holt, Rinehart and Winston, 1962.

Thompson, Jerry. "The Vulture over the Carrion: Captain James 'Paddy' Graydon and the Civil War in the Territory of New Mexico," *Journal of Arizona History,* vol. 24 (Winter 1983).

Thrapp, Dan L. *The Conquest of Apacheria*. Norman: University of Oklahoma Press, 1967.

_____ . "Stein's Pass, Gateway to Adventure," *New Mexico,* vol. 39 (June, 1961).

_____ . *Victorio and the Mimbres Apaches*. Norman: University of Oklahoma Press, 1974.

Wagoner, Jay J. *Arizona Territory 1863-1912: A Political History*. Tucson: University of Arizona Press, 1980.

Wallace, Andrew. "John W. Swilling," *Arizoniana,* vol. 2 (Spring 1961).

Wallace, Edward S. "The Gray-eyed Man of Destiny," *American Heritage,* vol. 9 (December 1957).

Waters, Frank. *The Earp Brothers of Tombstone: The Story of Mrs. Virgil Earp*. New York: Bramhall House, 1960.

Wharfield, H. B. *Fort Yuma on the Colorado River*. El Cajon, California: privately published, 1968.

Wiley, Bell Irvin and Hirst D. Milhollen. *Embattled Confederates*. New York: Harper & Row, 1964.

Woodward, Arthur. *The Great Western, Amazon of the Army*. San Francisco: Yerba Buena Chapter of E Clampus Vitus, 1961.

Wright, Arthur A. *The Civil War in the Southwest*. Denver: Big Mountain Press, 1964.

INDEX

Aguirre, Mary (Mamie) Bernard, 252 n. 1, 257 n. 7; and Dr. J. C. Handy, 179-80, 195

Ake, Anna Maria (Annie): at Cooke's Canyon ambush, 114-15; and Jack Pennington, 39; wedding of, 63

Ake, Charles Jefferson (Jeff): in Ake-Wadsworth party, 106; at Cooke's Canyon ambush, 113-14; and Jack Pennington and Fisher Scott, 120; describes Page's sawpit, 61-62; finds murder victims at San Pedro Mine, 86

Ake, Felix Grundy: abandons Sonoita Valley (1861), 101-02; at Cooke's Canyon ambush, 109, 113, 115-18; farm, Sonoita Valley, 68; family in Georgetown, Texas, 148; family migrates to Arizona (1856), 39-40, 43; hauls hay for Confederates, 120; helps Bill Ake escape, 100; leaves Tucson with Wadsworths, 104-07; lumber contracts, 43, 61; and Sonoita murders, 72

Ake, Lizzie. see Bacon, Lizzie

Ake, Mary: 39; at Cooke's Canyon ambush, 118; daughter's wedding, 63, 109

Ake, Virginia, 106, 118

Ake-Wadsworth party: ambushed at Cooke's Canyon, 110-18; persons in, 106-07; leaves Tucson, 104-07, 239 n. 46, 239 n. 48

Ake, William Riley (son of F. G. Ake): in Ake-Wadsworth party, 106; finds murder victims at San Pedro Mine, 86

Ake, William W. (Bill, nephew of F. G. Ake): at Annie Ake's wedding, 63; in California (1850-57), 40-41; and Crabb Expedition (1857), 42-43; described by Col. Reeve, 71; and Jack Pennington, 40; and John H. Page, 40-43; killed, 238 n. 13; kills Davis, 99; marries Lizzie Bacon, 99-100; as outlaw, 40-41, 43, 74, 99-100; and Sonoita murders, 68-76

American House, The (Tucson hotel), 44, 105

Anderson, John E. (Protestant minister), 182

Anderson, Samuel, 71, 73

Andrade, José, 154-55

Apache camp at Eagle Creek, 112

Apache depredations: affect on economy (late 1860), 88-89, (1874), 184; efforts to control, 137-38; suit for compensation of, 211-12; pioneers' perceptions of, 81, 85; legislative memorial to Congress about, 171

Apache depredations and killings (by year):
pre-1856, at Gándara hacienda, 59;
1857, at Apache Pass, 17, 18; livestock raid, Sonoita valley, 46;
1858, attack on Jack Pennington near Gila Bend, 60;